ANTISUBMARINE
WARRIOR
in the PACIFIC

ANTISUBMARINE
WARRIOR
in the PACIFIC

Six Subs Sunk in Twelve Days

JOHN A. WILLIAMSON

THE UNIVERSITY OF ALABAMA PRESS

Tuscaloosa

The University of Alabama Press
Tuscaloosa, Alabama 35487-0380
uapress.ua.edu

Hardcover edition published 2005.
Paperback edition published 2020.
eBook edition published 2020.

Typeface: AGaramond

Design: Michele Myatt Quinn

Paperback ISBN: 978-0-8173-6007-8
E-ISBN: 978-0-8173-9349-6

A previous edition of this book has been cataloged by the Library of Congress.
ISBN: 978-0-8173-1415-6 (cloth)

Publisher's Note: John A. Williamson passed away on May 2, 2004, after writing
and completing primary editorial work on *Antisubmarine Warrior in the Pacific*.
His extraordinary energy and enthusiasm made working with him a pleasure; The
University of Alabama Press is saddened by his loss and regrets his passing.

Contents

Map 1: Western Pacific Theater, World War II

Preface

ONCE UPON A TIME THERE was a ship called the USS *England*. She was a good ship. Built in the Bethlehem Steel Shipyard at San Francisco, commissioned on 10 December 1943, and dispatched to the Pacific the following February, she was a 1,200-ton, 306-foot-long vessel belonging to the long-hull class of destroyer escorts. Men on larger warships disparagingly dubbed her a tin-can destroyer. This misnomer didn't upset the *England's* crew. They laughed and remained steadfastly proud of their little ship, whose speed at full power was 24 knots and whose antisubmarine capabilities made her an indispensable piece of the protective shield cast around merchant ships and warship convoys crisscrossing the vast Pacific.

The *England* was a multipurpose ship—a screening escort with certain destroyer characteristics. To outsiders, that might have made her seem like a ship with no true purpose. But her fourteen officers and two-hundred-some enlisted men knew better. And they would have their chance to prove it during a single spell in May 1944. Over the course of twelve momentous days, the *England* was to amass a series of tactical successes that would make this humble tin-can destroyer one of the most accomplished ships to see action in the Pacific war, and indeed one of the legendary ships in the annals of antisubmarine warfare.

I should know, for I was the executive officer of the *England* in May 1944, and later, during the tumultuous autumn when kamikazes were raining down death on the U.S. Fleet off Okinawa, I was her commanding officer.

It all began on the morning of May 14, at 0800 on the dot, when a submarine designated the I-16 set out from Truk on a mission to resupply the beleaguered Japanese garrison at Buin, on the southeastern tip of Bougainville in the Solomon Islands. The I-16 was one of the largest subs ever built in Japan—348 feet long, with eight 21-inch torpedo tubes and a deck house that could be used to carry a dismantled float plane, a small landing boat, or a miniature submarine. But all the I-16 was carrying that morning was a cargo of rice. It must have been a grave disappointment to her skipper, Lieutenant Commander Yoshitaka Takeuchi, to be sent on a resupply mission when any day the U.S. Fleet was expected to make its long-awaited arrival in the waters of the western Pacific. Like any sub commander worth his salt, he must have wanted badly to go after warships.

Whatever his private feelings, Takeuchi kept them to himself and radioed his estimated time of arrival at Buin. Unbeknownst to the lieutenant commander, no sooner had this message gone out than American intelligence set about decoding it. The information wended its way down the South Pacific Area chain of command and finally worked its way into the following order for the *England*'s skipper, Captain W. B. Pendleton: "On or about 1700, 18 May, get under way in company with USS *George* (DE 697) and USS *Raby* (DE 698). . . . Proceed to position 15°10′S and 158°10′E. Japanese submarine believed . . . to be approaching this point from the north and should arrive that area by about 1400, 20 May. Good hunting."

In the Pacific, it was devilishly difficult to make any contact at all with enemy submarines, so you can imagine our reaction to this order on board the *England*. Three months at sea without engaging a single enemy submarine, and now, at last, we were being handed a pair of coordinates!

More was to come. While the *England* was steaming toward this encounter with destiny, seven additional Japanese submarines—the greater part of the offensive strength of Japan's advance submarine force—were dispatched to a scouting line between Manus and Truk, to arrive there no later than May 21. Again, U.S. intelligence was on the ball, and soon the *England* received what must be one of the most exhilarating communications ever addressed to an antisubmarine group: "Line believed to run from position 02°00′N, 150°22′E southwest on a line of bearing 216 true. Subs thirty miles apart on line. Seek out—attack—and destroy. . . ." These were the words of Admiral William "Bull" Halsey, our fleet commander.

Having had endless training, the men of the *England* were confident in their abilities; they would soon be put to the test. As for me, the impending encounters carried immense weight. They would reveal whether I could think under pressure, and whether I could lead men in the fog of combat. The moment of truth had arrived, both for the *England* and for me personally.

This is the story of a man and a ship. It occurred to me some years ago that as time marches on, as the events that distinguished the *England* recede further and further into the past, if I don't tell this ship's full story now, there's a good chance no one ever will. After all, I was with the *England* from the time of her commissioning until the time she was finally laid to rest at the Philadelphia Navy Yard. We were together through thick and thin—submarine chases, kamikaze attacks, and hurricanes. I deposited her at Philadelphia in July 1945, much the worse for wear, but not until after she had won the Presidential Unit Citation, after she had inspired Admiral Ernest King, commander in chief of the U.S. Fleet, to promise, "There will always be an *England* in the United States Navy," and after she had made a better man of me.

In exploring my memories of that distant past, I quickly realized that it would be impossible to tell the whole story of the *England* without delving into my own background. How did a kid raised in Depression-era Alabama, whose parents were so poor that at one point he actually lived in a tent with a retractable roof, come at the ripe age of twenty-six to be the commanding officer of a destroyer escort in the Pacific war? It seems to me that the traits necessary for leadership make themselves known in childhood and that the manner of a person's upbringing has much to do with whether those traits are later put to good use. At any rate, as I look back on my life, I can't help but feel that the events of my Alabama childhood during the Depression, when money was tight and opportunities were limited, and the events of that whirlwind year of 1944 in the far waters of the Pacific were two ends of the same trajectory. One end illuminates the other, and the autobiographical element makes this into the story of a ship with a face.

———

Prior to writing this book, I went to Washington to do additional research. The Office of Naval History supplied copies of the logs of ships I served on, including the *England* and the USS *Livermore* (DD 429). There, I also obtained the war diaries that I wrote while on the *England*. It was a custom in those days to put secret combat information in a ship's war diary. I wrote all the war diaries for the *England* during the time I was with her. I was also able to get the logs from the USS *George,* whose division commander commanded the ships in our screening escort when the sub operation described in these pages took place. (There were no logs from the USS *Tustem,* the armed guard ship on which I served, nor were there any from the Sub-Chaser Training Center I attended. My memory had to supply information about what happened during those assignments.)

The Office of Naval History provided me with another, equally significant and invaluable source—translations of the Japanese logs from the commander of Submarine Squadron 7, whose subs the *England* engaged in combat, as well as translations of the orders to those vessels from the Japanese high command. In addition, I had the opportunity to read translations of other information related to the Japanese sub operations described here, translations pertaining to both the I-16 and the scouting line.

The logs were invaluable in helping me bring back to life the events of May 1944. Of course, it is impossible to re-create the perspective of the Japanese submariners who were our enemy. Whenever I try to present their thoughts, it is pure speculation on my part. In attempting to see through their eyes, it did help to have had the opportunity, during World War II, to do thorough tours of several American submarines. This allowed me to see the world from the unique vantage point of a submariner, which considerably lightened the task of envisioning the actions a Japanese submariner might take to avoid attack.

Though it is long overdue, I would like to express my appreciation for the training I received from three special mentors who inspired me to achieve to the best of my ability those many years ago. As assistant first lieutenant on the *Livermore,* I was tremendously helped by Lieutenant J. G. Boyd, who outlined my duties and taught me the nuts and bolts of how destroyers operated. Our outstanding executive officer, then–Lt. Commander E. F. McDaniel, was also invaluable to me. He answered my endless questions about the ship with tact and patience, and later, when he was skipper of the Sub-Chaser Training Center and I was working there, his leadership was inspirational. Last but not least, I would like to thank Admiral Reginald Kauffman, who helped me as much as any other officer in the navy and who saved me from a future that might have been drab had it not been for him.

ANTISUBMARINE
WARRIOR
in the PACIFIC

The USS *England*

The *England* was named for Ensign John Charles England of Alhambra, California, who died on December 7, 1941, attempting to save his ship-mates on the USS *Oklahoma* during the Japanese attack on Pearl Harbor. The *England*'s keel was laid April 4, 1943; the vessel was christened by Ensign England's mother on September 26, and was commissioned December 10.

1

From Sweet Home Alabama to the Navy

I WAS BORN ON THE FRIGID morning of February 5, 1918, in Brighton, Alabama. My parents, proud to have a baby boy, named me John Alexander Williamson after my father's father. Mama and Dad, an electrician, came from deeply devout, dyed-in-the-wool Southern Methodist families. Between them, they had seven relatives who had fought for the Confederacy during the Civil War.

In 1920, the year my sister Rebecca was born, we moved to Birmingham, Alabama. The elementary school nearest to our house was Hemphill. I was skipped from second to third grade, then third to fourth, and later from sixth to seventh. Though it may have pleased my parents to see their son ahead of the pack, it wasn't thrilling to be younger and smaller than my classmates. Maybe that's the reason I used to get into fights all the time. Two or three times a week, I would come to blows with another boy, something that made Mama hopping mad. The scrapes gave me plenty of opportunity to exercise my powers of persuasion. Every time Mama found out about yet another incident, I would say, "But Mama, I didn't *start* the fight; I was just protecting the Williamson reputation!" The appeal to family honor inevitably placated her.

During my youth in Birmingham I learned to take risks, or as Mama liked to say, "unnecessary chances." After I got my bike, I would pedal to speed and then stand on the bar between the seat and the handlebars, zooming along with my hands outstretched in glee. I used to play Tarzan in the trees with my cousins, swinging from limb to limb by hanging by my heels and letting go. Once, I tumbled to the ground and broke my right shoulder. Another time, I landed on my head and was unconscious for three hours. Poor Mama suffered as much as I did, but no amount of lecturing from her could stop me.

In my mind, it was only by courting danger—or rather, not being cowed by the prospect of danger—that a person ever got anywhere. Risks required confidence, decisiveness, energy, and determination. Later, those traits would stand me in good stead in the Pacific, when that ocean became the battleground between the Japanese Empire and the United States of America.

—*νν*—

All those fights I'd gotten into as a child didn't do a thing to build up my confidence about physical contact. When I started Ensley High School, I was a year and a half younger than my classmates and too much of a shrimp to make the football team, but I did play for area teams. I liked to play offensive center and defensive linebacker—that way I could run around a lot, hoping someone else would make the tackles first. It wasn't until the captain of my football team made me play right guard that I learned to hit and tackle with a vengeance. It gave me a great feeling of freedom and confidence to lose my fear of physical contact.

Socially timid, I avoided girls the first two years of high school. Come junior and senior year, however, I started attending Friday and Saturday night shindigs in their homes—closely chaperoned, of course—and discovered that I had rhythm. Mother, ever the staunch Southern Methodist, discouraged me from dancing, but there was nothing she could do to stop me once I had tasted the joys of this "sin against God."

I also discovered that I liked girls, and that to take them out—and to have any hope of making my way in the world—I needed money. Thus at the age of fourteen I became an entrepreneur of sorts. For years I had been cutting grass for neighbors with Dad's push lawn mower. Now I shelled out three dollars for a secondhand bicycle, fixed it up, and used it to start a paper route in Bush Hills. If everybody paid me who was supposed to, I made a dollar fifty a week—an appreciable sum during the Depression. It gave me a taste for the satisfaction that comes of self-reliance, and in coming years I would branch out to other jobs: selling popsicles, mopping floors in a cafeteria, and working in the parts department of a General Motors parts warehouse.

———

After my graduation from Ensley in 1935, Dad and I figured that between what I had saved from part-time jobs and what he was able to afford from his earnings as an electrician, I could enter Birmingham-Southern, a liberal arts college a few blocks from home, and I enrolled that fall. A math major with a minor in English, I had no idea what sort of career to pursue. By the time I graduated in 1939, however, I did have confidence. My jobs had taught me how to make decisions and stick to them. Though not every decision I made was the right one, decisiveness seemed much better for making your way in the world than procrastination.

In the spring of 1939, a gentleman came to speak at our school chapel program about world affairs. He said that armies were being amassed all over Europe and that the world was headed for an inevitable clash. No nation in history had built an army like the one Germany was building without the intention of using it, he pointed out. War was inevitable.

The July after graduating from Birmingham-Southern I began selling Chevrolets for Drennen Motor Company. There were seven other Chevrolet salesmen in our division, all much older. During my first month there each one of them came to me separately and said, "John, you're a young man with a college education, why don't you get into something worthwhile?" I didn't pay them much attention. I was making good money. I had a new car, girls to date, good friends, and a nice family.

Then in September, German forces invaded Poland, and in spring of 1940 they overran Norway, Denmark, the Low Countries, and France. It didn't take a political science major to figure out that Hitler wanted to rule all of Europe and that if he weren't defeated by France and England, the United States would become embroiled in war. After the fall of France, President Roosevelt pledged that the United States would become the "arsenal of democracy" and would supply the allies with the material resources to fight. For all practical purposes, the United States was now an ally in a full-scale war. What, I wondered, was I going to do? I had no taste for war. I didn't want to kill other men, and I certainly didn't want to be killed.

Still, I felt a sense of duty toward my country. When I told Mom and Dad that I might join one of the services, they didn't like it. I knew, though, that if I didn't join now I would have to eventually. Better now than later. So the question was, which branch of the service should I join—army, navy, air force, marines? Though I had never been to sea, I leaned toward the navy.

In April 1940, I drove to the naval air station in Pensacola, Florida, to find out if I could join the Navy Air Corps. I got an appointment to take a flight physical, which I failed because of less-than-perfect eyesight. Then in May, the navy announced its V-7 Program, which sent college graduates to sea for thirty days as apprentice seamen, followed by three months of training, and after which—if they made the cut—they were commissioned as ensigns in the U.S. Naval Reserve. That seemed like the ideal program for me. I could get my commission, go to sea for a year, and then apply to flight school as an officer.

In June, I decided to join, took the physical, and once again was met with disappointment. I was eight pounds underweight. In college I'd been on the track team, and after graduation, to keep in shape, I'd taken to visiting the YMCA five days a week on my lunch hour. At six foot two inches tall, I was a skinny 142 pounds. Thwarted by the results of my physical, I decided to limit the workouts to three days a week and started chowing down. Bananas, meat, potatoes, ice cream—anything I thought might fatten me up went into my mouth. In July, with nine extra pounds added on, I took the physical again and was accepted into the Navy V-7 program. I was a navy man and proud of it! Although my parents hated to see me leave, they knew that sooner or later I would probably have to go, and they accepted their loss with good grace.

And so in September 1940 I got on a train for New York, boarded the USS *Tuscaloosa,* a heavy cruiser anchored in the Hudson River, and along with several hundred others began a thirty-day stint as an apprentice seaman. The ship's officers and crew would judge which of us were of officer caliber.

A friend of mine who was in the same program, John Hamilton, rode with me on the train to New York. On the way we met a good-looking gal nicknamed Skeets. She had a neat figure and a walk that turned heads. We had a day and a half together on that train, long enough to become well-acquainted. Skeets told us she was a stripper in New York, and she had the courtesy to give us her work address. The night before we reported to the *Tuscaloosa,* John and I headed over to the nightclub to see her perform. Boy, could she gyrate! In the middle of her act we yelled out, "Hey, Skeets!" She stopped moving for a split second, gazed around, and upon spotting us yelled back, "Hey, Bama!" then continued with her act.

The next day we were issued clothing at the naval base in New York, and in undressed blues, with our seabags on our shoulders, we climbed the ladder to board the cruiser. What a thrill it was to sail out of New York Harbor—me, a young man who had traveled little and hadn't even seen an ocean until he was sixteen. In my eyes, the USS *Tuscaloosa,* a heavy 8-inch-gun cruiser, was a beauty.

After operating at sea for a few days we steamed to Norfolk, Virginia, and boarded the *Wichita,* because the *Tuscaloosa* was leaving on a secret mission. With so many V-7 enlistees, the *Wichita* was one crowded ship. We had to sleep in hammocks. The officers weren't sure what to do with us, so we were given tours of the ship and duty assignments that included scrubbing the bulkheads. By the time my thirty days were over, I had learned two things: I was very good at scrubbing bulkheads and I didn't want to make a career of it. But tedious as the scrubbing was, I loved every minute on board and didn't have a hint of seasickness. As my brush went back and forth and back and forth, I would think to myself, What a wonderful life to be an officer on board a cruiser! The thought of going to flight school evaporated. I now wanted to serve my country on a cruiser.

There were about eight hundred V-7 enlistees in the Norfolk area, and five hundred of us were recommended as officer candidates. Some made their way to New York Harbor, where the *Prairie State* served as a V-7 school. There was another V-7 school on the downtown campus of Northwestern University in Chicago. I was accepted for a class at Northwestern that was to begin in the middle of December.

That left me October and November to spend in Birmingham. When I returned home, as not only one of the first guys in my peer group to join the armed forces but as an officer candidate accepted into the V-7 program to boot, I was the envy of my friends. Although I continued to sell cars, my heart wasn't in it. I was at the top of my game—in the navy and ready to go!

In December, with mixed emotions, I caught the train to Chicago. I hated to leave family and friends, but I was headed for adventure. Classes started on December 16. Northwestern had built a new dormitory, Abbot Hall, to house the V-7 midshipmen. I drew my midshipmen uniforms and was assigned to a room with a young man named Bob Scurlock, an interesting, fairly quiet fellow. In those three months we would get to know each other well. We decided from the beginning that we were going to have to study hard if we wanted to earn a commission in three months. Our subjects were primarily navigation (piloting and celestial navigation), gunnery, seamanship, and training in how to be an officer and a gentleman in the U.S. Navy.

Our classes were held in a building about a mile from Abbot Hall. We had to march back and forth in the cold Chicago winter. Some days, with the cold wind blowing off Lake Michigan, we almost froze to death making that trek. We marched in platoons, led by a petty officer whose responsibility was to assume command and make sure we proceeded on our way in fine military fashion. After a few weeks my platoon petty officer was released and I was appointed to take his place. It was no big deal, but I was pleased about the recognition. We were constantly being evaluated to determine our capacity to be naval officers, and every little bit helped.

Almost every day, someone fell from the ranks. That was an inducement to keep studying hard. Because I'd majored in mathematics and had taken a considerable amount of physics in college, gunnery and navigation came fairly easily to me. After six weeks I found myself tutoring some of the other men. Seamanship was fun. At graduation in mid-March I would rank seventh out of a class of five hundred.

Midshipman school wasn't all hard work and study. We were allowed liberty from 1200 on Saturday until 1800 on Sunday night, and we made the best of those thirty hours of freedom. On our first Saturday afternoon off, several of us went to a theater downtown that featured a movie and a stage show. On this particular day, a French girl by the name of Simone Simone was the stage-show headliner. She sang several songs in her thick, melodious accent, and we all fell in love with her. "The Last Time I Saw Paris" was especially moving. It left us a bit choked up and readier than ever to take on the Germans. We would free Paris and escort Simone back to her romantic city.

Inspections were held Saturday morning. During the first inspection, an officer came around and told our group that there was a Y WCA a few blocks away. He told us that each Saturday night the Y WCA had a party and dance, and they would like some of the midshipmen to come over as their guests. Most of us turned up our noses at that suggestion. Who wanted to go to a Y WCA? We had too many exciting things to do in our precious thirty hours than to go visit a bunch of hags at the Y WCA! However, a few of the boys who had nothing better to do decided they would go. On Monday morning they gave glowing reports of how beautiful the girls were and how much fun they had had. The next Saturday night I humbled myself and went.

That night I met two stunning girls, one named Pat and the other Barbara. That stroke of luck put me in a quandary. I couldn't decide which girl to fall in love with. After a couple of Saturday nights I decided I was in love with Barbara. The better choice would have been Pat, because she loved me and Barbara did not. But it was hard to resist Barbara Hale, a nineteen-year-old brunette from Rockford, Illinois. She was in Chicago studying art and lived at the Y WCA. She was beautiful and fun to be with.

At least Barbara cared enough to go out with me on weekends. We would get together on Saturday afternoons, usually go the Y WCA party Saturday night, attend church on Sunday morning, and spend the afternoon together. Sometimes we would skip the Y WCA and join some other midshipmen and their dates at the College Inn in the Sherman Hotel, where we would have dinner and then dance the night away. On two or three occasions, when we were ready to go and I asked for the check, the waiter said, "Your check is already paid. Some of the guests here wanted to give you and your friends a nice dinner and some fun. They don't want you to know who they are." That warmed our hearts! Chicago, unlike Norfolk, was good to navy men. I wish we had known who our benefactors were so we could have shown our appreciation personally.

One bitterly cold night as we left the College Inn about two o'clock in the morning, the girls waited in the lobby while we went out front to hail a taxi. There was a guy out there who had had at least three too many drinks. He came up to us thinking we were doormen and said, "Hey, doormen, call me a cab." We replied, "Sir, we aren't doormen; we're naval officers." He shrugged and said, "Okay, then, call me a boat!"

Near the end of the midshipmen school I heard of a hotel on Lake Michigan where Wayne King was playing a short engagement. I bought tickets, and one Saturday night Barbara and I went there for dinner and dancing. Wayne King was hot—he had one of the finest orchestras in the United States and was wildly popular with young people. Barbara and I had a wonderful time that night. As the evening closed, they turned the lights down low and we danced up close to the bandstand to the soft, romantic music. Seeing that I was a midshipman, Wayne leaned over to me and said, "I'm doing my best for you now, because after you leave here, it's up to you."

The three months at midshipmen school passed quickly. We were to get our duty assignments at graduation. My roommate Bob Scurlock's father was a navy admiral, and he had written Bob to suggest that he request a destroyer. "You'll learn more on a destroyer in six months than you will on a battleship or a cruiser in two years," he wrote. Although I had decided to request a cruiser, I thought maybe he was right. Those trim, deadly destroyers did appeal to me. With that advice to go by, Bob and I requested destroyers. In March 1941 we graduated and were commissioned ensigns in the U.S. Naval Reserve. Oh, happy day! I was even happier when I got my orders—to the USS *Livermore* (DD 429), a new destroyer.

There was only one problem: leaving Chicago meant separation from Barbara. I was deeply in love with her, even if she didn't return my love. Would I come back alive? And if so, would it be to Barbara? As the train moved out, I waved good-bye, hoping my view of her through the window wouldn't be the last.

2

Gearing Up for War

THE LIVERMORE WAS ONE OF the navy's newest destroyers. Built at Bath Shipyards in Maine and commissioned on 7 October 1940, she was a broken-deck, two-stack, 1,630-ton destroyer, one of the most beautiful destroyers the navy ever built. When I reported to her in the Norfolk Navy Yard on March 29, however, I was a bit disappointed. In the yard for restricted availability and upkeep, the *Livermore* was covered with hoses and lines and had workmen crawling all over her.

The *Livermore* carried five 5-inch 38-caliber semiautomatic guns, a number of 50-caliber machine guns, and a single-mount torpedo tube holding five torpedoes. In addition, she had two racks of six-hundred-pound depth charges on the stern and a Y-gun that would throw two three-hundred-pound depth charges about 150 yards on each side of the ship.

She was the division leader for Destroyer Division 21, under Commander Broadfoot, Naval Academy class of 1919. The *Livermore*'s commanding officer was Lieutenant Commander Vernon Huber, Naval Academy class of 1921, and her able executive officer was Lieutenant Commander E. F. McDaniel, class of 1927.

Our chief engineer was Lieutenant A. Gustov Beckman, Naval Academy class of 1931. Gus was from St. Louis, Missouri. He was a confirmed bachelor and about as fat as you could be without getting cashiered out of the navy. He said if he could find a woman who liked dogs enough, he might consider tying the knot. The biggest day of Gus's life was when the Sears and Roebuck catalog came. He would sit in the wardroom for hours at a time browsing through the catalog, ordering everything that a bachelor needed, from vitamin A pills to long underwear.

The ship's first lieutenant was Lieutenant Junior Grade Jake Boyd. I was assistant first lieutenant and torpedo and depth-charge officer, with a battle station on the torpedo tube.

My first two weeks were hectic. Time and time again, I combed the ship from stem to stern to learn all I could about her, about how to handle depth charges and torpedoes, about the division, about the people, and about the navy in general. The officers and petty officers tired of my constant questions, but they were helpful as I proceeded on my crash course.

The United States had agreed to give Great Britain a number of old four-stack destroyers on a lend-lease basis in exchange for naval bases in several places, including Bermuda. Upon departing Norfolk Navy Yard, the *Livermore*'s first assignment was to head to Bermuda to help open a naval base there. We got under way on April 6. Cape Hatteras, just outside the Chesapeake Bay, is infamous for storms, and when we passed the sea buoy there I realized that unless something changed, this passage was going to be a rough one. The storm, fierce even by navy standards, raged all the way to Bermuda. So much for my dreams of an exciting navy career. For three solid days I was seasick, and for three solid days I wanted out of the navy— oh, solid land! How could I fight a war—how could I man the torpedo tubes?—feeling like this? Sick or not, I still had to stand my watches and perform my duty.

And then on April 8 we pulled into Bermuda. Soft white clouds scudded across a brilliant blue sky. The seawater shimmered in the morning sun, a dancing kaleidoscope of blue, turquoise, and green, and a green carpet covered hillsides dotted with colorfully painted homes. This must be the most magical place on earth, I thought, hoping our stay would last. After the wretched passage, I could hardly wait to go ashore.

We anchored off Catherine's Point in Hamilton Harbor. As soon as I stepped ashore I saw that Bermuda's beauty was more than skin deep. Up close, the architecture was enthrallingly quaint, and flowers grew in lush abundance throughout the island. And everything was so clean! In those days no automobiles were allowed, so wherever you went you walked, rode a bicycle, or took a horse-drawn taxi.

Although the war affected Bermuda, it was not evident except for the navy ships in the harbor. Since we were not at war, three-quarters of our officers and crew could go on liberty at a time. I had a watch only one night in four. Someone told an officer on the ship about the Belmont Hotel, located on a hill across the bay from the town of Hamilton. This became our headquarters and watering hole. The view from the Belmont's terrace, which overlooked the bay, was breathtaking. There was no place at the dock for the *Livermore*, so we had to anchor and come in by boat. The officers from our ship and from the USS *Kearney*, our sister ship, would go ashore together or meet ashore and head for the Belmont, which had a great bar, excellent dining facilities, and a jovial atmosphere. The last boat ran late enough for any sober individual to make it back in time. Anyone who missed that boat caught the milk boat as it came in the next morning at 0600.

The Waterfront, the main street in Bermuda, boasted a number of intriguing British stores. Good perfume was inexpensive, and all of us bought perfume to take back to our girlfriends, wives, or mothers. One afternoon an officer bought a bottle of Khus-Khus (pronounced *kush-kush*), a famous West Indian fragrance. He was so delighted with his purchase, and so tipsy, that when he got back to the ship he took half of the bottle of Khus-Khus and sprinkled it on Chief Engineer Gus Beckman's bunk. Gus aired his bedding for five whole days trying to get rid of the smell of that perfume. Finally he gave up and got his hands on another mattress.

Bermuda at that time was very Victorian. I found later after visiting more British islands that the farther away people got from England, the more Victorian they became. That suited me just fine, for the Bermudans were charming people.

—◊◊◊—

Only a week later, on April 15, we were ordered to return to Norfolk. Such a short time in paradise! We departed Bermuda with the *Tuscaloosa* and the *Wichita*, both 8-inch-gun cruisers. During the trip back to Norfolk, our duty was to be the antisubmarine screen for these two ships. En route we conducted various training exercises, including simulated torpedo attacks on cruisers.

In late April and early May we operated between Norfolk and Newport, Rhode Island, with several destroyers and cruisers, and sometimes with the destroyer *Ross* (DD 563) and the carrier *Ranger*. The days passed with more training exercises and with all kinds of drills, such as man overboard and damage control. I seized every opportunity to learn, soaking up all I could about the *Livermore* and the various duties we would be required to perform.

Then—hallelujah!—we got orders to return to Bermuda in company with the *Kearney;* the *Quincy,* an 8-inch-gun cruiser; and the *Wasp,* an aircraft carrier. The purpose of going back was to begin so-called neutrality patrols. The patrols varied. On one we would sail with an aircraft carrier and two destroyers, conducting exercises and training for two weeks. On the next we would sail with a light cruiser and two destroyers. This gave us experience with sundry ship operations and various types of formation steaming.

Fortunately, I hadn't suffered any more bouts of seasickness. Every minute at sea was a joy to me. Each time we rattled the anchor chain in port, I was ready to go! Our patrol would proceed from Bermuda to within twenty miles of the coast of Africa, continue northwest to within twenty miles of the Azores, and then head back to Bermuda. As a new officer on board, I had been standing junior-officer-of-the-deck watches, but now I qualified for officer of the deck in port, and I anxiously awaited the opportunity to stand top watch.

Jake Boyd, a good first lieutenant and an able division officer, was also an outstanding mentor. He knew so much about the *Livermore* and was invaluable to me in my quest for knowledge. I learned much about leadership from him, as well as from Lieutenant Commander McDaniel, our exec. As I learned to trust each of our officers and crew members, I knew that if we ever found ourselves in combat—and as time went on, this seemed more likely—I could count on them. I hoped that they could count on me, too.

I was proud of the *Livermore* and liked my fellow officers, the crew of the ship, and the many petty officers who did so much to educate me. There was one thing that didn't appeal to me, however, and that was profanity. Everyone has heard the expression "curse like a sailor." Jake Boyd, the first lieutenant, didn't like it any more than I did. Every time we heard someone spouting off we suggested that he cut out the foul language, and he would—at least while around us! But neither Boyd nor I tried to civilize our chief boatswain's mate, Henry. Henry, who had been in the navy for thirty years and was set in his ways, could use foul language and make it sound like a Sunday school lesson.

Now that I'd learned so much about seamanship, I felt more and more at ease when we got under way. I also learned to appreciate the beauty all around me. At sea no two days are ever alike. Water, waves, wind velocity, humidity, sky and clouds, sun and moon—all these variables are like chips of glass in a kaleidoscope, jumbled together to make each day unique. Days and nights go on one after another seemingly without end, ever changing. At times the sea was so calm that I could see the canopy of heaven reflected in the ocean, and each star shone distinctly. Other times, the sea was so rough that the ship would be pitching and rolling, and I would be awestruck by the power of wind and waves. (If the sea's mighty power could be harnessed, humans would never lack for energy!) My favorite type of day was when clouds scudded across a blue sky and whitecaps skittered across the water's surface. I'll never tire of going to sea, I often thought. Later on I would learn to endure fighting, but I would never like it. My love for the sea has never ceased.

A sailor could become absorbed in the sea life all around. Against the vast backdrop of the sky, the horizon a fine line, I would spot porpoises and flying fish. During this period of the neutrality patrols we cruised with running lights on and lights on deck, and it was not unusual to find several flying fish on deck in the morning. At night they would jump toward the lights and crash into the bulkhead. Breakfast often consisted of flying fish. The porpoises loved to sport around the ship, groups of eight or ten of them diving in and out of the water. Sometimes we'd be steaming at 15 or 20 knots and there would be a porpoise directly in front of the bow, staying just ahead of the ship. What wonderful, playful creatures!

It was not unusual for the mid-Atlantic to be buried in fog. On one occasion it was so dense we could barely see the ship's stern from the bridge, and it was impossible to see a ship more than three hundred yards away. Since none of the ships at that time had radar, international maritime rules required that each ship give a prolonged whistle every minute to prevent collisions. The "position buoy" also helped. This was a simple mechanism, a piece of wood ten to twelve feet long with fins. The fins guided a metal device that shot a spout of water up twelve or so feet into the air. The carrier—the lead ship in the formation—would tow this object a thousand yards astern, and the following destroyer would position her bow just alongside the buoy. The destroyer in turn would pull a buoy three hundred yards astern so that the following destroyer could position herself, and so on down the line.

One densely foggy day, the carrier bellowed out two blasts, indicating that she had stopped. The destroyer ahead of us also came to a halt and gave two blasts. We were the third in line, and so we halted and signaled with two blasts. However, the ship on our starboard bow still gave one blast, signaling that she was proceeding ahead. Suddenly we heard three blasts from the carrier, indicating that she was going full speed astern. The destroyer ahead of us gave three blasts on her whistle and backed down full speed. The only thing we could do was back down full speed to starboard. The destroyer ahead of us came backing down full speed to port, and the carrier passed between the two of us, also backing full speed. That was the closest I ever came to a collision at sea. The carrier had been forced to back down, so she thought, to avoid collision with the ship on our starboard bow that had given that single whistle.

You might think backing down at sea is no big deal, and normally it wouldn't be. However, on this occasion we were concerned and scared. Relatively speaking, a carrier is a huge monster, several times larger than any destroyer.

When a carrier ahead gives an indication of full speed astern, backing down on three little destroyers, and you can't see where she is in a dense fog, you need to be vitally concerned. On our destroyer we *were* concerned! I'm sure the officers on the bridge of the other two destroyers felt the same way.

When the carrier gave three blasts on her whistle to indicate she was backing down full speed, all three destroyers gave three blasts and backed down—hoping against hope that they would not see that carrier coming down on them out of the dense fog.

Fortunately all ships escaped harm.

If a ship backed down with a position buoy in place, there was a danger that the buoy would get tied up in the screws as the hull backed over it. This time, for some lucky reason, this didn't happen to any of the ships in the formation. After the ship on our starboard bow had passed ahead of the carrier, we were able to proceed as usual. I must admit I was a little nervous after this incident, and Captain Huber was jumpy for the next two days.

———~~~———

From the newspapers, it was obvious that the United States was gearing up for war. Though our stance was officially one of neutrality, as the "arsenal of democracy" we were already furnishing the Allies with ships, planes, tanks, guns, and other war matériel. And we were mobilizing our armed forces at every turn. With the draft instituted in the latter part of 1940, the services were building manpower as rapidly as training facilities would permit. New ships were coming off the lines, new airplanes were being built at a steady pace, and the newest and best tanks were being churned out by former automobile manufacturers. Before long, our neutrality patrols would be combat patrols.

My romance with Barbara began to cool. I wrote her regularly for a while, and for every two letters that went out, only one came back. She informed me she had been at the bus station in Chicago, about to go home for the weekend, when a couple approached her. They were talent scouts for a Hollywood studio, and they wanted her to take a screen test. Did she harbor dreams of becoming a starlet? Two weeks later, I got another letter from Barbara saying they had given her the screen test and were offering her $150 a week to go to Hollywood as a "potential starlet." She wanted to know what I thought. As an ensign I was only making $144 a month; $150 a week sounded really tempting. I wrote her and told her regardless of what advice I might give, she would probably take the offer. The prospects of a future together were dimming. "I hope we see each other again one day," I wrote wistfully.

So Barbara was whisked away to Hollywood. Though I longed for her, it didn't keep me from dating in Bermuda. One night at the Belmont, I spotted two navy nurses at a table alone. We got to chatting and I asked if I could buy them a drink. The next night I had a date with one of them, and again a few nights later. After that second date, as we were saying goodnight, we began to kiss each other with warmth and emotion.

"You're pretty good at this, Jill," I said. "We ought to see each other more often."

"I'd like to see you, too," she remarked, "but I'm not sure my husband would go for it."

"Your husband! You aren't wearing a ring—why didn't you tell me you were married?"

"Well," she said, "my friend and I are stuck here in Bermuda, our husbands are far away, and we're tired of staying at home by ourselves. So we decided to take off our rings and go out for dinner the night you met us. Now I'm concerned that we might get to liking each other too much, and that wouldn't be fair to you, me, or my husband."

That was the end of that. She was an attractive girl and we were both lonesome, but I agreed that we shouldn't go out anymore. Our hormones might get the better of us.

Another night at the Belmont, while I was sitting on the terrace with some fellow officers, a crowd of men in uniform collected around the bar. We sent Max Burns, our scouting officer, to see what all the excitement was about. Some thirty or forty minutes later, Max, who had a way with women, came back with one of the most beautiful girls I'd ever seen in my life. It turned out she was a French-Egyptian who had been living in Cairo, where she'd met some wealthy British businessman at a cocktail party. He was much older—fifty-five years to her twenty-one—and quite susceptible to her charms. He told her that if she would marry him he would go back to England and change his will, leaving her half of his estate and leaving his family the other half. He planned to divorce his wife so he and the new beauty could live together in Bermuda. The girl, who had been raised in Egypt under rather straitened circumstances, jumped at the proposal. The Brit gave her spending money, bought her clothes, and put her on a ship to Bermuda, where she arrived safe and sound to await his arrival.

Her fiancé did as he promised. He went back to England, changed his will, divorced his wife, and caught a ship for Bermuda. But the prospect of the enchanted life that lay in store for him proved to be too much—he had a heart attack en route. So there she was in Bermuda, a French-Egyptian girl who was beautiful and now rich. Max had several dates with her, for which he was greatly envied by the rest of us.

———

Around this time, the navy, having determined that personnel on small ships had little chance to exercise, hired Gene Tunney, a well-known boxer, as a physical fitness officer. One of his innovations was the Gene Tunney Exerciser for shipboard use. This could be used just about anyplace on the ship. It consisted of a bulkhead-mounted bracket with foot straps and handgrips. When you put your feet in the straps and pulled down on the grips, it would raise your feet. If you did this exercise two hundred or three hundred times a day, so it was said, you'd stay in decent shape.

Our tubby chief engineer, Gus Beckman, was coming up for his physical and decided he'd better shed some pounds. Rather than the recommended number of pulls on the exerciser, he did five hundred or six hundred a day. Over a period of weeks this turned his lard into muscle and gave him more of an appetite than ever. Finally the day arrived for his physical. He went over to the doctor on the *Kearney*. When he came back he was furious. He stormed into the gunnery-handling room where the Gene Tunney Exerciser was and got ready to yank it off the bulkhead.

"Chief, what are you doing?" said one of the officers.
"I'm taking this damn thing down," he replied. "It's no good."
"What are you so angry about?" I said, as soon as we'd calmed him down.
He said, "Since I've been using this damn thing I've gained twelve pounds!"

Though we managed to salvage the exerciser, Gus never went near it again.

Since we were on the brink of war and the navy could ill afford to lose qualified Naval Academy graduates, Gus was allowed to pass his physical. We were delighted because we liked the guy, and he was a good chief engineer.

'Though war was looming, we still steamed at night with our lights on. Whether we were with the carrier or the cruiser, the *Livermore's* usual position was on the starboard or port bow, in an antisubmarine screening station. In the daytime we would use our echo-ranging equipment to detect submarines and at night we would listen. In listening mode, our sound gear was so ineffective that if we were going over 10 knots we couldn't detect a submarine unless it was proceeding at a high speed and was very close to us.

—⁓—

On May 20, after another wonderful week's layover in Bermuda, we got under way with the carrier *Wasp,* the cruiser *Quincy,* and another destroyer. Little did we know that our neutrality patrols were now a thing of the past.

At 1930 on May 22 a reconnaissance aircraft off Bergen, Norway, noted that the giant German battleship *Bismarck* had sailed on her maiden voyage with the *Prince Eugene,* an 8-inch-gun German cruiser. It would be a huge boon were the Royal Navy to sink Hitler's new battleship, and her majesty's fleet set out to do just that. At this time HMS *Hood* and HMS *Prince of Wales* happened to be at sea, south of Iceland.

Between 2200 and 2300 on the twenty-second, a British battle group sailed from Scapa Flow in northern Scotland. The group included the *King George V,* which carried the flag of the commander in chief of the home fleet, the carrier *Victorious,* seven cruisers, and seven destroyers. In the meantime the *Bismarck* and the *Prince Eugene* had sailed around northern Iceland, come through the Denmark Strait, and encountered the *Hood* and the *Prince of Wales.* A few salvos from the *Bismarck* sank the *Hood,* and the *Prince of Wales* came away from the encounter damaged.

At around 2400 on May 24, planes from the *Victorious* attacked the *Bismarck* and claimed to have scored one torpedo hit. At 0306 on the twenty-fifth, the British fleet lost all contact with the *Bismarck.* For thirty-one hours and twenty-four minutes the German ship was nowhere to be seen. The British high command wanted to prevent the ship from entering a French port or returning to Bergen.

Contact was regained on the twenty-sixth, at which time we received the shock of our lives. The commander in chief of the Atlantic Fleet sent our task force top-secret orders to attack and to try to sink the *Bismarck* if we ran into her. We were also to report her position. Our task force was quite a ways from the position where the *Bismarck* was lost—several hundred miles south—so we changed course and headed north in search of the elusive ship.

It was a tall order. The *Bismarck*, with her 15-inch guns and their range of thirty thousand yards, had the ability to sink our cruiser and two destroyers, and maybe even our carrier. Our orders were to attack with torpedoes in an effort to divert fire from the *Quincy* while she got in close enough to train her 8-inch guns on the *Bismarck*. The range would have been between six thousand and eight thousand yards. We knew our torpedoes didn't have much of a chance against the *Bismarck* unless we could get within four thousand yards. Though we were unaware of it at the time, the German ship, unlike ours, had not only radar but also fire-control radar. A formidable would-be foe! As we turned north into the fray, our feelings were ambivalent.

Had we actually met and attacked the *Bismarck*, it would have been the first naval battle between Germany and the United States—and it would have been the spark that started war between us. It's tempting to ponder the consequences, had the United States declared war in May 1941 instead of later that year, in December, after the Japanese attacked Pearl Harbor. Surely Japan would have joined Germany had we declared war on that country, or had Germany declared war on us. Our battleships would not have been lying idle at Pearl Harbor on December 7, and the Japanese attack there would probably have been prevented.

Fortunately or unfortunately for us, the *Bismarck* was found again at 48°N 16°W, apparently heading for the coast of France. On May 26, torpedo planes from the carrier *Ark Royal* attacked her and claimed one hit amidships and possibly one torpedo hit on her starboard quarter. The next day, between 0122 and 0141, destroyers attacked the *Bismarck* with torpedoes and claimed two hits.

An overwhelming British force was now in contact with the *Bismarck*, including the battle cruisers *Rodney*, the battleship *King George V*, the carrier *Victorious*, and seven destroyers and cruisers that had left Scapa Flow on May 22. On the twenty-seventh, the *Rodney* and the *King George V* opened fire on the *Bismarck* with their 15- and 16-inch guns at ranges as close as four thousand yards. The only reason they could get that close is that the *Bismarck's* big guns had been damaged and she couldn't fire back. This let the British ships get into far closer range than they otherwise would have been able to. Several hundred rounds later, and with additional fire from the destroyers and cruisers, the *Bismarck*, though limping, was still afloat.

With the *Bismarck* badly damaged, the *Rodney* and the *King George V,* low on fuel, headed back to England. The *Dorchester,* a heavy cruiser, was ordered to sink the German ship with her torpedoes. She fired one on the starboard side and one on the port side, and at 1039 on the twenty-seventh, the *Bismarck* finally disappeared below the waves. The British picked up the few survivors.

The saga of the *Bismarck* is a remarkable story of a ship that fought to the death with amazing courage and seamanship. Hardly any other battleship in the world could have matched her record against the massive array of forces that confronted her on that fateful day of May 27.

We heard the news of the sinking and proceeded on our normal patrol, arriving back in Bermuda in early June.

———

New destroyers like the *Livermore* were equipped with 5-inch guns for antiaircraft fire and two sound gears and depth charges for antisubmarine operations. Our 5-inch 38s were not only effective antiaircraft weapons, they were also effective against ships and as fire support for troops ashore.

Since I had been on board, we had not used our sound gear to practice with a live submarine. The only training we received for antisubmarine warfare and echo-ranging with our sound gear was on other surface ships. Occasionally we would use another destroyer as a substitute submarine. At that time we didn't have a way to figure range rate, but we did have Doppler. Using Doppler, we could tell if the "submarine" was coming toward us or heading away. And by the change in bearing rate, we could tell whether it was moving to the right or the left.

Since we had no idea of the depth of a submarine, a depth-charge attack would probably be ineffective. Depth charges could be set to detonate at any depth from thirty to six hundred feet. If a submarine were at two hundred feet and depth charges exploded at four hundred feet, it might shake the occupants up a bit but it wouldn't do much damage. It would have been possible to pass over the submarine and get a reading on the ship's Fathometer, but I don't believe that had occurred to anyone. (Later, of course, we discovered this and were then able to find the depth of the submarine accurately.) We couldn't get an accurate range rate on the submarine, either, and because of this we couldn't tell whether we were close to a submarine in a lateral area. Under these circumstances, a submarine probably had a better chance of escaping us than we did of sinking it.

One antisubmarine warfare procedure we practiced was the so-called depth-charge baker attack. This attack didn't utilize sound gear; rather, it was based on the premise that a submarine periscope had been sighted. Two destroyers were involved. One destroyer would attack an imaginary submarine. The other destroyer would fire a shell from her 5-inch gun within 45 degrees of the attacker's bow from two thousand to three thousand yards away. The location of the splash marked the imaginary periscope sighting. The attacking ship would speed toward that point and simulate dropping depth charges in a semi-elliptical pattern in the area where the submarine could be, assuming the submarine was traveling at speeds of 3 to 6 knots.

Depth-charge baker attacks were practically futile for us. Since we had sound gear, we could probably pick up contact on the submarine prior to the time depth charges were dropped. Rather than guessing where the submarine might be on this curve of 3 to 6 knots, we could make a much more accurate attack using our sound gear to echo-range. For other ships, many of which still had no sound gear, the depth-charge baker attack was their best bet against subs.

At night, I later found out, submarines would often attack by firing torpedoes from a surface position. To get an accurate target angle, ship course, and speed, the sub would have to show its periscope. The chances of sighting a submarine periscope in daylight were greater than the chances of making contact by sound gear, especially if you had good lookouts. Oftentimes, water conditions were so bad you could not pick up a sub using sound gear within six hundred yards. If you were echo-ranging under good water conditions, you might pick up contact as far away as two thousand yards.

Even with sound gear, then, we weren't an effective antisubmarine weapon. An aggressive submarine skipper might have a better chance of sinking a destroyer than the destroyer would have sinking a submarine. However, most submarine skippers were more anxious to escape depth-charge attacks than to sink destroyers. Few submarines were aggressive enough to attack a destroyer while being attacked by one.

—∿∿∿—

As the beautiful days of summer passed, so did the busy but quiet days on neutrality patrol and the dreamlike spells in Bermuda. August gave way to September, and September changed our lives.

The summer of 1941 had been disastrous for the Allies and for the United States, which was still officially neutral but gearing up for war. The United States was shipping planes, tanks, ships, and guns across the Atlantic at an ever-increasing rate. The Germans knew that winning the war depended on stopping ships laden with matériel from reaching Britain. German submarines in the North Atlantic, operating in coordinated attack groups called wolf packs, were becoming more aggressive and more effective at sinking Allied ships. Most of the shipping went across in convoys protected by British and Canadian destroyers and corvettes, and many of these merchant ships were going down. The British and Canadians had far too few vessels to properly protect transatlantic convoys. It was not unusual for a slow convoy to start out with forty ships from Halifax, Nova Scotia, and straggle into England with only ten or fifteen left. During the summer of 1941, the Germans sank 10 percent of the ships that crossed the North Atlantic.

The Germans had so many submarines in the North Atlantic that no convoy was safe. Too few escorts were available. It was very frustrating for the officers and men on the escorts to know that the protection they gave the convoys wasn't adequate.

President Roosevelt and the U.S. high command knew that the United States could not build planes, tanks, ships, and guns fast enough to achieve an aggressive counterattack against the Germans unless something was done about the submarine threat in the North Atlantic. The United States had established a so-called sphere of influence in the Atlantic. A line was drawn from the southern tip of Greenland southeast to within four hundred miles of England, then straight south. It included most of the North Atlantic. Within this area the United States claimed the right to engage in commercial shipping and to use her military ships for peaceful missions and self-defense, including matériel transport to the Allies.

In the summer of 1941, Germany began infringing on America's right to use the seas freely. Among several other acts of aggression, a U.S. merchant ship, the *Robin Moor,* was sunk by a Nazi submarine in the South Atlantic in violation of international law. Then on September 4, one of Hitler's U-boats attacked a U.S. destroyer conducting a peaceful mission within America's sphere of influence in the North Atlantic. On that day, the USS *Greer,* carrying mail to Iceland and flying the U.S. flag, was torpedoed in full daylight and without warning. She sank almost immediately.

On September 11, in response to this event, President Roosevelt gave an impassioned radio address to the American people. He detailed the several acts of German aggression against ships flying U.S. flags in the Atlantic and the Red Sea and then explained to an American public, some of which was still reluctant to go to war, that

these acts of international lawlessness are a manifestation of . . . a Nazi design to abolish the freedom of the seas and to acquire absolute control . . . of the seas for themselves. . . .

[W]hen you see a rattlesnake poised to strike, you do not wait until he has struck you before you crush him.

These Nazi submarines and raiders are the rattlesnakes of the Atlantic. They are a menace to the free pathways of the high seas. They are a challenge to our own sovereignty. They hammer at our most precious rights when they attack ships of the American flag—symbol of our independence, our freedom, our very life.

Upon our naval and air patrol, now operating in large numbers over a vast expanse of the Atlantic Ocean, falls the duty of maintaining the American policy of freedom of the seas—now. That means, very simply, very clearly, that our patrolling vessels and planes will protect all merchant ships—not only American ships but ships of any flag—engaged in commerce in our defensive waters. They will protect them from submarines; they will protect them from surface raiders.

[L]et this warning be clear. From now on, if German or Italian vessels of war enter the waters the protection of which is necessary for American defense, they do so at their own peril.

The orders which I have given as Commander-in-Chief of the United States Army and Navy are to carry out that policy at once.

Ships convoying war supplies to the United Kingdom were declared to be ships of commerce, and they would be protected in the delineated sphere of interest. That very day of September 11, even before President Roosevelt gave this famous speech, the *Livermore* and the *Kearney* received an urgent, top-secret dispatch to proceed to the North Atlantic and begin convoy duty between Halifax and England. Twenty-seven other U.S. destroyers received a similar message.

At 0759 on that fateful day of 11 September 1941, we got under way from Bermuda and headed north with our sister ship. Our orders were to proceed to Placentia Bay, Newfoundland, and await further word. Though it was undeclared, we were at war.

3

North Atlantic Convoys

OUR ORDERS SAID THAT WITH or without a convoy, we were to attack any submarine we encountered in the U.S. sphere of influence. Of course, only German submarines patrolled that area. None of us on the *Livermore* had experienced shooting to kill, nor had any of us ever been shot at. We came to recognize, however, that war was the business of killing. You took the most destructive weapons you could find and used them to bring the enemy to his knees, making him surrender unconditionally so you could impose your will on him rather than let him impose his will on you.

Like our politicians and our high command, we knew that somehow, someway, we had to defeat Hitler. We just didn't know it would start so soon. Yes, we were ready and anxious to sink German submarines, but we headed north with mixed emotions.

Exactly what sort of warfare was it that we would be waging? The Germans had the benefit in the Atlantic (a much smaller ocean than the Pacific) of going after concentrated areas of commerce. Although German submarines eventually operated throughout the Atlantic, they concentrated in the north, where the main arms supply routes between the United States and Britain were, and along the U.S. East Coast. Slower ships, usually those that traveled less than 12 knots, proceeded along well-defined convoy routes across the North Atlantic—sitting ducks for German U-boats. The shortest route to England from the United States was the Great Circle Route, which is what convoys usually traveled. And then there were numerous commercial ships traveling along the U.S. coast; later, after war was declared, the Germans would concentrate submarines along the coast and sink hundreds of American ships.

To disrupt convoy lines across the North Atlantic, the Germans stationed a scouting line of submarines running southeast from the southeastern tip of Greenland. When a convoy headed for Britain passed this line, the convoy's disposition and speed were broadcast to other submarines scattered along the convoy routes ahead. German wolf packs traveling in groups of two or more would try to home in on the slower convoys, picking off their ships sometimes by day but mostly by night. (German aircraft would also attack convoys headed for the Soviet Union.)

Convoys usually ranged in size from thirty to sixty ships. Protecting a convoy of forty ships would require approximately eight escorts. At this stage in the war, because of a shortage of escorts, most convoys had a maximum of only five, either destroyers or corvettes. In time, the United States would build hundreds of destroyers, destroyer escorts, and sub-chasers to better protect the convoys from submarine and air attack. Once we had enough escorts to protect our convoys, the navy then organized "hunter-killer" groups to seek out and destroy enemy submarines. These groups enjoyed a high success rate because German submarines were under orders to surface and report by radio at regular intervals to the German high command. By the middle of 1943 the United States and Britain were using radio-direction-detection devices to locate U-boats as they broke radio silence to make their routine reports. By crossing the results from two or three separate direction-detection devices, the location of a submarine could be pinpointed and hunter-killer groups could be guided to that area. This would eventually break the back of German submarine warfare.

In conducting their warfare, both submarines and surface ships depended on sound detection, or sonar. At the time there were two technologies for doing this: listening devices and active gear. Listening devices (rudimentary by today's standards) allowed a ship or submarine to determine an enemy vessel's location. For example, by the sound of propeller noise a submarine could often determine what kind of surface ship it faced. A submarine running silently at 3 knots or lying on the ocean bottom could sometimes hear a propeller thousands of yards away. After tracking the sound for a few minutes, it could determine the approximate course and speed of the target. Usually, a periscope was used to confirm enemy course and speed and to identify ship type.

Surface ships and submarines also made use of active gear that produced a subsonic ping. When used as a listening device, sonar was silent, but when it was used actively and produced a ping, it could be heard by other surface ships if they had the same or close to the same frequency. The ping could also be heard by submarines. This technology had been invented in the 1930s by the British and was being installed in U.S. ships by 1939. The ping could be emitted manually, at irregular intervals, or set to ping at regular intervals by the sound operator. The sound would travel through the water at certain speeds; when it hit an underwater target, it would bounce back to the sending vessel. Since the speed of sound through water was known, it was easy to determine the range to target by determining the time between the ping and the echo. The subsonic ping was translated into a sonic sound heard through a speaker in the submarine control room or in the surface ship's antisubmarine battle station.

During World War II, although listening devices were valuable to submarines, they were almost worthless to surface ships proceeding at speeds over 3 knots. Most surface ships relied on echo-ranging or pinging to find submarines.

The distance at which an antisubmarine vessel could detect submarines using sound gear varied widely. You could gain sound contact at a maximum of about 2,500 yards if you knew there was a submarine present and if water conditions were good. In some areas water conditions were poor, particularly where freshwater flowed into saltwater, such as around Trinidad. In these areas you were lucky to get a sound contact at five hundred yards. Water temperature varies according to depth and usually occurs in layers. Temperature gradients often made it difficult to detect a submarine because the ping would bounce off a layer of water back toward the surface. Destroyers and destroyer escorts had on board a temperature-measuring device called a bathythermograph, which indicated the temperature at various layers and gave some idea of whether a submarine could be detected close by or at great distances. In some areas, a submarine could not even be detected at four hundred yards. By measuring the temperature of the water and the various gradients, submarines could hide under a layer to avoid detection.

Because surface ships traveled at speeds of 10 to 15 knots, listening technology was highly ineffective, so they would ping instead. Most ships had only one sound gear. Their submarine search would usually be a beam-to-beam search. The sound gear would be trained to the starboard or port beam, 90 degrees from the bow, and a search would begin by sweeping forward in 5-degree increments. Once the bow was reached, the sound gear would sweep to the other beam, 90 degrees to port or starboard, and again proceed in 5-degree increments.

For the few ships with two sound gears, both sides could be searched simultaneously. Destroyers built between 1939 and 1941 had two sets of sound gear on board. The sound gear was located in a dome that was lowered from the bottom of the ship so that it could send pings and receive echoes, which were then transported to the speaker. The sound gear operator would normally sit in a room adjacent to the bridge and operate the system from there.

When an antisubmarine vessel contacted a submarine, the normal approach was to head for the target and control the pinging intervals as you approached, decreasing them in order to receive more rapid echoes from the target. This way you could acquire more accurate information. Sometimes, as the range closed, the echo and the ping would be only seconds apart.

During the early part of World War II, and for many years prior to that, the primary antisubmarine weapon was the depth charge. The depth charge was a drum loaded with three hundred or six hundred pounds of TNT. Normally, the larger depth charge would be dropped from the stern of the attacking vessel, while the smaller one would be thrown from starboard or port with a Y- or K-gun. The gun could throw a three-hundred-pound depth charge about 150 yards to the starboard or port side of the ship.

The Y-gun was shaped like the letter Y and had a three-hundred-pound depth charge on each tip, with a black powder charge in the bottom that would explode when ignited, hurling the projectiles to starboard and port simultaneously. K-guns, which mounted single three-hundred-pound depth charges, were located on the starboard and port sides of the ship. Usually a destroyer or destroyer escort would have four to six K-guns, two or three to starboard and two or three to port. A normal attack pattern for a ship with K-guns would be to drop six six-hundred-pound depth charges from the stern and fire both K-guns from starboard or port.

The depth at which the charges would explode had to be manually preset before they were dropped or fired. Depth charges could be set to explode from thirty to fifty feet or in fifty-foot increments, down to six hundred feet.

The depth charge attack was generally not accurate for the simple reason that you had to have a fairly good idea of the depth of the sub and be able to predict its movement. If you didn't know, chances were the depth charge wouldn't explode close enough to damage the submarine.

Using sound gear, you would usually lose contact anywhere from 200 to 400 yards, depending on the depth of the submarine. The destroyer or the destroyer escort was typically 100 yards long. If you lost contact at 300 yards and dropped your depth charges from the stern, you would be 400 yards from the submarine. If you were traveling at 10 knots, you were traveling 330 yards a minute. That meant the submarine had at least one minute to maneuver between the time you lost contact and the time the charges were dropped.

With all the technological limitations, sinking a submarine in the early days of World War II took a lot of perseverance. You had to stay with that contact until it was sunk or until all hope of sinking it was gone. Many more subs were attacked than were sunk or badly damaged.

When ordered to the North Atlantic, we had never practiced convoy escort. We would have to proceed by trial and error. Our primary mission was to protect convoys from submarines. Since there weren't enough destroyers and corvettes to perform this role, we were told that if we made a submarine contact, we should let the convoy commander and the other escorts know immediately.

When a submarine was discovered by one of the escorts, the convoy commodore would turn the convoy away from the direction in which the submarine was contacted. As the convoy turned, the contacting vessel launched an attack against the submarine. This left the area previously covered by the contact vessel open for surprise attacks by other submarines.

Because of the inadequate number of escorts, our primary mission was to protect the convoy, not to destroy the submarine. Once the convoy was free from attack, even if just temporarily, the contacting ship had orders to rejoin the convoy and take its station.

Submarines were usually not sunk in the few minutes it took the convoy to turn and maneuver clear of the threat. Sometimes it would take an hour; other times it would take many hours to sink a submarine. At first our antisubmarine ships weren't scoring many kills on U-boats. An escort would make one or two attacks and then return to station. It didn't take the high command long to recognize this problem, and after a couple of months our orders were changed: "Your primary mission, as long as you are with the convoy, is the protection of the convoy. Once you make contact with an enemy submarine, your primary mission changes from the protection of the convoy to the destruction of the enemy submarine, *and you stay with it until you sink it or until all hope of sinking it is gone.*"

—◦◦◦—

When we headed north on September 11 in company with our sister ship, the *Kearney,* we knew we were heading for combat, but we had enough confidence in ourselves and our ship not to be anything but excited. It took two or three days to get to Newfoundland, our first point prior to being assigned to a convoy. On September 13 we anchored in Placentia Harbor. The surrounding area was barren—no trees, no grass, just rock, or so it seemed. Not knowing what our assignment would be, we kept our engines on standby so that we could get under way on a half hour's notice. There wasn't much to do except work on the ship, play cards, listen to music, talk, and watch movies. We would gather on the fantail every night, weather permitting, to watch movies. That's how we got introduced to the northern lights. While waiting for the movie operator to change reels on the projector we'd gaze up at the sky and see the marvel of those lights pulsating across the sky.

Finally on September 23 we got under way in company with the USS *Plunkett,* whose division commander, the commander of Destroyer Squadron 27, was officer in tactical command (OTC) of our group—the *Livermore, Kearney, Plunkett, Greer,* and *Decatur.* All ships were darkened as they headed into the North Atlantic night. And how very dark it was! Without radar, the officer of the deck had trouble keeping station on the other ships.

On September 24, several hundred miles from Halifax, we sighted our convoy and relieved the Canadian escorts that had brought the convoy thus far. The escorts were switched this far away from Halifax because the Allies didn't want the Germans to know that U.S. destroyers were involved in convoying. I suspect the Germans did know. To preserve the secret, if it was one, we were scheduled to meet British escorts at a mid-ocean meeting point about four hundred miles from the English coast. British escorts would take the convoy the rest of the way.

The *Livermore* took position ahead of the convoy, proceeding at 076 degrees true. We patrolled at 9.5 to 12 knots, while the convoy, constrained by the speed of its slowest ship, cruised at 8 knots.

During the entire passage the weather was rough. The *Livermore* was bouncing around like a cork on the choppy sea, and almost every day someone fell and injured himself. This didn't deter us from doing our duty. There were sixty ships with us, which only magnified the sense of importance that we attached to our job. Here we were protecting a huge convoy of ships loaded with guns, planes, and tanks as it wended its way across the North Atlantic. We knew we had to get this equipment and supplies to our allies if they were going to hold off the Germans until the day the United States actually declared war.

During war, time at sea is long stretches of boredom punctuated by short bursts of action. For four days nothing much happened. Then at about 1833 on September 29, while patrolling on a base course of 110 degrees true, we made sound contact on a submarine bearing 120 degrees true, distance 800 yards. Hearts pounding in our chests, we changed course toward the submarine, increasing our speed to 15 knots. With the bearing roughly changing, we could tell that the submarine was on an opposite course. Then at a range of 160 yards contact was lost. We dropped three six-hundred-pound depth charges, the first one and the third set to detonate at 150 feet, the second at 250 feet. The second depth charge might have met its mark—it wasn't clear. As we were pondering the outcome, a second submarine suddenly appeared bearing approximately 130 degrees true at a range of 340 yards. This submarine was also on an opposite course. Again we lost contact at a range of 200 yards, whereupon we dropped three six-hundred-pound depth charges with a setting of 150 feet. We believed that one or more of these depth charges were effective. The submarines when first contacted were apparently just maintaining steerageway, but as soon as we made sound contact, they ratcheted up their speed to dodge whatever we were going to throw at them.

Much as we would have loved pressing these attacks, we were prevented by the proximity of the convoy. Neither submarine fired torpedoes at our convoy. Why? Had we damaged them? It was a question we would never answer. Taking up station ahead of the convoy, we resumed our patrol.

On October 1 we sighted the British escorts at the mid-ocean meeting point. They took our screening stations while we took station astern of an Iceland-bound convoy of four ships that broke off from the main convoy. On October 3 we anchored in Helguvik Bay off Hvalfjordur, Iceland.

Iceland made Newfoundland look like a green paradise. The harbor was ringed by rocky, somber cliffs, and we weren't sorry to get under way a week later. We headed for Reykjavik in company with the *Plunkett, Kearney, Decatur,* and *Greer,* picked up a convoy of two vessels, and headed back out into the Atlantic to rendezvous with a convoy returning from England. The next few days were uneventful. We made a couple of sound contacts with what might have been subs—or large fish, which can give off sub-like echoes. We responded to these contacts with depth charges and had no idea whether they had any effect.

Convoy duty quickly settled into a routine. By day we patrolled and zigzagged with the sound gear going; by night we listened. It was cloudy, cold, and dreary, with little sunshine and few stars. With winter advancing, the days grew shorter. We stood our watches, disappointed at the lack of submarine contacts, and when we were relieved we braced ourselves in our bunks against the motion of the turbulent seas. The weather was steadily taking its toll.

That routine was about to change. By October 15 we had safely escorted our 8-knot convoy through most of the submarine gauntlet in the North Atlantic. On that day, however, there was a slow 4-knot convoy heading toward England under a Canadian escort of one destroyer and three corvettes, and it was in deep trouble. A wolf pack that had launched two successive nighttime attacks on the convoy was thought to be still lurking in the area. Our escort group got orders to go to the relief of this convoy, which had as many as sixty ships.

From the *Plunkett* our OTC, the commander of Destroyer Squadron 27, ordered us to form column on him, and at 0025 on the sixteenth, a terribly dark night, we set out for the beleaguered convoy. Considering the urgency of the situation, we proceeded at a speed of 20 knots, which the

OTC then ordered increased to 25. We were the second ship in column, with the *Kearney* and the *Decatur* following us. The *Greer* we lost.

The ships had three conditions of readiness. The most battle-ready condition was general quarters, during which all watertight doors were closed and every officer and man was at his battle station. Condition 2 was the next most ready, with some watertight doors closed and half the crew on watch. During condition 3, watertight doors were open and only one third of the crew was on watch.

We set out for the convoy at 0540 under condition 2. Soon the OTC ordered us to form a scouting line at a distance of six miles between ships; spread out like this, we would have a better chance of finding the convoy. At 1043 we sighted the convoy bearing 121 degrees true, and within half an hour the *Livermore* had taken station on its starboard bow. The convoy now had eight escorts to protect it, all stationed ahead or on either side—none astern.

Tension was in the air, our excitement palpable. Finally, we were on the enemy's scent! At 1710 we began making a sweep ahead of the convoy. After dropping two depth charges, we completed our sweep and resumed our station on the convoy's starboard bow. The idea behind sweeping ahead of the convoy and dropping two depth charges wasn't entirely clear to us. Of course, if there were U-boats in the area and they heard depth charges, they might think a submarine was being attacked and it might make them wary about launching further attacks of their own. In my opinion, however, dropping depth charges at no known target just to make underwater noise and create confusion was ineffective. The tactic would prove to have no deterrent effect on the submarine attacks that were to occur later that night.

All was quiet, and we began to wonder if our depth charges had scared the enemy off. Then around 1943 two flares shot up into the darkness—a merchant ship signaling the presence of a submarine in the vicinity. This was followed by a series of star shells that one of the escorts fired to try to illuminate the enemy. Sounding general quarters, the *Livermore* closed on the convoy, all hands at their battle stations.

Zigzagging on our base course, we fired four star shells in the area where a submarine was thought to be, made no contact, and at 2125 reversed course toward the convoy because we had an indication that another ship was in trouble. Minutes later, an explosion ripped through the sky, and we saw flames erupt from one of the merchant ships we were protecting. Its hull torn apart by a torpedo, the ship sank like a stone.

Once again quiet settled over the convoy. Then, just before midnight, we sighted a huge blaze coming from a ship on the other side of the convoy. It too had been torpedoed, and it too went under.

Imagine our frustration: we had been chomping at the bit for days, waiting for real action, and here was the enemy under our very nose sinking the ships we were supposed to be defending. What made it doubly frustrating was that we could do nothing to save the merchant ships in our convoy. When they went down, all hands went with them, because it was impossible for escorts to pinpoint where ships had sunk. Even if we had been capable of locating the site of a sinking, we wouldn't have had time to rescue the survivors—the North Atlantic was so cold that survivors didn't live for more than a few minutes.

It was our custom not to echo-range at night because a submarine could pick us up much farther away if we were echo-ranging than if we were just steaming silently with our sound gear and listening. But because the sound gear was so ineffective, and because on this particular night several submarines obviously knew our exact location, we did echo-range. At 0110, now October 17, the echo-ranging device seemed to indicate the presence of a submarine in our vicinity. We fired a series of three star shells to starboard, but we saw nothing. Then at 0205 another merchant ship, this time on our port beam, exploded violently and slipped beneath the waves. All we could do was shake our fists at the sky.

Finally, at 0230, the *Livermore* made her first sound contact with a submarine. Hoping against hope, we dropped five six-hundred-pound depth charges and two three-hundred-pounders. Again it was shooting in the dark; we had no idea whether we'd scored a hit. Ten minutes later another sound contact was made, perhaps with the same submarine. Here again the *Livermore* launched a full attack, dropping four six-hundred-pound depth charges, after which we were so close to the convoy that we had to change course to avoid collision. That was yet another source of frustration—we couldn't hang around to see whether our depth charges had met their mark or to launch additional attacks.

Presently one of the merchant ships turned on her lights, calling for an escort. As we were turning toward that ship she blew up, and the bright light of the explosion illuminated the track of a torpedo across our bow. Some of us on the bridge saw it. Startled, we realized that had we not turned toward that ill-starred ship and moved our bow out of harm's way, the *Livermore* would have met the same fate. As the seconds ticked by, tension mounted. Then one of our signalmen said, "Well, I guess we're going to have to paint a target on the side so the sons of bitches can hit us." Everyone chuckled, which helped ease the tension.

In the early morning hours we made three more submarine contacts, each time dropping depth charges without knowing whether they had hit home.

What a night—attacking submarines, watching merchant ships go under, getting torpedoed! All of this took place in the classic fog of battle. Although we had seen three merchant ships blow up, we couldn't be sure how many had been lost. It wasn't until dawn broke that the dimensions of the devastation became clear, and we were shocked. Not only had eight merchant ships been lost, but our sister ship, the *Kearney*, was badly damaged from a torpedo attack. A torpedo had hit her number 1 fire room, and soon it and the number 1 engine room were flooded. Still able to make way, she limped back to Iceland. Deeply saddened to hear our sister ship was hurt, we were anxious for information about casualties, not least because we knew so many of the *Kearney*'s crew from our stays in port. When the *Livermore* later returned to Iceland I would have a chance to visit the *Kearney* and see the damage firsthand. All the men in the engine room had been killed.

The destruction was horrific. Few of us on the *Livermore* had ever seen combat, much less combat on this scale. Eight merchant ships were lost with their entire crews and all their cargo—cargo that was vital to Britain as it tried to hold out against the Germans. It was a severe blow. Our spirits lifted a little when someone on a Canadian corvette radioed the Canadian destroyer and commented cheerily, "We gave the Jerries hell last night, didn't we?" Still, it seemed that our convoy had caught more hell than it had given. We didn't know whether any submarines had been sunk. Later we found out that at least one had gone under—not exactly "hell."

Most convoys crossing the North Atlantic steamed at around 8 knots.

However, because a convoy could go no faster than its slowest ship, some convoys, like the one that unfortunate night, were as slow as 4 knots. World War II submarines had a maximum speed when submerged of approximately 9 knots, but they relied on batteries and could only run about an hour at 9 knots before they had to surface to turn on their diesel engines and recharge. So, a sub would cruise at only 3 or 4 knots underwater unless there was some reason for additional speed. A sub traveling under the surface could keep up with a 4-knot convoy, then surface under the darkness of night and close in for an attack.

If a sub dropped behind and could not catch up with a convoy under the water, it would often surface to make faster time. Subs could go at least 15 knots on the surface. German submariners felt perfectly comfortable on the surface at night unless it was bright. In this particular convoy, we escorts would probably have been much more effective stationed astern instead of ahead of the convoy. If we had made runs astern of the convoy, echo-ranging during the day, we might have been able to pick up the submarines that were following the convoy and sink some of them. The advantages of this tactic would become clear to me later in the war.

At 1045 on October 17, we were close enough to land-based airplanes that three U.S. patrol planes joined the convoy and commenced circling it, looking for submarines. A little over an hour later, the *Livermore* made sound contact with a U-boat at about one thousand yards and launched two six-hundred-pound depth charges. Again there was no evidence of results, and we were unable to regain contact.

Later that morning we got orders to break off from the convoy and form a scouting line on the *Plunkett,* with the *Decatur* five miles to port and the *Livermore* five miles to starboard. We headed away from the convoy, and while reloading depth charges in one of the racks we sighted a large oil slick, two empty life rafts, an overturned lifeboat, and widespread debris. Some time later we sighted a submarine hull turned turtle. Because the hull would be a menace to navigation in the convoy lane between Nova Scotia and England, the *Decatur, Plunkett,* and *Livermore* fired on it to sink it and then headed back to Newfoundland. At last, we had sunk a German submarine. It wasn't a very good trade for that horrible night.

The next few days passed uneventfully. Then in the late morning of October 20 the wind began to whip up. By 1400 we were in the midst of a terrible storm, force 9 winds coming in on our starboard beam as we steamed on our westerly course. Our fuel was just about spent, making us much less stable in the water, and our chief engineer didn't like to put water in the fuel tanks to stabilize the ship. And so she began rolling wildly—40, 45, 50 degrees to port—while the waves rose into threatening walls that threw off a spray so heavy we couldn't see beyond a thousand yards. The captain should have insisted that the chief engineer fill a tank with water as soon as it was empty. If we had rolled a few more degrees, the whole ship could have capsized. I didn't know this until much later. We fledgling officers were like children on an amusement park ride, having a grand old time, oblivious to the danger.

Suddenly we found ourselves smack in the middle of a convoy heading northeast to England. Without radar, we hadn't detected it earlier. Fortunately for us, we ended up between two rows of ships and there was no collision. But that sobered us up a bit. The wind began to abate that night, and by daylight of the next day it was down to a force 3.

After refueling in Little Placentia Bay, Newfoundland, we got under way for Boston, delighted to be heading back to the States. More ready than ever for liberty, we could go ashore with our heads held high because we were now battle-hardened veterans. I was given a week's leave to go home while the *Livermore* underwent repairs for minor damage sustained in the stormy Atlantic. What a joy to visit all my friends and to see Mother and Dad and Sis once again.

In early November we departed Boston with twelve officers on board, including our division commander, Commander Broadfoot, and our division doctor, Lieutenant Junior Grade Stephens. Poor old Doc Stephens—he got sick just about every time we rattled the anchor chain. Fortunately for him and for us, everyone else remained in pretty good health. We got under way with Destroyer Squadron 7 and headed for Casco Bay, Maine, steaming at 25 knots in column. The passage only took a few hours, but it was significant for me because it was on this trip that I stood my first top watch as officer of the deck under way. (The officer of the deck is the person responsible for operating the ship in the absence of the captain and executive officer.) Before, I had only been standing these watches in port. Boy, was I proud!

On November 9, after fueling in Placentia Bay, Destroyer Squadron 7 got under way to pick up a convoy headed for England. The next day we found our convoy and began the escort.

In the Boston Navy Yard our diesel generator had been removed to reduce topside weight, which left an empty space. This gave the captain an idea. All the officers slept in officer's country, which was under the ship's bridge. If a torpedo hit in that area, it was possible that all the ship's officers would be killed at once. To eliminate that danger, the captain decided that four of us would move to the newly emptied space and sling hammocks there. This was fine, except that the hammocks hung some six feet off the deck. One night I dreamed that it was time to go on watch and that I was in my old bunk. I tumbled out of that hammock so fast that there was no time to register what was happening before I slammed down onto the steel deck. Making matters worse, at that very moment the ship was rolling, and the force of the roll flung me against the bulkhead. Although I sustained no serious injuries, for the next several days my body was a little bruised.

When our convoy duty was over we proceeded to the harbor of Reykjavik, Iceland's biggest city. We had one night of liberty. I was very impressed by a singular local custom: at that time, Icelandic couples who wanted to get married would have a trial marriage and live together before the wedding. If things worked out well, they were officially married. Interestingly, our divorce rate in the United States was higher than the rate of separation following trial marriages in Iceland. The Icelandic people considered divorce far more serious than we did in the States, even in those days.

The next day we got under way for Hvalfjordur, our regular anchorage, and waited for a return convoy. Earlier, few ships had anchored in the area other than destroyers and escort vessels, but the preceding weeks had seen a buildup of both British and American ships, including the USS *Wichita,* where I had passed my seaman apprenticeship.

We Americans were overjoyed to see the buildup of British ships, and not just because Allied teamwork warmed the heart. Though the U.S. Navy had a strict rule that no alcoholic beverages were to be served on board at any time, the Royal Navy did allow alcohol on its ships. British sailors were given a drink each day if they wanted it, and wardrooms were amply supplied with liquor. British officers were great hosts and would invite their American counterparts to visit British ships. We usually went at cocktail hour. And because our food was better than the food on British ships, we would reciprocate by inviting the Limeys over for dinner. It was not unusual to see a fleet of small boats going from U.S. ships to British ships at cocktail time and then returning to U.S. ships at dinnertime. This was known as a cooperative war effort.

What pleasure we had was more than tempered by the weather. Days in the North Atlantic were getting much shorter as winter approached. On November 23 sunset came at about 1630, and shortly afterward the wind began to pick up. We were anchored in about four and a half fathoms of water with thirty-five fathoms of chain to the port anchor. By 2000 the wind had grown so strong that we put a lead over the side, near the starboard forecastle, to be sure we were not drifting and pulling our anchor. We also stationed an anchor watch and a drift-lead watch on the forecastle. At 2200 the barometer fell dramatically and the wind whipped up to force 9. Minutes later, we commenced warming up the boilers in preparation for getting under way on immediate notice if necessary. When the wind climbed to force 10, a British destroyer passed on our starboard side, dragging anchor. By 2400 the wind had peaked at force 11, much fiercer than the wind during our last storm at sea. Soon we too began dragging anchor, and at 0055 we decided the wisest course was to get under way.

By now the wind was so powerful that even with both anchors down and power on the engines, we couldn't maneuver the *Livermore* into the wind. She was dragged from her anchorage at a speed of 6 knots and deposited on the beach. Shortly after we ran aground, the captain asked me to take a sounding on our port quarter. I found that we were in water only six feet deep; our propellers were buried in the mud.

Once again, the *Livermore* had had a close call. The place we ran aground happened to be the only section of beach for miles where there was any mud at all. The rest of the shore was solid rock, which could have shredded our hull.

The wind died down in the early morning, and the *Badger*, anchored off our starboard beam, began running a towline to us. It was a ten-inch manila line that we were going to secure to a bitt on our fantail so the *Badger* could tow us stern first. As designated officer in charge on the fantail, I was sent for an ax and was ordered, when we were free of the beach, to cut the manila line and get it free as quickly as possible.

At 0450 the towing line was secured and we were afloat. An inspection the next morning indicated that the *Livermore* had sustained no damage, which was confirmed by a post-grounding trial run.

We weren't given much of a respite from the weather. Two days later the wind began to pick up rapidly, and by 2130 we had made all preparations for getting under way. Within the hour a merchant ship dragging anchor passed close to starboard, and the ship anchored on our port bow began dragging anchor, too. We didn't waste any time; we got the hell out of there and rode out the storm without mishap.

In late November we helped escort a slow, 5-knot convoy coming from England and bound for Halifax. The weather continued to plague us, a situation aggravated by the presence of stragglers in the convoy. Usually, a destroyer would go to the stern of the convoy, urging a slowpoke merchant ship to catch up with the other ships and to stay in formation. December arrived with shorter days, darker nights, and fierce winds. The harder they blew, the more stragglers we had.

December 2 turned out to be the roughest day I'd yet encountered at sea. The waves were so high it took my breath away. Standing on our bridge, we were forty-two feet above sea level—and still looking up at waves cresting at seventy-five or eighty feet. It was not unusual to see the bow of the ship on one wave and the stern on another, with empty space below the hull, in the trough between waves. The weather was so rough it scattered the convoy; each ship had to steer the course safest for her. A few hours into that storm all semblance of a formation had disappeared, and we were on our own.

The next day we managed to find the *Plunkett* and the *Decatur,* but with the storm still upon us, the other ships were nowhere to be seen. It took two more days for the winds to relent. A damage assessment revealed that considerable havoc had been wrought on the *Livermore,* though none of it life-threatening. Mooring line and towing line reels had torn loose from their pivots, and one depth charge rack had fallen overboard. The rest of the damage was minor—two lengths of fuel hose damaged beyond use, several life rafts beat up, some fire hoses carried away, and life jacket bins dented.

For the next three days we looked for the rest of the convoy, and by December 7 we had found only one missing ship, the *Rapidan.* Then news came that made the storm we had just lived through seem like small potatoes. At about 1800, while we were speculating over the whereabouts of the other ships, a priority dispatch arrived from the commander in chief of the U.S. Fleet:

THIS IS NO DRILL, THIS IS NO DRILL, THE JAPANESE HAVE ATTACKED PEARL HARBOR, SEVERE DAMAGE TO THE AMERICAN FLEET. THIS IS NO DRILL, THIS IS NO DRILL.

Each day our radio room would listen to regular news broadcasts and print up a report of happenings around the world to distribute to the officers and crew. As soon as the shocking news of Pearl Harbor came in, we flocked to the board where the radiomen had posted a news report:

Flash—Pearl Harbor, Manila and Honolulu and other points in the Pacific were attacked today by Japanese bombing planes. At a late hour this afternoon the State Department at Washington said that the attacks were still in progress. . . .

Honolulu—It was announced that a considerable amount of damage had been done at the Pearl Harbor Naval Base and the City of Honolulu by Japanese aerial attacks.

San Francisco—Federal Bureau of Investigation authorities announced today that the FBI was fully mobilized to prevent any attempts of sabotage on the west coast by the Japanese.

Washington—The unexpected attack on the United States by Japan galvanized the British government into immediate action. Soon after the first news of the attack on Honolulu and Manila were flashed to London, Prime Minister Churchill called United States Ambassador John Winnat to Ten Downing Street.

Washington—State Department reports heavy damage and loss of life in Japanese raid on Hawaii.

Another report was printed a short time later and read in part as follows:

Washington—President Roosevelt summoned his cabinet and congressional leaders into an emergency war conference for 8:20 p.m., the cabinet will assemble at 8:20 and the leaders of both parties will join them at 9 p.m.

London—Both Houses of Parliament were called to meet in an emergency session at 10:00 A.M. tomorrow.

Tokyo—The Imperial government announced a state of war exists between the United States and Japan.

Flash—It was reported tonight that the Japanese government considered itself at war with Britain as well as the United States.

Washington—The War Department clamped down a tight wartime censorship this afternoon on all information regarding the strength, location and movement of United States troops outside the continental limits. The Department said that such information will hereafter be secret and will be so considered under the law.

Billings, Montana—The isolationists' leader, Senator Wheeler, indicated this afternoon that he would give full and unquestioned support to the administration in the war with Japan. Said Wheeler, the Japanese attack means war and we have to see it through as a United States of America.

And then a third news report:

The United States moved swiftly toward setting her guns in action to back the reply, which Japan invited. At a late hour, and with censorship clamped down over Army and Navy movements, these things are certain: the USS *Oklahoma,* one of Uncle Sam's proudest battleships, is on fire in Pearl Harbor; . . . oil tanks in Honolulu have been destroyed; houses blown up; a considerable number of civilians killed; at least five Japanese bombers have been shot down by anti-air fire defense; and more than 100 Army men have been killed.

Police guards have been thrown all around Japanese consulates and even restaurants, as the temper of the crowds in American cities has grown fierce with each new bulletin. All men in active service have been ordered to report to their bases by tomorrow morning. . . . The Panama Canal is blacked out, with all Japanese in the area under military arrest. Those things are certain.

It is known that Canada has massed all her aircraft strength in the provinces of British Columbia and the Yukon territory. Modest estimates were that the Maple Leaf Dominion had assembled at least three thousand attack planes and bombers along the Pacific shores of the country, waiting for a possible Japanese invasion attempt.

The U.S. Navy had been unofficially at war in the Atlantic since early September; now it would be officially at war in the vast Pacific. On December 9 at 0430, we were released from escort duty to proceed to the Boston Navy Yard for repairs to the damage sustained in the recent North Atlantic storm.

As we headed down the coast of Nova Scotia, the *Livermore* steamed at 15 knots into a 15-knot wind—the most bone-chilling cold I've ever experienced. The wind was on our starboard bow, and spray was coming over on the forecastle. It was snowing and we were collecting ice like mad. The snow and the wind considerably lessened visibility. Once we thought we were coming upon another ship and we backed down full in order to avoid collision. It turned out to be a ghost ship—a figment of our imagination. Rerouted to Casco Bay, Maine, we were heading in that direction when we unwittingly steamed into the midst of Destroyer Squadron 2, proceeding along a parallel but opposite course. Between the perils of ice and the danger of collision, the days and nights left little time for relaxation.

At Casco Bay we refueled and underwent repairs. By December 14 we were en route again for Reykjavik to continue convoy duty until the end of December.

Thus ended the year 1941. From midshipman at Northwestern University in Chicago to ensign on the USS *Livermore* in the North Atlantic—I had learned more in that year than any year in my life. For a new ensign I'd seen my share of excitement, but that was just the beginning.

4

Armed Guard

THE REPAIRS THE *Livermore* received in Casco Bay in mid-December were not adequate for all the damage suffered in the North Atlantic. So, in early January 1942, we headed to New York Navy Yard for final repairs.

Our executive officer, Lieutenant E. F. McDaniel, had recently received a promotion to lieutenant commander. We were proud of him and delighted about the promotion, which reflected well on our ship. Little did I know as we steamed toward New York that this would be the last trip I would make on the *Livermore,* and the last time I would see some of her officers and men.

When we arrived at New York I had orders to proceed to Damneck, Virginia. My assignment: armed guard officer on a merchant ship. Needless to say, the orders came as something of a disappointment. I loved the *Livermore* and thrived on destroyer duty. Armed guard duty, whatever it entailed, couldn't possibly be as exciting as going to sea on a great destroyer. I had learned a lot and had made many friends. I was a battle-hardened veteran, or at least I felt like one. The gold on my cap and on my uniforms had taken on the greenish tinge of a man who had been to sea. So it was with reluctance that I proceeded to Damneck and reported for duty.

Most merchant ships that the United States armed in World War II were supplied with at least some firepower to protect against surfaced submarines. Most merchant ships were given one antisubmarine gun; some of the more modern ones were given two or more. Most of these were 3-inch 50-caliber guns or 4-inch 50s. Antiaircraft machine guns were given to merchant ships vulnerable to attack by enemy aircraft.

Naturally, armed ships required a contingent of navy people on board to handle the care and firing of weapons. It wasn't exactly glorious duty. At first the navy decided that it would be good to have a reserve officer with limited experience to be the officer in command of firepower handlers. And because reservists who had been on a destroyer for at least six months were the ideal candidates, the navy trained its sights on me.

I reported to Damneck on January 11 for four weeks of training on guns and small arms. I already knew about 5-inch 38s and 50-caliber machine guns because we had them on the *Livermore*. At Damneck, part of my time was spent learning how to disassemble and assemble a .45 automatic pistol while blindfolded. I also went to the pistol practice range regularly.

At the end of the training period, I was given an eight-man crew consisting of one second-class boatswain's mate and seven seamen. We were assigned to a slow 8.5-knot tanker, the SS *Tustem*, which we boarded in Mobile, Alabama, on my twenty-fourth birthday, February 5, 1942. The only weapon we had was one 4-inch 50-caliber gun, which was mounted on the *Tustem*'s stern. Our objective was to go to Texas, fill up with oil, and bring it back up the East Coast to Philadelphia or New York.

This was about two months after Pearl Harbor, and German submarines were beginning to lurk off the U.S. East Coast in search of the rich harvest of ships plying that route. At that time the southernmost of the sinkings were occurring around the Chesapeake Bay. As far as we knew, there were no German submarines south of that area and none in the Gulf of Mexico. This was soon to change.

The skipper of the *Tustem* was one Captain Wolf, an old salt who had been in every port in the world. Wolf was an excellent seaman and a fine captain. He did everything he could to make his navy contingent comfortable—everything short of paying us more. I hadn't given much thought to my salary on the *Livermore*, but now that I was sailing with the merchant marine I couldn't help but think it was paltry. My ensign's salary was $137 a month, and the salary of a navy apprentice seaman was about $37 a month. The merchant marine seamen on the *Tustem* were raking in a minimum of $400 a month because their jobs were considered hazardous duty, and her petty officers and officers made far more than that!

As you can imagine, serving on an 8-knot tanker going from Texas to the northeast coast was not very productive duty for me. And it didn't take my men long to be trained on our 4-inch 50-caliber gun. They could operate that gun night or day, in rain or shine, under any conditions of weather or sea. The only real purpose of the gun was to fire at surfaced submarines in the daytime. It was no good against aircraft, but then, running up and down the East Coast, submarines were our only threat.

Our trips began in Houston, where we would load up with fuel and head for the East Coast. After coming through the Gulf of Mexico, we rounded the cape at Key West and turned north. On the second trip, because of some engine trouble, Captain Wolf decided to anchor off Miami, which was safe from submarines at this time, to have the engine repaired. Without the repair our maximum speed would have been reduced to 6 knots. Since U-boats were now sinking ships as far south as northern Florida, we wanted to steam at maximum speed to improve our chance of getting through safely.

While steaming up the coast, we would receive radio reports at night of the sinkings. I'd stay up with Captain Wolf to plot the sinkings so that we could dodge danger zones. It was impossible to dodge them all. In some cases, we passed through an area only a few hours before or after a submarine sinking. The captain and I agreed that we would hug the beach, staying as close as possible to avoid sinking if we were torpedoed. As I remember, we drew about thirty-two feet of water when fully loaded. We used to kid about it, saying that if we got sand in our condensers, we would haul farther out into the water. If we didn't get sand in our condensers, we would close back toward shallow water. By the time we departed Houston for the third trip, submarines were infesting the entire East Coast.

Again we anchored off Miami for engine repairs. One day I was on deck when a boat carrying a young man and a pretty young lady in a white bathing suit came sailing by. Spotting me, they came close aboard and we started talking. I found out that he was the son of a Ford dealer in Miami and she was a French girl whose family had escaped from France. They had come to live in Miami, where her father's brother lived.

"Hey," I said, "I've got a Brownie camera. I'd be glad to take some pictures of ya'll in your sailboat. I'll send them your way as soon as they're developed."

"Much obliged," said the man. He gave me his name and address and introduced the young lady as Didi. I had no idea that someday I'd deliver those pictures personally.

With the engines back in shape, we resumed our course up the coast. As we approached Cape Fear at about 0100 we were trying to decide whether to go inside or outside the flashing light of the sea buoy there. We had just enough water to go inside the light if we chose to do so.

I said to Captain Wolf, "You know, if I were a submarine skipper I would lie off that cape, and when the light didn't flash I would know there was a ship passing by. I could listen to the propeller noises and estimate speed. I would also know about the course it was on, and I would have my torpedoes ready. If I was a submarine skipper, that's exactly what I would do."

"Let's go inside the light," the captain said without further ado.

And we did. There was another tanker about four thousand yards astern of us that decided to go outside the light. I happened to be on the wing of the bridge gazing out at sea when suddenly a brilliant blue flash erupted from the tanker. Torpedoed tankers make huge bonfires.

I hustled over to the chart house and called Captain Wolf. He came running out on the bridge, took one look at the conflagration, and started yelling, "Go to general quarters! Go to general quarters!" Meanwhile, I sounded the alarm for battle stations. We manned our gun, but being too far away to see the sub we weren't much help. I suspected the marauder skedaddled from that area as fast as his engines could take him, out to the safety of the open sea. However, with the Americans short of antisubmarine vessels at this stage in the war, he might have felt perfectly comfortable right where he was, lying in wait for the next sitting duck to happen by.

Had we chosen to go outside the light, you probably wouldn't be reading this story.

After that isolated moment of high tension, it was back to the same old dull routine. With just one gun and so little to do, I felt completely out of the navy loop. I missed the bustle of the *Livermore,* missed my shipmates, missed military readiness and the possibility of a different kind of action in this war. My second-class petty officer was perfectly qualified to handle the crew manning the *Tustem*'s single gun.

When we arrived at Philadelphia, I was determined to request reassignment back to active duty. I asked the navy port captain for permission to go to Washington to see the people at Navy Personnel. "Williamson," he said, "you're just the guy I'm looking for. I need someone to take officer messenger mail to the Navy Department. While you're there," he winked, "maybe you could drop by Navy Personnel and get assigned back to a real ship." The next day I picked up the officer messenger mail and caught a train to Washington.

The navy, realizing the seriousness of the submarine threat, had decided to build hundreds of sub-chasers that would require thousands of officers and men to operate. Two types of sub-chasers would be built: one was a 110-foot wooden hull carrying a 3-inch 23-caliber gun, two or three 20-millimeter machine guns, sound gear, and depth charges; the other was a 173-foot steel hull with a 3-inch 50-caliber gun, more machine guns, depth charges, and sound gear. Both vessels would be powered by diesel engines and equipped with radar. The 110-footer was designated SC (for submarine-chaser), while the 173-footer was the PC (for patrol vessel, submarine-chaser).

The crew of the 110-footer would be approximately thirty-two men and three officers. The crew of the 173-footer would be about sixty-five men and five officers.

Because thousands of men would have to be trained for sub-chasers, the navy decided to establish a training center on pier 2 in Miami. Many navy captains coveted that command because they saw it as an outstanding opportunity. Admiral Ernest King, the chief of naval operations, said, "The only people who know anything about fighting submarines today are the men who were commanding officers of destroyers in the North Atlantic. I want someone who has been a commanding officer of a destroyer in the North Atlantic to head that school."

It just so happened that my old executive officer from the *Livermore*, Lieutenant Commander McDaniel, had for some months been in command of his own destroyer in the North Atlantic. And it just so happened that McDaniel's division commander was in Washington at that time. Navy Personnel discussed the sub-chaser school with the division commander, who heartily recommended McDaniel for the job.

The captain in charge of recruiting someone to head the school phoned Commander McDaniel, whose ship was in the Boston Navy Yard at the time, and told him about the assignment. "Would you like to take this on?" the captain asked. "No, damn it!" replied McDaniel. "I'd rather stay at sea, but you people down there know what my qualifications are, and if you think I should go down there to command that school and that is what the navy needs, then send me orders, and I'll go." And so they did.

McDaniel made his way to Washington to arrange for personnel. The Navy Department suggested he ask for reserve officers since regular navy people were in short supply and badly needed at sea. "There's one reservist I'd especially like to have," Commander McDaniel said. "He was transferred from the *Livermore* some months ago. I have no idea where he is now, but his name is John A. Williamson."

At the same time, I was in the Navy Department looking for the office to which I was supposed to deliver the officer mail. There are hundreds of offices in the Navy Department building, and by coincidence, or fate, just as Commander McDaniel was saying he wanted me, I opened a door to ask for directions. "That's the young man I'm talking about," he said, pointing to me!

I was as startled to see him there as he was surprised to see me. Of course I had no idea what he was talking about. "Johnny," he went on, "where are you and what are you doing?"

"I'm an armed guard officer on a merchant ship that's tied up at Philadelphia. I want back in the navy and I've come to request destroyer duty."

He asked, "Do you need an officer to replace you?"

"No sir," I replied, "my petty officer can do what needs to be done on that ship."

"Go back to your ship, turn your command over to your petty officer, and meet me in Miami in a week," he said.

It sounded too good to be true. "But Commander McDaniel, where are my orders?"

"You just got them," he said.

I still couldn't believe it. "You mean I take verbal orders to go to Miami and I go there in a week?"

"That's right," he replied. He told me to meet him at pier 2 when I arrived. "The navy will pay your expenses and get your orders down once you arrive."

I could hardly believe my good luck. It's been said that a coincidence is a miracle in which the hand of God is not evident. Little did I know how dramatically this miracle would change my life—and what a difference it would make in the war against Japan.

I delivered the mail, returned to Philadelphia to turn in my command to my petty officer, and then caught a train to Birmingham to spend a couple of days at home. Then on April 1, 1942, I headed for Miami—the *real* navy—and an assignment I would never forget.

5

Sub-Chaser Training

W HEN I REPORTED TO Lieutenant Commander McDaniel (or Captain Mac, as we now called him, since he was skipper of the Sub-Chaser Training Center), he and I and a lieutenant by the name of Don Kerr were the only officers there. Only a few enlisted men had reported. Despite the dearth of personnel, the site of what was to be the training center was hopping. Construction workers swarmed all over the place converting pier 2 into classrooms, training areas, offices, and storerooms. The pace was hectic.

Ours was a daunting task, but we undertook it with confidence that this was going to be the best school the navy had ever had. In addition to converting pier 2 into a school, we had to get our hands on some 110- and 173-foot sub-chasers to train our people and to develop a curriculum for classroom teaching. The subjects included submarine tactics, seamanship, attack procedures, gunnery, and convoy operations—an enormous curriculum. I was appointed head of two departments, seamanship and anti-submarine warfare. I would also be an instructor in both.

Thanks to the character and dedication of Captain Mac, the Sub-Chaser Training Center turned out to be one of the most rewarding and most challenging organizations of which I have ever been a part. "Don't ask me how to do the job," he would say, "just get it done!" And because he expected us to get it done, we did.

The ensuing months were bustling with activity. Soon officers and men were arriving by the train- and busload to attend the Sub-Chaser Training Center. While cobbling together a curriculum, we were also scrambling to get accommodations in Miami hotels for all the newcomers. I don't know how we did it. Between us and the air force, we ended up taking over all the hotels in the Miami and Miami Beach area, which greatly depleted Miami's tourist industry. At any given time the Sub-Chaser Training Center had several thousand students enrolled for month-long courses. We had to arrange for sub-chasers for all these personnel to train in.

It was our responsibility to rate the officers who came through, determining their qualifications for positions on the sub-chasers, both 110-foot SCs and 173-foot PCs. Most of the officers and men were reservists, few of whom had been to sea long enough to command either ship. If an officer had limited experience at sea, such as sailing, we usually made him skipper of an SC. If an officer had had a lot of experience at sea, we made him commanding officer of a PC. It was amazing how fast people were assigned to man the hundreds of sub-chasers rolling out of various shipyards on the East and West Coasts and the Mississippi River.

As time went on, not only were we training crews to man the PCs and SCs being produced in the hundreds, we were also shaking the ships down. A shakedown for a ship is a training time to get the ship ready to fight.

Officers and men who were experts in training the ship's people on the ship would ride it to sea and conduct many drills and firing of the guns. These drills would continue until the experts felt the ship's people were ready to fight effectively. The ship would then proceed to its assigned warfare duties.

Various types of ships have different areas of shakedown. All the sub-chasers built on the East Coast came through the Sub-Chaser Training Center for shakedown. They were usually there for two weeks. I was part of the team that helped these ships shake down and prepare for combat.

Both kinds of sub-chasers had diesel engines. The 110-footers had pancake diesels and the 173-footers had regular vertical in-line diesels. The pancake diesel was a flat engine whose pistons operated in a horizontal position. The two main propulsion diesels for the PC were the Fairbanks Morse diesel and the General Motors diesel. To reverse the propellers, these engines had to be stopped and then started in reverse. Every time you made a landing, you held your breath to be sure the diesels were going to reverse in time to prevent the ship from slamming into the dock or the vessel being tied up alongside.

Both SC and PC sub-chasers had sound gear and surface radar. This was my first experience with radar, and I was delighted to have it after all those blind nights in the North Atlantic. With radar, our sub-chasers could tell where convoys were, keep station on convoys, and pick up surfaced submarines.

I had been in Miami for six weeks before I had a single day off. Even though courses were a month long, we launched a new course every week. When officers and men arrived for the first time, it was Captain Mac's procedure to give a hellfire-and-damnation talk, getting the newcomers so worked up about the Germans and the Japanese that they would learn all they could in sub-chaser training. The following, dated April 1944, conveys the flavor of these legendary deliveries:

> Gentlemen, before this training center was started, I was at sea. And in my experiences at sea, there was absolutely no doubt in my mind as to what this war was all about and why we're fighting it. That's in view with the experiences that I had personally. After I came ashore and began to come in contact with the civilians in this country, and, yes, many of our service people here in Miami, I came to the conclusion that there was a percentage of our people, both in and out of the service, who did not know why we were fighting this war. . . .
>
> What the Germans have done and how they have run this war, for some reason beyond my comprehension, has not been publicized the way the Japs' actions have been. But let me tell you, as a result of my own personal experiences, there is absolutely no difference between the Germans and the Japs. As a matter of fact, the Germans are even far more dangerous to this world than the Japs are because the Germans are more intelligent in their savagery.
>
> Let me give you [an] illustration. After we had gotten in the war, one of our American tankers proceeding independently was torpedoed and sunk. The submarine evidently didn't know that there were any escort vessels anywhere in the vicinity. The destroyer just blundered up on the scene by bull luck. That submarine had come to the surface and found our sailors, both regular and merchant marines from the torpedoed ship, swimming in a regular sea of oil and gasoline. Those bastards had set the oil on fire with incendiary bullets. The submarine was lying on the surface, out on edge of that pool of fire, and the German officers were walking up and down on deck, smoking cigarettes listening to those American sailors scream with agony, frying in oil.

At the beginning of this war, gentlemen, things like that were going on all of the time. There was only one answer, and that is that the German people who were running this war had been converted, by some means, into a nation of complete and utter savages. A German Lt. Commander, for instance, one that corresponded in writing to one of our Lt. Commanders, who had been in command of a submarine, was a prisoner of war and had been captured because his submarine was destroyed. That Lt. Commander was an educated man, a fellow about forty-five years old, one of the leading scientists in Germany. As a matter of fact, he had a degree from one of our colleges here in this country—an exceptionally intelligent man. He was asked the question, "Fellow, what on earth has happened to the German nation to make them hate the entire world the way they do? What has the world done to Germany to make them hate it the way they do?" And, I wish anybody in this world who claims a smart civilization could have heard his answer. He sneered and said, "It's almost impossible for me to get my language down to the low intelligence that you have to try to explain something to you." The German Lt. Commander said, "The German people have always been known as the only race of people on the face of the earth that are naturally efficient. . . . "

We did not ask for this war, it was forced down our throats, we had to get into it. But now that we are in it, the sole purpose of fighting this war is to prevent Germany or Japan from winning. Just that simple. And the reason we must prevent them from winning is because, if they did win, our civilization in this world would be gone. Therefore, in the last analysis, we are fighting this war to save civilization itself. That's all, just that. . . .

The issue is so plain, as plain as the nose on your face, if you just stop and think. The world is fighting a desperate war, a desperate war to save civilization itself. Every human being on the face of this earth who's got a spark of manhood or an iota of civilization in him has a job cut out for him to help save their civilization. And it doesn't make any difference whether he is an apprentice seaman or a full Admiral in the Navy. He still has a job to do. And it certainly should not be necessary for somebody to trick him into doing it. And, he certainly should not have any strings to his service, stating that I will help to save civilization if you will let me fight according to my personal pleasure. Can't you see how silly that is?

And, even if it wasn't such a silly thing, suppose we tried to reorganize our fighting forces today to give every officer and every enlisted man just the type of duty that pleases him today? If he changed his mind tomorrow, change his duties accordingly? These "I" men haven't stopped to think of that. If we ever tried any such damn fool thing as that, we might as well fold up our tents and surrender that day, because we will never win this war with people motivated by any such selfish influences. . . .

I wish that every one of you could stand shoulder to shoulder with me and say, as though you never meant anything more on the face of this earth before, "I have an individual mission assigned to me to help save our civilization, and I intend to see to it that no man, woman, child or circumstance will in any way reduce the efficiency with which I perform my mission." See if you can say that and really mean it. When you can, you are fit to wear that uniform you've got on. Be proud of that uniform, men. Some of the finest people this world has ever known have died in it. . . .

Although I loved Captain Mac and thought he was a great leader of men, I didn't always agree with the way he expressed himself. In my opinion, a person doesn't have to use questionable language to get a point across and to influence others. Naturally, being a different person, I wouldn't have made the same speech. But I would have tried to achieve the same effect on our officers and men. In both his speeches and his actions, Captain Mac was as dedicated to winning as any individual I've ever met in any arm of the military. He made that Sub-Chaser Training Center into one of the best schools the navy had ever had, and he was well respected for it.

Captain Mac didn't care about the means so much as the end. To give you an example, a couple of months after the center was set up, we were assigned two PCs and two SCs for training. By this time German submarines were haunting not only the Caribbean but also the East Coast and the Gulf of Mexico. When a submarine sank a ship within three hundred miles of our training center, the admiral in charge of the Caribbean Sea Frontier, headquartered in Key West, would order our sub-chasers to go after the submarine. More often than not this was a fruitless search, because by the time our ships got there, the submarine was long gone.

When our sub-chasers were ordered to sea, they'd be gone for several days, and we'd have to shut down the seagoing part of our training. Captain Mac felt that in the long run it was more important to train people to sink submarines than to send four sub-chasers out on futile searches for them. So he picked up the phone and called Admiral Ernest King, then commander in chief of the U.S. Navy. "Admiral," said Captain Mac, "I've got a problem," and he related what had been going on. Admiral King agreed that it was better to use the sub-chasers for training and told him to keep his ships.

A week after that conversation, Captain Mac happened to be in Key West at a meeting with the commander of the Caribbean Sea Frontier. While he was there, a call came in indicating that a submarine had sunk a ship some two hundred miles south of Miami. The admiral got off the phone and said, "Mac, hate to do it, but I'm going to have to take your ships again."

Captain Mac replied, "Admiral, you can't have them."
The admiral, shocked, looked at McDaniel and said, "You heard me; I said I was going to take your ships."
McDaniel repeated, "Admiral, you can't have them."
"McDaniel," bellowed the admiral, "you are a lieutenant commander of the United States Navy! You know that when an admiral tells you to do something, you damn well do it."
Captain Mac said, "Admiral, may I use your phone?"

Surprised, the admiral gave a hesitant go-ahead.
Captain Mac picked up the phone. "Operator, this is a navy flash; get me Admiral King in Washington, D.C." A minute later he had Admiral King on the phone. "Admiral King, I'm here with the commander of the Caribbean Sea Frontier and he wants to take my ships." Then Captain Mac handed the receiver over to his superior and said, "Admiral, do you want to take my word for it or do you want to talk to Admiral King?" I doubt if E. F. McDaniel ever became a close friend of that admiral.

From then on we kept our school ships. And before long we had five or six 110-foot sub-chasers and five or six 173-foot sub-chasers as school ships, which were put to good use every day.

Captain Mac didn't care whom he threatened, as long as he knew he was right. Another time, a fresh trainload of sailors was due in for training. They were supposed to be transported from the main line railroad several miles away by way of a spur that connected with the training center on pier 2. A couple of days before the train was scheduled to arrive, the railroad manager called Captain Mac. "Mr. McDaniel," he said, "the train isn't going to be able to leave the main line to bring the troops to your training center." He told McDaniel to have them picked up at such-and-such a place, which was several miles from pier 2.

"Sir," said Captain Mac, without a moment's hesitation, "those troops will be brought to pier 2, and if you don't bring them to pier 2 I'm going to take over the whole damn railroad clean up to the main line. If you don't want the spur taken over, you better have those troops delivered to pier 2." As soon as the troops arrived on the main line, they were promptly delivered to our doorstep.

And then there was the time our mess halls were operating at full capacity and we had several thousand additional troops due in. Sometime before that, we had taken over the Ungar Buick Company to transform it from a dealership to a mess hall. The work was supposed to be completed two days in advance of the additional troops' arrival. About three weeks before the mess hall was to be finished, the supervisor of the construction company dropped in on Captain Mac and announced, "Captain, company workers are going on strike tomorrow and we won't be able to finish the mess hall in time. I'm sorry, but there's nothing I can do about it."

"Sir," said Captain Mac, "you go back up to Ungar Buick and get your union leaders together with your supervisors, and I'll be up there in fifteen minutes."

We had been assigned a company of marines to guard the Sub-Chaser Training Center. As soon as the construction company supervisor left, Captain Mac called the lieutenant in charge of the marines to his office. "Get all of your men together," he ordered, "double-time up to Ungar Buick, fix bayonets, and surround the facility."

Captain Mac walked over to Ungar Buick, which was a few blocks away from pier 2, and went into a conference room. By now all the union leaders and the company supervisors had gathered. Through the open windows of the boardroom, they could hear men marching up at double time. A voice barked, "Fix bayonets! Surround the building!" A minute or two later, Captain Mac turned to the gathering and said, "Gentlemen, this building is surrounded by marines with bayonets. They have orders not to let any man

leave the premises who doesn't promise to meet back here tomorrow morning and finish the job. Now, I'll give you gentlemen thirty minutes to decide what you want to do." With that, he turned on his heels and walked
out of the room.

Fifteen minutes later, they called him back in and said, "Sir, we'll finish
the contract on time." And they did.

A month or so after I arrived at the training center, I rented a house in
Coral Gables with a friend of mine on the staff, Lieutenant John Boy, and
our training center doctor, Lieutenant "Doc" McKinnes. Around the time
we rented the house, I began seeking out female companionship. One of
the first people I called was the young Ford guy who had pulled up alongside my tanker with his French girlfriend Didi. You'll recall that I'd taken
some pictures of them. I told him I had the pictures and asked him if he
was dating Didi exclusively. "No," he replied, "she's just one of several girls
I'm going with."

"Do you mind if I call her for a date?"
"Go right ahead," he said obligingly.

So I called her. She was living in a nice home that her family had picked
out after escaping from France. Her parents spoke only French, but Didi
and her siblings were conversant in English. Didi had a thick accent but
her English was quite good—certainly better than my painful French. She
remembered me when I called her, and after we'd chatted for a while she
invited me to her home. I had to spend a couple of evenings talking with
her father in my poor French before he would let me take his daughter out.
Didi was charming, with a small, neat figure, and I loved her French accent. She was my favorite girlfriend until I had the good fortune to meet
Betty Lou Kauffman.

Around the time I was dating Didi, Admiral Reginald Kauffman relieved the admiral who had been commander of the Caribbean Sea Frontier. Admiral Kauffman shifted its headquarters from Key West to Miami
and moved his family into a lovely home on Miami Beach. Somehow I
managed to meet his daughter, Betty Lou. Didi's lovely French accent
couldn't compete with Betty Lou's charm. From that point on, all my spare
time was spent with Betty Lou Kauffman, a warm, delightful young lady

and one of the best dancers I've ever known. We went dancing every chance we could in the various nightclubs around Miami. In going with Betty Lou, I got to know Admiral and Mrs. Kauffman well, and they invited me to dinner on several occasions. At the time, I didn't realize how valuable that friendship with Admiral Kauffman would turn out to be.

Before the United States entered the war, Betty Lou's brother, Draper Kauffman, had been doing bomb disposal work in Britain as a reservist with the Royal Navy. Once the United States was drawn into the conflict, he was selected to set up a school for underwater demolition teams (UDTs) in Florida. Later in his career, Draper Kauffman would become superintendent of the U.S. Naval Academy.

Although Barbara Hale, my girlfriend from Northwestern days, was still in the back of my mind, our regular correspondence had dwindled to the occasional letter. We were so busy that personal time was at a premium, and that premium didn't include writing letters. Betty Lou was too near, too dear, and too much on my mind.

I had learned a lot in the North Atlantic. I had learned about German submarine tactics, how to conn a destroyer in a submarine attack, and how sound gear worked in the detection of submarines. But it was at the Sub-Chaser Training Center that I learned how to sink submarines.

There were three things you needed to know about a submarine to make an accurate depth-charge attack. First, of course, was the depth of the submarine. The second was his speed. And the third was his course, or the direction in which he was going. This information helped to determine range rate, which was vital in determining firing time.

Captain Mac and some of the other officers and I worked out an attack procedure on a submarine using a stopwatch to determine both range rate and the submarine's movement (toward us or away from us). Although it was a rudimentary method, at that time we had no other way of figuring out range rate.

A knot is a measurement of nautical miles per hour. A statute mile is 5,280 feet, and a nautical mile is 6,000 feet or 2,000 yards. A ship going one knot covers 33 yards per minute. Normally our attack speed on submarines was 10 knots or 330 yards per minute. If a submarine was coming toward us, the range would change more than 330 yards per minute. If he was heading away from us, the range would change less than 330 yards per minute. If the sound operator called out range 900 yards and you started your stopwatch, then by counting the number of seconds that had elapsed when he called out 800 yards or 700 or 600 yards, you could determine range rate.

Doppler technology was a much more sophisticated, accurate way of determining the direction of submarine movement. Doppler measured changes in sound pitch. The pitch of a sound is determined by its wavelength. Higher-pitch sounds have shorter wavelengths than lower-pitch sounds. For example, an approaching train has a higher-pitch whistle than a train that has passed. That's because as the train comes toward you, the sound waves are compressed. Once it passes you, the sound waves become longer.

The same thing is true for a submarine. A submarine coming toward you would have a higher-pitch echo than a submarine heading away from you. You would determine the pitch with your sound gear, which emitted sound that bounced, or echoed, off of the enemy sub. Because submarines moved slowly, differences in pitch were slight. But with training and practice, you could detect them.

To determine sub range rate, at first we had only the stopwatch and the Doppler. Then a mechanical device called a range-rate recorder, which gave more accurate measurements, became available and resulted in a higher success rate for attacks.

Trickier than determining range rate was determining the depth of a submarine. We could get rough estimates of depth by the range at which we lost contact with a sub. If he was deep, we lost sound gear contact at greater distances than if he was shallower. Often, in attempts to sink a sub, we would make a nonfiring run and try to pass over the sub. If we did we could often get an accurate depth of the sub using our Fathometer (depth recorder).

To practice sinking U-boats, we used an "attack teacher" on which simulated submarine attack runs could be made. One officer would control the submarine and another officer would operate a sub-chaser or a destroyer escort. The attack teacher was an effective means of learning antisubmarine warfare. It provided a real-life or almost-real-life situation. With the teacher, we could learn how to determine range rate and the direction of a submarine's movement, though the situation lacked the tension of live combat.

Playing with the attack teacher was fun and games for most of the officers who came through the training center. Unfortunately for them, the course being only a month long, this practice was limited. I had plenty more practice because I taught at the training center for nine months. During that time I played with the attack teacher just about every spare minute I had, except when out dancing with Betty Lou. Various skippers would do their best to frustrate me by using different submarine tactics. After a while, no matter what a submarine skipper did, I could usually score a hit on him. A few other diligent souls who also had extra time at the training center also became proficient at sinking subs.

In theory, I could now sink submarines. The question was, Could I do it in combat? And would I ever have the chance?

After I'd been at the training center about four months, I went to see Captain Mac and requested a transfer to command a PC. "Johnny," he said, "when you can provide for your replacement here, you can go to sea as skipper of a PC."

As officers came through the antisubmarine warfare and seamanship departments, I would talk them into staying and instructing at the training center. The problem was, we were growing so fast that every time I picked someone to replace me, that person would be needed elsewhere at the rapidly expanding center.

Finally I did get someone to take over the antisubmarine warfare department. And soon after that, I got a boatswain who was an outstanding seaman to take over the seamanship department. He had had at least twenty-five years' service. His name was Dusty Shouldice, and he was one fine warrant officer, well qualified to head seamanship training.

One day when Dusty was in my office, a lieutenant junior grade, an executive officer on one of the PCs, dropped by to ask for some eight-inch line to tie up his sub-chaser. Now manila line was in short supply because most of it came from the Philippines, which the Japanese had seized, and we normally used six-inch line to tie up the 173-foot sub-chasers. But this lieutenant insisted on the eight-inch. "Lieutenant," I said in no uncertain terms, "you'd better be glad you have six-inch line. We don't have enough eight-inch to spare."

This junior grade was something of a wiseacre. He'd been on a carrier in the Pacific, and because he'd been close to combat he thought he knew everything. On his way out, he stopped and said, "This isn't the old navy I used to know."

"Son," Dusty piped up, "I've been on the clap list longer than you've been in the navy. Forget about eight-inch line!"

That shut him up; he never came back with a request for eight-inch manila line.

—◦◦◦—

While at the Sub-Chaser Training Center I developed a new man-overboard procedure for the navy. Just beyond the Miami sea buoy, the Gulf Stream flows north anywhere from 3 to 5.5 knots, depending on the weather. Sometimes a wind from the north bucks the Gulf Stream current, making the sea off Miami choppy and making it difficult to see a small object on the water's surface.

On one such day, I was instructor on a PC and we were doing man-overboard drills. Our normal procedure was to throw a cardboard box over the side and say to the talker on the fantail "man overboard starboard side" or "man overboard portside." From the fantail, the talker would report man overboard to the bridge. Then the officer of the deck would turn to starboard or port, depending on where the box was, and try to find it.

Because of the choppy water that day, it was difficult to spot the box. On board there happened to be an "elderly" lieutenant commander who was one of the trainees. He was probably only forty-five, but I was twenty-four, so he seemed old. "Wouldn't it be great," he said, "if we had a point of reference to go back to when we dropped over the box? If we could go back down our own wake, it would be much easier to find the box."

"What a great idea!" I said.

At lunch I took a maneuvering board and, using the turning circle of a sub-chaser, figured what you would have to do to run back down the wake—and to *know* that you were running back down the wake. That was important, because if you thought you were running back down your track and you weren't, you might never recover a man overboard.

My maneuvering-board calculations indicated that on a PC, with its unique turning-circle characteristics, you would have to turn approximately 65 degrees to starboard or port, then reverse your rudder, and then come to the reverse of your original course. If you did this, you would run back down your exact track.

Hence, if "man overboard starboard side" was reported to the officer of the deck, he should immediately order right full rudder. Then he should let the ship swing 65 degrees and order the rudder shifted to left full. In the process of shifting the rudder, the ship would swing an additional 5 degrees to a total of 70 degrees. The officer should then bring the ship to the reverse of the original course so that she was running back on her original track. This would maximize the chance of recovering a man overboard.

After lunch we tried this procedure several times, and every time it made the box much easier to spot. Our wake was the point of reference for finding our man overboard.

When I got back into port I made a report to the seamanship department and all instructors, telling them to use this new man-overboard procedure for night and low visibility. It would eventually come to be known as the Williamson turn.

After I'd gotten the antisubmarine and seamanship departments squared away, Captain Mac finally agreed to let me go. My orders were to proceed to New York and assume command of the PC 1196.

Again I left an assignment with mixed emotions. I admired Captain Mac for his dedication and the way he motivated those around him. As an instructor, I was fortunate to have had a close association with many fine officers and men who had come through the training program. Many of these friendships would later be cultivated in assignments on the PC 1196 and still later on destroyer escorts. Such bonds went deep, not least because most of us were reserves. It was because we were all dedicated to a much higher purpose than in civilian life. We were dedicated to winning a war, and that required the utmost responsibility: learning to fight a war.

My only sentimental regret was leaving Betty Lou. We had developed a wonderful relationship and I knew I would miss her.

I was detached from the Sub-Chaser Training Center on December 18, 1942, and was told to report for duty at Consolidated Shipyard in New York on January 1. That allowed me to spend Christmas at home. I was delighted at the prospect on the horizon: commander of my own ship! All the training I'd received so far—midshipman school, destroyer duty in the North Atlantic, armed guard duty on a tanker, and the Sub-Chaser Training Center—had prepared me well for the challenges that lay ahead. And it developed in me a deep respect for the navy, which I felt had given me far more than I had ever given it.

6

PC Commander

WHEN I LEFT BIRMINGHAM ON December 30 by train for New York, I felt the flu coming on, and by the time I arrived the next afternoon I was wretched. I stumbled out of the train, hailed a taxi, and started the long search for a hotel. It being New Year's Eve, most of the hotels were filled, but at last I found a room in a small hotel just off Times Square.

Times Square on New Year's Eve was a madhouse. The noisy revelry only aggravated my condition as I lay in bed with a fever of 103 degrees, feeling sorry for myself. On a chill New Year's Day, still weak, I reported to the commandant of the naval district as the prospective commanding officer of PC 1196. "Prospective commanding officer" simply meant that I would be skipper once the sub-chaser was commissioned. The person who was supposed to be my executive officer just happened to be the world-famous piano player Eddy Duchin. He had joined the navy and I'd gotten to know him at the Sub-Chaser Training Center.

PC 1196 was built at the Consolidated Shipyard on the Harlem River, which runs between the Hudson and East Rivers. After reporting for duty I called my good friend Terry Jackson, whom I had met in Miami as he came through the Sub-Chaser Training Center. A lieutenant commander at this time, Terry had been assigned as prospective commanding officer of a sub-chaser built at Consolidated Shipyard just before mine.

"John," said Terry, "where are you going to stay?" When I said I didn't know, he asked me to stay with him. What a stroke of luck! Terry's family owned a building on the corner of 58th Street and Central Park West, and he was living on the top floor in a penthouse. So for three months I lived in the lap of luxury—a delightful apartment with a great view. Being roommates drew the two of us even closer, and we remained good friends until he died of cancer in the 1950s. Another good friend of mine from

Miami days was Lieutenant Commander Ambrose Chambers, prospective commanding officer of the ship built right after mine. Terry and I called him Brose.

Brose Chambers gave me a spectacular introduction to New York. For a boy from Alabama, it was thrilling. Brose was married to a girl by the name of Virginia, who was a good friend of Minnie Astor (Vincent's wife), Marie Harriman (Averell's wife), and two or three other New York socialites. These patriotic ladies operated what they called a Ship's Service Committee. They gave a party for the officers and crew of every ship that was commissioned in New York, paying for it out of their own funds and going to great effort to make each of the parties a smashing success. The parties were given at various hotel ballrooms, usually with bands playing. I don't know how many thousands of dollars this cost the sponsors. Probably none of them missed the money, but still, it was a wonderful thing to do for the war effort, not least because it helped a crew bond prior to their ship's commissioning. Of course, one of the ships being commissioned was mine, so the Ship's Service Committee gave a party for my officers and crew. Our PC affair was much smaller than a cruiser or carrier party, but nevertheless it was great fun.

During my four-month stay in New York, I spent a lot of time with my friends at the Stork Club, one of the most popular nightclubs in the country. One of the socialites introduced me to a woman named Dolly, who had a small advertising agency and produced a publicity newspaper for the club that was sent to army, navy, and marine customers. Just about every night I wasn't working on my ship or on some aspect of the commissioning, I had a date with Dolly at the Stork Club. There she would slap together articles about current customers and happenings at the club.

At that time Sherman Billingsley operated the Stork Club. He was a man who reveled in grand gestures. When I arrived with Dolly or other friends—Marie Harriman, Minnie Astor, Brose and Ginny Chambers, Terry Jackson, or my exec Eddy Duchin—Sherman always made a point of sending us a magnum of champagne. He took excellent care of good patrons. It was a good thing, too, because those four months of living the high life in New York took a toll on my lieutenant junior grade's salary; I would need about six months at sea to make up for it.

Eddie Duchin was a great friend for a night on the town. He made quite a splash in New York, and at every nightclub and restaurant we went into, we got the best seats in the place. Maître d's and waiters fawned over Eddie. His life wasn't all gay, though. Eddie's wife had died during childbirth, and his son, Peter, about two or three years old then, was living at the Harrimans' apartment under the care of a nanny. While Eddie was in New York, he stayed there with his son.

Averell Harriman was traveling all over the world for President Roosevelt and was rarely in town, which is why his wife Marie often joined our group for dinner. After dinner we would often repair to Marie's apartment, and Eddie would tickle the ivories for us, working his magic.

One evening at the Stork Club a famous publisher was to join us for dinner. His wife, a beautiful young lady, was already there with us. A phone call came for the publisher and since he had not yet arrived, his wife agreed to take the call. After a few minutes she came back to the table with a sad, worried look.

"What's the matter?" I asked.
"Oh, it's terrible," she replied. "First they bomb Paris, then London, and now Tokyo!"
"But that's great news!" I said. "Tokyo is an enemy city—Tokyo is in Japan." That was the night Jimmy Doolittle led sixteen bombers from the U.S. carrier *Hornet* on a bombing raid over Tokyo—the first U.S. attack against the Japanese homeland. She was so relieved!

As it turned out, Eddie and I never went to sea together. At the time I was a lieutenant junior grade and he was a lieutenant, and I didn't think it would be fair for him to be my exec when he was senior to me. So I had him transferred to another ship commanded by a lieutenant commander. Giving up Eddie wasn't as big a sacrifice on my part as you might think—there was no place on a sub-chaser for a piano. But I was sorry to part ways with him.

———

One thing that the Sub-Chaser Training Center did was to recommend improvements on the SCs and PCs that were being built. The PCs built at

Consolidated and other shipyards were sent down to a repair base in New York Harbor, where the navy would spend $200,000–$300,000 incorporating the improvements into them. Since I had been at the Sub-Chaser Training Center and knew what the improvements were, I had Consolidated itself put the improvements into my ship as she was being built. This, I thought, would shave between three and six weeks off of the time it took before we went to sea.

Despite my efforts to avert it, the Navy Department insisted that we spend several weeks at the repair base in New York Harbor anyway. In frustration, I called Washington and talked with the admiral in charge of the Bureau of Ships. "Admiral," I said, "the navy is going to waste a lot of time before sending me to sea with my ship. We don't need more than three or four days in New York Harbor before heading to Miami for shakedown. Can you do something about this?" Now I know this admiral had better things to do than worry about one little sub-chaser in New York commanded by an impudent whippersnapper. But by golly, he got it handled! We would stay in the harbor for one week and then head along the coast for Miami. Maybe because I was reservist rather than regular navy I didn't have any fear about bucking tradition.

On April 7, 1943, the USS PC 1196 was commissioned at New York Navy Yard's berth 14, pier G. We had a total of four officers and fifty-nine men. Lieutenant Junior Grade Charles "Pat" Morgan was to be the executive and communications officer; Ensign Karl R. Shuttle, the first lieutenant and engineering officer; and Ensign Robert Sharp, the gunnery, commissary, and supply officer. In addition to these three superb officers, the ship was given one of the best crews any PC ever had. The men included our first class boatswain's mate par excellence, E. W. McGaughy; M. L. Titis, our indispensable chief machinist's mate; and L. Gruber, our quartermaster third class. Thanks to our outstanding crew, never during my time on that ship did we fail to get under way when ordered to do so, nor did we ever fail to carry out orders as directed. Not all PCs were so reliable. I couldn't have done better with another crew.

In the next few days after commissioning, we cruised around the New York/New Jersey area, loading ammunition, fueling, compensating our magnetic compass, and generally learning how to handle our ship.

On April 16 it was time to start turning the PC 1196 into a fighting ship. That day we got under way from Tompkinsville, Staten Island, and entered the lower bay of New York Harbor to go through all the drills—general quarters, fire drill, man overboard, and collision drill. The next few days were taken up with more drills and the test firing of guns. We dropped depth charges and fired our single 3-inch 50-caliber and 20-millimeter guns. The crew was operating efficiently, and I felt completely satisfied with our gun and depth-charge tests.

My days with the high-society crowd in New York were coming to an end. While waiting for the shakedown cruise to commence, we would drill by day and anchor at Tompkinsville by night. Two-thirds of the crew would get liberty, but I didn't go ashore much anymore. We were too far away for easy access to the Big Apple.

It was the responsibility of the gangway watch to be sure that each man who went ashore had his liberty card and was authorized to leave the ship. It was also their responsibility to check each man when he came back on board to see that he had no liquor or other unauthorized material. One crew member was seventeen years old, but he looked like he was fourteen, which earned him the nickname Baby. Baby was a strikingly good-looking redhead. One late afternoon Baby appeared on the gangway to go ashore. He showed the gangway watch his liberty card, and they asked him, "Well Baby, what are you going to do tonight?"

In the toughest voice he could muster, he said, "Oh, I don't know; I think I'll go ashore and get shacked up with some old bag twenty or twenty-one years old."

When we were ready to proceed to Miami for shakedown, our orders called for us to go south along the coast. I didn't want to travel along the coast. If we cruised outside the Gulf Stream I could give my crew the at-sea training they needed, and I could do my own celestial navigation rather than piloting along the coast. I got in touch with the admiral in charge of ship routes and persuaded him to change my orders.

On Saturday, April 24, the greatest PC that ever sailed the seas got under way for Miami on her shakedown cruise. We crossed the Gulf Stream and headed south. Our estimated date of arrival was April 27.

On the trip to Miami we ran drill after drill. We encountered very little traffic, for there weren't many ships in that area. On the twenty-sixth we were conducting a drill that involved a generator failure, which required us to stop all engines. The repair was made to the generator and the engines were restarted.

I had estimated that we would pick up Cape Canaveral on radar about 0500 on the twenty-seventh on our starboard bow. At 0450 radar reported a contact on our port quarter about fifteen miles away and gaining on us. We were going along at 15 knots, and I assumed it was another ship coming up on our port quarter. About fifteen minutes later we began to pick up other contacts on our port quarter, including land. This was mystifying. All the land was supposed to be ahead, on our starboard bow.

We put our heads together and finally figured out that when we had restarted the generator the day before, we reversed the polarity on it, and everything that appeared on the radar on our port quarter was actually on our starboard bow. And so we stopped the engines again and reversed the generator's polarity. When the engines were restarted the radar was back on track, mystery solved.

We arrived at Miami that same day and moored at pier 2. I was glad to be back on my old stomping grounds at the Sub-Chaser Training Center. While there, we picked up several new men, which gave us a total crew of five officers and sixty-five men.

We stayed in Miami for shakedown approximately two weeks, during which we were put through various drills that included firing at surface and aircraft targets. Our antiaircraft practices consisted of firing at a sleeve towed a thousand yards behind a navy plane. The sleeve was some four feet in diameter and about twenty feet long. The plane would fly overhead and as soon as it passed we would begin firing at the sleeve.

At the end of our vital shakedown, we were ready for sea. As a reward for completing it, we were given the opportunity to go to Havana, Cuba, to enjoy one night of liberty. So on May 10 we got under way. In those days Havana was a wild town. Anything a sailor wanted could be found in Havana. I went ashore with Karl Shuttle and one of the other officers. We covered about as much ground as you could in one night. At about 1230 we ran into two of our guys on shore patrol trying to keep up with disorderly sailors. "Captain," they said, tired out from the night's patrol, "this is a bad part of town. I'm not sure you want to be here," and they directed us to a nicer section of the city. I appreciated their consideration, but we had gone to this district like tourists, out of curiosity—which was quickly squelched. Havana was no New York.

I wasn't sorry when the PC 1196 got under way the next morning. We were heading off for adventure, and it quickly came our way—or so we thought. That night, May 13, a German submarine sank a U.S. cargo ship southeast of the Bahama Banks and east of Cuba. Searches had gone out but found nothing.

The Bahama Banks, which lie south of the Bahamas, is an area of shallow water some ten to fifteen miles wide and fifteen miles long. It was thought that the submarine might try to escape by cutting across the Bahama Banks at night, entering the Gulf Stream, and then heading north along the U.S. coast. To prevent this from happening, on May 14 the navy ordered us to proceed to the banks and stay there overnight, intercepting the elusive sub if it tried to come across. Since the water was only thirty feet deep, the U-boat would have to cross on the surface. So at about 1500, we anchored in the middle of the banks.

All was quiet. The hours dragged on. Then suddenly at 0200 the radar began to pick up a contact. The contact, southeast of us, was heading west across the banks. It had to be the submarine, we thought. As the target got closer we went to general quarters and waited, everyone silent, watching. Based on the course it was currently on, the contact would pass about a thousand yards from where we were anchored.

We hoisted anchor and started the engines to give ourselves the mobility for an attack. Expecting the U-boat to pass on the surface, we intended to sink it with gunfire. Since U-boats carried 4-inch guns, more firepower than we had, we would have to maneuver close enough to the sub to unleash our machine guns on the enemy gunners before they had a chance to be in a position to open fire on us.

Peering through my binoculars, I watched the target approach. It was sitting low in the water, just like a surfaced submarine, and the conning tower was located just where a submarine's would be. Suddenly I lowered the binoculars, rubbed my eyes, and took a second look. To my amazement, as the vessel drew nearer, it dawned on me that this wasn't a submarine at all, but an old four-stack destroyer with its stacks cut off and no running lights. What I had thought was the conning tower was the pilothouse.

I challenged the ship, but she didn't answer. Nor did she respond when we illuminated her with a searchlight and ordered her to stop. She might be a tanker fueling submarines in the area, I thought. Maybe that was why she was running across the banks at night with no lights.

"Stop your ship!" I yelled through my megaphone. We were close enough by now for them to hear. "We're coming aboard to conduct a search!"

This time she did stop. We lowered our boat and sent over a well-armed search party. As I'd suspected, the ship was an old four-stack destroyer converted into a small tanker. But the captain had the proper papers, and the crew was mostly Bahamian. All we could do was to declare her friendly. The captain said they were heading for the Bahamas with oil—that they always cut across the banks after refueling at the Caribbean island of Aruba.

What a letdown for PC 1196, primed for action! By May 18 we were in Key West to practice runs with live submarines. My crew was performing commendably, even on the submarines, and our confidence had peaked. If we ran across a German submarine, we knew we could sink it.

On May 22 we escorted a ship to Guantanamo Bay, Cuba, which was to be our base for the next several months as we performed convoy duty in the Caribbean. Our operating area stretched from Guantanamo Bay to Trinidad.

Guantanamo Bay had a decent officers club and good places for the men to have a beer and to exercise on the beach, but there wasn't much to do. Across the bay was a barrio called Caimanera, nothing but houses of prostitution and bars. I went over one night with a couple of officers from the ship to see what it was like. Caimanera was so low-rent that I wouldn't even go into a bar for a drink. I was afraid to associate with any of the girls there. One officer going over in the boat with us said that he and two other guys had paid a girl to sleep exclusively with them. She was their "private" prostitute. I didn't need that kind of privacy and I never went to Caimanera again.

At the end of May we got under way to meet our first convoy. Convoys traveling between New York and Recife, Brazil, passed close by Guantanamo Bay. Normally, convoys left New York with one group of escorts, dropped off those escorts at Guantanamo Bay and picked up new ones (us), and then proceeded with the new group to Trinidad, where they dropped those escorts and picked up yet another new group for the voyage to Recife. The escorts were changed because, unlike the merchant ships being escorted, they didn't carry sufficient fuel supply for the entire trip. Convoys usually included a few tankers as well, which would be dropped off or picked up at Aruba.

The Caribbean has a westerly trade wind of varying intensity that whip up waves anywhere from six to twelve feet. Our route to Trinidad took us east, into the trade wind, and our little sub-chaser would bounce along, taking lots of saltwater over the bow. Now over time, saltwater wreaks havoc on metal, and whenever we were at Trinidad we'd be busy as ants cleaning and painting our ship for the return trip to Guantanamo Bay.

The trip from Guantanamo Bay to Trinidad lasted some eight days. Our first convoy consisted of four PC escorts and a single destroyer. We arrived at Trinidad on June 5, and we were relieved by the escorts that would accompany the merchant ships on the next leg of their voyage. Then we proceeded through the "Dragon's Mouth" into the Gulf of Paria. In the gulf there was a section base where we tied up to wait for a convoy heading back to Guantanamo Bay.

Trinidad was an unusual place. Its mountains jutted straight up out of the sea. During one of the early voyages of discovery, a seaman wrote, "The world is not round as we have always believed. It is in the shape of a woman's breast and Trinidad is the nipple on that breast." Once in a while the enlisted men ventured into Port of Spain, and I occasionally went there to have drinks and dinner with a couple of officers.

The section base was less exciting. There was a place for the men to go ashore and eat, as well as an officers club perched on a high hill overlooking the bay. At night, if we didn't want to go all the way into town, we would hike up this hill and drink rum punch and watch a movie under the palm trees. By day we stayed busy getting the ship ready for the return trip to Guantanamo Bay.

June and the first half of July were largely uneventful. Then one beautiful afternoon in mid-July, en route from Trinidad to Guantanamo Bay, I was standing on the wing of the bridge. We had been detached to investigate something astern of the convoy and we were on our way back when all of a sudden I saw a periscope some 500 yards ahead, moving from port to starboard. We headed a little starboard of it, and I had the men set depth charges at fifty feet. Using my stopwatch, I estimated the time it would take us to come within range of the U-boat. Once we were within range, we dropped a five-charge pattern and fired the Y-gun, which sent the charges out about 150 yards from each side of the ship.

At that time we were not far from Trinidad, and the water around that island, a mixture of saltwater and freshwater, was not conducive to carrying sound. In fact, conditions were so poor that we couldn't pick up the submarine at all on our sound gear, although we did continue to search for some fifteen minutes after dropping the depth charges. Since we couldn't hear anything or get another contact, I saw no point in dropping more depth charges. After our first attack, we had no idea whether we had damaged the sub or, if not, where it might be.

A few days later, a plane did spot a submarine in the area that had been damaged and couldn't submerge. Was it the one we'd attacked? We never found out.

After that we settled back into routine convoy duty and had no submarine sightings at all. On August 7 we got under way from Trinidad to help escort a twenty-ship convoy to Guantanamo Bay. Little did I know that on this trip, the greatest miracle of my life would take place.

It happened en route to Aruba, where we were to drop off a couple of tankers before proceeding to Guantanamo Bay. It was one of the darkest nights I've ever seen—pitch black, no stars, no moon, no rain, no lightning. You could hardly see your hand in front of your face. Suddenly, radar reported a contact about two miles astern of the convoy. Right away, I suspected that a U-boat had surfaced with the idea of closing in on the convoy and firing torpedoes. This was a common tactic of submarines. You'll recall that submerged, they could travel only 3 to 4 knots for any extended time—not fast enough to keep up with an eight-knot convoy like ours. On the surface, however, subs could go 15 to 16 knots.

We had gone over this scenario many times at the Sub-Chaser Training Center and decided that a good tactic would be simply to ram the submarine. Hitting it broadside at a high enough speed, we could slice into the sub's three-quarter-inch rolled-steel hull with our bow and sink it. If that damaged our ship and we sank, so be it—the navy would swap a 173-foot sub-chaser for a German submarine anytime.

Our PC 1196 turned and headed for the stern of the convoy where the enemy was trailing. Ringing up flank speed, we went to 18 knots and tracked the U-boat, which was traveling at 8 knots, the speed of the convoy. Presently we rounded the stern of the convoy and headed directly for the submarine.

To retain an element of surprise, I decided not to use a searchlight. We knew the Germans had a radar-detection system that told them when they were being tracked by radar, but we didn't think their radar could indicate how far away an antisubmarine ship was or in which direction it was coming.

Excited and nervous, I was determined to hit him broadside. We continued tracking while the range shrank: 1,000 yards, 900 yards, 800 yards, 700 yards, 600 yards. In another minute we would be ramming that submarine at a speed of 18 knots.

I was on the wing of the bridge with my binoculars glued to my eyes, trying to make out the target. Five hundred yards, 400 yards, 300 yards. . . . Then, with only thirty seconds to go before crash time, a brilliant blue flash of lightning pierced the sky and illuminated the water just ahead of us. It was a silent bolt, no thunder. And in that single burst of light, to my horror, I saw a native outrigger sailboat with ten to twelve people on board.

"Left full rudder!" I yelled at the top of my lungs, praying that we would miss the boat.

I was shocked at what I had almost done. If our 173-foot steel hull had rammed that fragile sailboat, it would have sliced right through it and probably killed most of the people aboard. Those that it did not kill would certainly have been wounded, and it would have been almost impossible to pick them up without turning on a searchlight and possibly attracting German submarines to our convoy. I'm sure I would have felt obligated to turn on the light and rescue survivors—but then what would we have done with them? We had a pharmacist's mate but no doctor on board.

These and a host of other hypothetical questions swirled through my head. The thought of what had almost happened was horrifying. Not only would all those natives have perished, but we would have been disgraced, the laughingstock of the Caribbean convoy group. I could almost hear officers and men from the other ships saying, "When are you guys going to hit another sailboat?"

Thankfully, the flash came thirty seconds before we hit the sailboat. It was the only lightning bolt that entire night.

The Lord sent that lightning just in time, I thought, to save the lives of those people and to save me from a disastrous mistake. How grateful and humbled I was.

The suddenness of the radar contact is what led me to believe a submarine had just surfaced. Why we didn't get a contact on the sailboat earlier, and why another ship didn't pick it up, I don't know. Two other things made me think the contact was a sub: it was on the same course at about the same speed as our convoy, and we were some forty miles from land. I had never seen a native sailboat that far from land in the Caribbean. At any rate, a sailboat as large as that one should have had some kind of light to distinguish it from an enemy ship, for in the Caribbean at that time there was little if any neutral shipping.

We arrived back at Guantanamo Bay on August 12. While we were in dry dock there, one of the officers from the local command came aboard and asked me if I would like to make a special trip. "Would you be willing to take an aircraft engine on your fantail to Jamaica?" he said. He indicated that ninety-four mail pouches also had to go along for the ride. "If you do this for me," he promised, "I'll arrange special liberty for your officers and men in Jamaica."

"You bet," I said, thinking of the limited opportunities for fun in Guantanamo Bay. So we had his engine loaded on the fantail, and on August 18 we set off for Kingston Bay, Jamaica.

As soon as we docked, I made a beeline for the shore to find out about entertainment for the officers and crew. The Jamaica Country Club graciously offered guest passes for the officers, and the Myrtle Bank Hotel, which was the best hotel in town, agreed to organize a dance for the crew that very night. I was amazed that they could get enough women together for a dance at such short notice.

Early in the evening I stopped by the country club with two other officers. At the bar, decked out in dress whites, was a big British colonel with a walrus mustache. Just as I discovered on my trip with the *Livermore* to the British island of Bermuda, he confirmed that the farther the British got away from England, the more Victorian they became. I ordered a scotch and turned to him. "Hey, sir, this scotch is a great drink, isn't it?"

"Young man," he replied, "scotch is not a drink; it is a way of life."

After drinks, we repaired to the hotel to check on the dance. It turned out to be great fun for the crew, who had had no decent liberty up to this point. Then we spotted some officers we knew in the dining room and decided to join them for dinner. The dinner was excellent—all the trimmings and accompanied by a profuse amount of wine. Afterward I suggested that we "king bee" for the meal, which hadn't been cheap. In king bee, you end up with an odd man out, who has to pay for everyone. There was an escape hatch, however—the loser could match each one of the other players for the price of the dinner. I was the loser, but in matching the other players—six of them—I won from all but one guy. In other words, I made five times the price of the dinner that night. We also king-beed for the wine. My exec, Pat Morgan, lost in the match but won from everyone except me. We both came away from that dinner better bankrolled than we'd been in months.

That was my last hurrah as commander of the PC 1196. Back in Guantanamo Bay on August 20, I was surprised—and elated—to find orders awaiting me. At that time, destroyer escorts were coming off the line fast and furiously. The Sub-Chaser Training Center had been designated to train the officers and men for these great ships. My orders were to proceed to Miami for training in destroyer escorts. My exec, Pat Morgan, would relieve me as commander of the PC.

Since I had a few days' leave before heading off to Miami, I decided to go to New York and visit my friend Dolly for a few days, then to Birmingham to see my family. I'd gotten to know the skipper of a Coast Guard ship that was performing escorts from Guantanamo Bay to New York, and I hitched a ride with him. As soon as I reported on board, I told him that I wanted to stand watch as a regular officer while en route. He said, "Heck no, John, you've been busy as you could be running that PC 1196 and you're not going to stand watch. Consider yourself on a cruise."

"Aye, aye, sir!" I enjoyed those days at sea, soaking up the sun and visiting with his officers and crew. At the end of August we arrived in New York, where I spent several delightful days with Dolly before returning to my hometown. Then on September 12, I was on my way to the Sub-Chaser Training Center to start a new life.

7

The Birth of USS *England*

THE SUB-CHASER TRAINING CENTER had an excellent destroyer escort training program. Training was hands-on, with lots of days at sea. One day we were on a destroyer escort performing different drills and exercises when the officer in charge said we were going to do a man-overboard drill using the Williamson turn. "What's that?" I said, with a start.

"You should know," he said. "You developed it."
"Yeah, I remember developing it, but I called it 'man overboard for night and low visibility.'"
"After you left, we decided to make it standard procedure for all man-overboard situations. And since you developed it, we decided to call it the Williamson turn."

Well, wasn't I pleased! By the end of the war, all the ships in the U.S. Fleet were calling their man-overboard procedure the Williamson turn.

The program lasted a little over a month. During that time, the Stork Club publicist from New York, Dolly, came down to Miami to visit me, accompanied by Marie Harriman. Every night when I got through I would have a date with Dolly. We would go dancing or go to the theater and dinner; occasionally Marie would join us for dinner. Dolly and I had a terrific time together, and we confessed our love to each other, though there was no talk of marriage.

At the end of training, I got orders to proceed to Norfolk in late October as executive officer of the destroyer escort USS *England*, which was being built at San Francisco and would soon be commissioned before heading off to the Pacific. Imagine my surprise when, only two weeks after I had arrived in Norfolk, I got a telegram from Dolly saying she was getting married. Apparently she had found another guy and had fallen in love almost immediately after she left me. I managed to get over the blow, though it did leave me bruised for a while.

What made up for Dolly's betrayal was my new assignment, a dream come true. In Norfolk I helped assemble the crew and began five weeks of intensive training. Our commanding officer, Captain W. B. Pendleton, the chief engineer, and most of the chief petty officers were in San Francisco during the ship's buildout at Bethlehem Steel Company. One of their tasks was to write the ship's organization book. So in Norfolk I was in charge of the crew. Those few weeks would be critical, and I wanted to start them running.

There were about a dozen destroyer escort crews training in Norfolk at that time. We would be judged on two things: barracks inspection and personnel inspection on the drill field. I assembled the crew and gave a little speech:

> Guys, we have a lot of work to do before going off to fight the Japanese. We want to have the best destroyer escort in the Pacific, and we're going to start now. After personnel inspections, all of the officers and crew get liberty. There is one exception—the crew of the USS *England.* You may have liberty only if we come first in barracks and personnel inspection. If we don't, you're going back to the barracks and clean them up again. Then I'll personally conduct another personnel inspection and barracks inspection. If I think these second inspections are satisfactory you may go on liberty.
>
> I want you to get in the habit of coming in first! When a plane and a ship are fighting each other, or a destroyer escort and a submarine are fighting each other, there is one first and one second. Second place is death and destruction, so we must get in the habit of winning.

I stuck to my guns. The first week we came in second in both the barracks and the personnel inspection. The crew went back and cleaned up the barracks, and I conducted another personal inspection. The barracks looked good, as did the men, so they went on liberty. The following week I inspected our barracks carefully and everything looked shipshape. Out on the drill field I looked the guys over and they presented themselves commendably. When the captain came around to inspect them, I saluted and said, "Lieutenant Williamson, executive officer, USS *England,* sir! We have the best looking crew on the field." He gave me a funny look, then proceeded with his inspection. "You may be right," he said.

That week we came in first in both the barracks and the personnel inspection, and we repeated the success each week thereafter. The guys were beginning to get the idea.

Without preparation for war, you were the loser; with preparation, you stood a fighting chance of prevailing—and of controlling yourself in combat. One day in Norfolk a young seaman came up to me who had just finished boot camp and was now assigned to the *England.* "Lieutenant Williamson," he said, "I'm afraid that when we go into combat I'll be scared."

I said to him, "Son, you may be scared, but remember, you'll be so well trained that whatever your job is—machine gunner, loader on a machine gun, or part of a 3-inch gun crew—you'll go ahead and do it. You'll be so well trained you'll react automatically."

That seemed to satisfy him, and I think he went away a little more confident.

Our five-week training period went well, and when it ended we were off to San Francisco to get the *England* in shape for the Pacific war. We caught the train on December 2, our morale high. The crew was anxious to get on with the show. That wasn't true of all ships' crews. Several prospective crew members of other ships who were on that train deserted while en route.

We arrived in San Francisco on December 5. The *England* was still berthed at Bethlehem Steel in the final buildout phase, her commissioning scheduled for the tenth, but the living quarters on board were ready, so we went directly from the train to the ship. When I arrived on board I discovered that the organization book, which was to explain in detail to the officers and crew how the ship would operate, hadn't been written. That started a mad scramble to get the job done in the few days left before we got under way for the first time.

At 1600 on December 10 the USS *England* was commissioned. The U.S. Navy district operations officer read the commissioning orders from the secretary of the navy, and then Captain Pendleton read orders marking the official start of his command. The ship was put into commission by order of the chief of naval personnel, and at 1630 watch was set.

On the morning of December 15, after a few more days of construction work, the *England* got under way for the first time, departing Bethlehem Steel and mooring at pier 54 in San Francisco Bay to take on fuel. The next few days were hectic, as we conducted drills, took on torpedoes, and performed various tests on the ship.

There wasn't much time for liberty, or to think about women. And that was a good thing, since I was still getting over Dolly. But I hadn't forgotten about Barbara Hale, the gal I had met in Chicago in 1941 who had come to California to be an actress. One weekend she was in San Francisco and called me from her hotel. I invited her out to the ship for dinner, and she arrived late in the afternoon, as beautiful as ever. I fell in love all over again and forgot all about Dolly. Barbara invited me to Los Angeles for a weekend before we set sail for the Pacific.

Most of the time I busied myself getting the ship ready for war. The workload was heavier than it should have been, on account of our lax commanding officer. Captain Pendleton lived in Oakland, California, with his wife and spent little time aboard ship. He would report in occasionally, sign any papers I had ready for him, and then go back home saying, "I'll see you in a few days, Williamson."

One day he pulled this and I said, "Captain, we have to get under way in the morning to test the sound gear."

"Well, take her out, and let me know if anything happens," he said. This struck me as a little too hands-off. Captain Pendleton didn't know me very well and had no idea whether I could handle that ship or not. The few times he had come with us for underway tests and drills, I had done the piloting, but he had brought the ship alongside. Fortunately for him, I loved handling ships and had had ample experience conning a 173-foot sub-chaser.

In fact, I was glad to be given the responsibility. An incident in late December was typical. Radio inspectors and technicians came aboard and we got under way to compensate our magnetic compass at the compensating range. Once again, Captain Pendleton was absent, so the pilot took over as conning officer. As the ship's navigator I was keeping track of where we were at all times. At one time during the compensation, we came, I thought, too close to shallow water. I took the control away from the pilot, guided the ship out of that water, and then turned the control back over to him.

On December 22, Captain Pendleton did join us for weapons-firing tests. Among other tests, we fired plastic hedgehogs from our Mark 10 projectors on the bow. The Mark 10 projector was a relatively new antisubmarine weapon that could rocket-fire twenty-four hedgehogs two hundred yards ahead of the ship in a semi-elliptical pattern. Each projector was filled with thirty-five pounds of TNT. (Remember, the depth charges we dropped from the stern contained six hundred pounds of TNT, while those fired from our K-guns contained three hundred pounds of TNT.) The hedgehogs were much more effective than preset depth charges because they would not explode unless they actually came into contact with a submarine.

You'll recall that the depth charge attack was not very accurate because the submarine could move out of range well before the charges sank to their preset depth. Moreover, you had to guess the depth of a submarine unless you could pass over it and get a Fathometer (depth indicator) reading. A hedgehog had to be very accurately fired, but if it hit, the concentrated power of its thirty-five pounds of TNT was enough to blow a two- or three-foot hole in a submarine's three-quarter-inch rolled-steel hull. With an accurately fired hedgehog, you knew you had scored a hit, and a devastating one; with depth charges, you couldn't always be sure that you'd even made contact with the target.

In the latter part of December, we returned to Bethlehem Steel for some additional work on our turbo-electric engineering plant. Then on the thirtieth it was off to San Diego for shakedown. Finally! As we departed San Francisco and sailed under the Golden Gate Bridge, we were one happy crew, proud of our ship—which at full power had a speed of approximately 24 knots—and were raring to fight the Japanese. Of the fourteen officers among us, only five had been to sea on a navy ship, and of our more than two hundred enlisted men, I would guess that no more than forty had any experience at sea.

New Year's Day 1944 was a day of celebration, not just for our ship but also for many other ships at San Diego that were going through shakedown or just returning from the Pacific. For me, it was the start of the most eventful year of my life. But I didn't know that then, and anyway, there wasn't much time to contemplate the future. I was busy as a cat on a hot tin roof. The next few weeks were a dizzying whirl of activity. The *England* had to prepare to fight not just submarines, but also airplanes and ships. During all the underway training I continued to navigate, and because Captain Pendleton, even when he was aboard, didn't do much, I took on the responsibility of running the ship.

An example of the sort of training we were doing was zigzagging. On January 4 we went to sea with two patrol escorts, the *Coronado* and the *Morris,* to practice this. A submarine had a better chance of getting close enough to attack a ship on a steady course than if she was on a zigzagging course. It was extremely difficult for a sub to score a hit if it fired a torpedo just as the target was about to change course. When we finally got under way for combat, we would usually follow a zigzagging course.

It was a lesson that the USS *Indianapolis* didn't take to heart. The *Indianapolis* was the cruiser that delivered the nuclear bombs to the planes that would drop them on Japan. While returning to a harbor in the Philippine islands, she was keeping a steady course. It just so happened that a Japanese submarine spotted the ship. Quickly jockeying into position to fire, it launched a torpedo and sank the *Indianapolis.* Fortunately, some of the crew survived. The captain was court-martialed primarily because he was not zigzagging—that is, he wasn't taking all precautions to avoid a submarine torpedo. No doubt he believed the war would soon be over and that no enemy sub could possibly be in the area.

The next few days were taken up with antisubmarine warfare practice against live submarines. Though my regular battle station was in the combat information center, Captain Pendleton let me conn many of the submarine runs during these practices—invaluable training for the future. Returning to San Diego Harbor from antisubmarine practice on the night of January 5, we tied up alongside the USS *Whitehurst,* one of our sister ships. This was the first time the *England* had been with a sister ship, and it was a joyous occasion meeting her crew.

In the ensuing days we had a lot of station-keeping practices with other ships, which was important for officers because practically all of our shipboard life we would be sailing with other ships, either keeping station on them or having them keep station on us. We also practiced the three different conditions of battle readiness: general quarters, condition 2, and condition 3.

As I mentioned, under condition 2 one-half of the crew was on watch at any given time. It was called Watch and Watch. Watches were usually four hours off and four hours on, except for "dog" watches, which were two hours. We had tried condition 2 on the *Livermore,* but it wore us out. We found we were much more effective under condition 3, with one-third of the crew on watch at a time. This meant you were on one watch and off two. A ship's crew could do this for many days and still perform other shipboard duties. For most combatant ships, condition 3 was the normal war cruising condition. When enemy action was imminent or probable, you would go to general quarters.

Our officers and men were given liberty as time permitted. One night three of our officers had had too much to drink at a tavern and couldn't find a taxi to get back to the dock. An army jeep with the keys in it happened to be sitting outside the tavern. So they commandeered the jeep and drove it back to the dock in time to catch the ship's boat.

When I heard about this the next day, I didn't think it was conduct becoming officers from the USS *England,* so I decided to put the fear of God in them. A friend of mine once joked that in Birmingham there was a street named for me, and it was called One Way. I learned in the navy that you must have standards to live by, and standards of leadership to go by, otherwise anything goes. These standards were often non-negotiable. It would be foolish for a leader not to insist on standards that help people achieve their potential, that help them be what they are capable of being.

I faked a message from the commanding officer of Pacific training, which was the operational command in San Diego, indicating that three navy officers had been seen stealing a jeep outside a tavern. Each ship was to report the names of any of its officers who had been ashore the previous night.

When I showed this message to the three officers, it really shook them up. Then I produced two more fake documents: one reported their names to "Commanding Officer, Pacific Training, Shore Patrol Command" and another ordered the officers to report to him the next day. With each successive missive, they withered a little more.

I let them sweat for a few hours before letting the cat out of the bag. "Look guys," I said, "what you did was not in keeping with the conduct of officers from the USS *England.* Now I'm not going to say that you can't have too much to drink again, but I am going to tell you not to get so drunk that you end up doing something stupid like this." The ploy must have worked, because those officers never caused trouble again.

The latter half of January was spent in additional drills and practices. Voice radio, radar tracking, laying smoke screens, antiaircraft firing, night training—you name it, we went over it. Several times we fired practice torpedoes that would float at the end of their run. All of our torpedoes ran hot and straight, and we got good at firing and hitting our target ship. This and all the other work was getting us ready for protracted days at sea in combat areas. It was critical to train the officers and men in their various duties so that no matter how rough the sea, how fierce the enemy, or how rapid the heartbeat, they would still be able to perform. Operating the *England* to the limit of her ability and ours was a life-and-death matter. But no matter how hard we practiced, we wouldn't know what real combat, or protracted periods at sea, was like until we joined the war in earnest.

That day would soon come. On January 25 an inspection party from the commanding officer of Pacific training arrived on board, observed us as we went through various drills, and gave us the green light. The very next night in San Diego Harbor we swapped practice torpedoes for real ones and loaded the tubes for real.

We had one more availability at Treasure Island in San Francisco before heading off to Pearl Harbor. During our last stay there, Nelson Granzella, chief quartermaster, reported on board for duty. I badly needed a chief quartermaster to help me with navigation, and in the months to come Nelson would prove invaluable.

In early February my personal life brightened. Barbara Hale, you'll recall, had invited me to Los Angeles for a weekend visit before the *England* set sail for the Pacific. So with just a couple of weekends left, I took a plane down from San Francisco. In those days a common means of commercial flying was the DC 3, a small propeller plane that carried some twenty or thirty people. The plane had an aisle in the middle, with two seats to either side. As I settled myself into a window seat, I noticed a number of female passengers scrambling to get a seat next to a vacant seat.

"What are they doing?" I asked the stewardess.

"Didn't you know?" she said. "Robert Taylor is getting on the plane in Oakland, and these ladies are hoping he'll sit next to them." Robert Taylor was one of the best-known, best-looking Hollywood stars, and he also happened to be a navy lieutenant. At the time he was married to the movie actress Barbara Stanwyck. I was starstruck by her.

We landed in Oakland, and sure enough Robert Taylor came on board. All his would-be companions were craning their necks and looking around anxiously, hoping against hope that he would deposit himself into the adjacent seat. Imagine their disappointment when, appearing to prefer the companionship of a fellow navy man, he lowered himself into the seat next to mine.

I seized the chance to talk with my neighbor, not so much because he was Robert Taylor, but because he was married to Barbara Stanwyck. After we introduced ourselves, I pretended not to know who he was. "Robert, I've seen you somewhere before. You look very familiar."

"Well," he responded, "I've been in a number of movies. That's probably where you've seen me."
"Yes, that's right. Well, I'm glad to meet you. You're one great actor."

We hit it off just fine, and when we arrived in Los Angeles, there was Barbara Stanwyck, waiting to meet him. He introduced me to her, and they invited me to come spend the weekend with them. I said thank you, but I was in Los Angeles to see my girlfriend, the actress Barbara Hale, hoping they would know who she was. They didn't. Barbara Hale, young starlet, wasn't in the same league as Barbara Stanwyck.

Nonetheless, she was thriving as a starlet in Hollywood—getting paid well and loving her work. She was glad she had gone to Hollywood and was looking forward to a good career in the movies. It just so happened that Barbara Hale's dad was in Los Angeles visiting her the weekend I flew down. When I got to the hotel he invited me to stay with him, since there were two double beds in his room. To be polite I accepted, but I was sorely disappointed at the prospect of not having my own room, which always left open the possibility that I could lure Barbara into it. No way I wanted to room with her father.

Still, we had a great weekend. On Saturday we toured Hollywood and ate lunch at one of the best restaurants in town. That night we went to a hotel for dinner and dancing. Yes, I was still in love with Barbara Hale, and she was still *not* in love with me, though she enjoyed my company. My only consolation was that she wasn't romantically interested in anyone. Sooner or later, I thought, this gal is going to fall in love with me. Little did I know that when I left on Sunday afternoon, that would be the last time I would ever see Barbara Hale, except in the movies and on the *Perry Mason* show, where she played the secretary.

The fact that I was heading off to war made my parting from Barbara a little easier than it would otherwise have been. I was anxious to get back in the saddle! On February 14, the *England* departed Treasure Island for Pearl Harbor. We were a heavily laden ship. A few days before our departure, a commander at the San Francisco Naval Base contacted me and said, "Williamson, how many extra men can you take on your ship to Pearl Harbor?"

"What do you mean, Commander?"
"Well, every ship that leaves here we try to load to full capacity in order to get everyone as far west as we can."
"We don't have but a few extra bunks," I said, "though we do have lots of cots. We could probably put thirty men on cots if necessary."

So we ended up with an extra twenty-eight navy men and eleven marines—one crowded ship. I had all these people put on watch stations so they would have something to do for the five or six days en route to Pearl Harbor.

Loaded to capacity with personnel, supplies, fuel, and ammunition, we joined up with the destroyer escort *Cloues* and sailed in column under the Golden Gate Bridge. Finally, it was off to war.

8

Pollywogs in the Pacific

FROM THE TIME WE SAILED under the Golden Gate Bridge in company with the *Cloues* and hit the open ocean, the weather turned rough. Winds blew from 15 to 30 knots all the way to Pearl Harbor, and sea swells were ten to fifteen feet. As the two destroyer escorts bounced along, one after another of our marine guests fell sick, and they remained in misery all the way to Pearl. One day I heard a green-faced marine saying to another, "You know, they can keep me out here in this Pacific for fifteen long years, and when they tell me I can go home, if they're planning to send me on a destroyer escort, I'll tell them to hell with it. I'll stay on the island." The other marine readily agreed.

I had to hand it to our marine guests—as sick as they were, they stood their watches as assigned. On February 20, 1944, right on schedule, we contacted the high mountain on Oahu, Hawaii, 111 miles away. At dawn, planes from Pearl Harbor came out and let us practice antiaircraft firing at sleeves they were towing. Later that morning we moored in outer Pearl Harbor Bay and immediately set about transferring our supernumeraries to shore. With great relief, they dragged themselves off our crowded little ship, never looking back.

The very next day we got under way for Funafuti in the Ellice Islands, escorting the attack transport *Yarmouth.* The skipper of that ship was officer in tactical command and we were the screen. We took station about fifteen hundred yards ahead of the *Yarmouth* and patrolled back and forth, protecting her from any submarine that might be lurking in our path.

The reason we weren't part of a larger convoy, which would have been the case had we been operating in the Atlantic, was the different war environment in the Pacific. Here the Allies had far-flung supply points for waging a war by land, sea, and air. Allied shipping was not heavily dependent on convoys because it was difficult for the Japanese to concentrate submarines over an ocean as vast as the Pacific. The wolf pack formations that terrorized Allied shipping in the Atlantic were rare in the Pacific. In terms of mission, too, Japanese subs were stretched thinner than German U-boats. Although one of their main missions was indeed to destroy enemy shipping, Japanese submarines were also used equally for scouting and, in some cases, for the resupplying of beleaguered outposts lying far from the homeland. In the Pacific war, then, Allied ships ran less of a risk from submarines than in the Battle of the Atlantic. But there was one big disadvantage that antisubmarine warriors faced in the Pacific, and that was the problem of detection. Japanese submarines, which didn't do radio reporting, were much more difficult to detect than German U-boats.

The Japanese submarine mission of resupplying outlying garrisons had grown critical by early 1944. From the beginning of the Pacific war, U.S. strategy to overcome the Japanese involved a dual thrust: army general Douglas MacArthur would push up through the islands of the southwest Pacific while Admiral Chester Nimitz led his naval forces on an island-hopping drive westward across the Pacific. The two thrusts would converge south of Japan for the final assault against the homeland. By the time the *England* was steaming toward Funafuti in the southwest Pacific, the turning point in the war had already occurred. The Americans had secured Guadalcanal and the other Solomon Islands, as well as the Gilberts and the Marshalls, and planning was under way for the final leg of the campaign in New Guinea. The U.S. strategy was working; the Americans were closing in on the Japanese homeland from two directions. By now whatever hopes Japan had harbored of further advances in the Pacific were dashed. So the Japanese concentrated on forming successive rings of defense against attacks on the homeland. That involved reinforcing their far-flung island garrisons with the help of their submarines.

———✦———

During the voyage to Funafuti, we finally adjusted to our skipper's hands-off leadership style. It certainly took some getting used to, especially for those of us who had gone to sea with commanders who believed in an iron rule. Lieutenant Commander Pendleton—"Doc" to his peers—had graduated from the U.S. Naval Academy in 1921. From the day of his commissioning to the day he arrived in San Francisco to take command of the USS *England,* Pendleton had gone through a string of unusually short tours of duty. One of his tours was as executive officer of the USS *Stewart,* a destroyer on the China station. Then lieutenant Pendleton reported to the *Stewart* on October 6, 1934, and was detached on January 16, 1935, at the request of the commanding officer and the division commander. In remarks attached to his fitness report, the *Stewart's* commanding officer noted this about Lieutenant Pendleton:

> This officer is below average as an executive and navigating officer, particularly in view of the length of his commissioned service. He has demonstrated inability to function as an administrator. He shows but little foresight in even simple matters. He is unreliable in carrying out the orders of the commanding officer, due either to forgetfulness or lack of comprehension. He has failed to execute too many orders, and has executed too many others incorrectly. He is very slow to grasp fundamentals of piloting and his working knowledge of celestial navigation is too limited.

The commanding officer did concede, however, that Pendleton was "even-tempered and loyal" and that his personal conduct was exemplary.

Perhaps this fitness report was the reason Pendleton had remained a lieutenant for seventeen long years before being appointed temporary service as a lieutenant commander in 1942. He commanded the destroyer escort *Smart* from May 13, 1942, until October 9, 1943, at which time he was transferred to the precommissioning detail for the *England* as she was being built in San Francisco. When Lieutenant Commander Pendleton took command of the *England,* it was after a long and checkered career.

Prior to commanding the USS *Smart,* Lieutenant Pendleton had had four years in and around the South Pacific. He had commanded the USS *Tern* (AK 31), which had been a minesweeper and was converted to a seagoing tug. Pendleton's ship was at Pearl Harbor on December 7, 1941. His ship fought fires raging on board the battleship *West Virginia* and his crew rescued its survivors.

Our skipper's lackadaisical attitude about almost everything clearly indicated that he didn't want to go back to sea. Though he felt the navy had treated him badly by keeping him a lieutenant for so long, he wasn't keen on being commanding officer now that he'd made it. In fact, after we had been on board for two weeks, Captain Pendleton asked me to draft a letter recommending me for command of the vessel. "I'll sign it," he said. "Yes sir!" I responded, surprised and barely able to disguise my delight. So off I went and penned the letter, and as promised, Captain Pendleton signed it. Alas, if it sounds too good be true, it probably is. The Navy Department never responded, and Pendleton remained our captain.

My disappointment quickly faded, for in a sense I became commanding officer by default, running the ship in the absence of instructions from the skipper. My normal battle station was in the combat information center, where we tracked the courses of enemy ships, subs, and planes. But because of my antisubmarine warfare knowledge—and Captain Pendleton's lack of it, despite his tour of duty as commander of a destroyer escort and a course at the Sub-Chaser Training Center—my station during a submarine attack was with the captain on the bridge, by the sound repeater.

On those occasions when Captain Pendleton did exert a semblance of leadership, his decisions could be arbitrary. For example, there was the time we were proceeding with another destroyer escort from Guadalcanal south to Noumea, in New Caledonia, for availability. Now, the *England* was a 306-foot destroyer, but this other ship had a shorter, 292-foot hull. The sea was choppy, with twelve- to fifteen-foot swells.

Captain Pendleton, the officer in tactical command, was in a hurry to reach Noumea to get our boiler firesides cleaned, so he rang up a speed of 20 knots. The other ship, two thousand yards on our port beam, also increased speed to 20 knots. The *England* was riding the swells without much trouble, but the shorter-hull destroyer escort began pitching badly.

A half hour later the skipper of the other ship, Hank Vaughn, requested permission to slow down. He was taking too much of a beating at this speed in a medium-heavy sea. I was on the bridge with Captain Pendleton. "They're not being hurt," said Pendleton. "We'll continue at this speed." About fifteen minutes later we got another message from Vaughn: "We are in danger of breaking longitudinals. May we slow down?" When Captain Pendleton saw this dispatch, he said, "Tell him 'Bullshit.'"

"Now wait a minute, Captain," I intervened. "That's a short-hull destroyer escort. You can see she's taking much more of a beating than we are. You're in charge of that ship. If she does break a longitudinal, you'll be responsible for it and could face a court-martial. Hank Vaughn is a very competent skipper."

Captain Pendleton paused, then turned to the signalman and said, "Tell him 'Proceed independently.'" So the other ship slowed down and we left her behind.

We arrived at Noumea around dusk. The next morning Captain Pendleton was up at the break of dawn looking for the other destroyer escort, which hadn't come in yet. When she finally did arrive, at 0930, he was greatly relieved. He knew he should have slowed down and stayed with her.

Now you might think that on account of his leadership style, the officers and petty officers didn't like Captain Pendleton. Far from it—we loved him! He let us run the ship the way we felt it should be run, and that built our confidence, and confidence in combat would be a crucial element in the later successes of the USS *England*. Partly because of our skipper's hands-off approach, the *England* would become a legend in the Pacific.

Yes, we grew fond of Captain Pendleton, quirks and all. Unlike most skippers, he never suggested we have a matériel inspection, and I had to prevail on him before he agreed to hold an inspection every Friday afternoon, which was standard in the navy. But there was one thing Captain Pendleton was a stickler about, and that was equipment—all equipment on the ship should work. He had an odd way of enforcing this rule. One afternoon at matériel inspection, we came across a submersible pump that didn't work. He turned to me and said, "Throw the goddamn pump over the side." I didn't argue with him, but behind his back I made sure the pump didn't get tossed, because submersible pumps were in short supply and were very expensive. The men had that pump working by the afternoon.

Another quirk of our skipper's was his insistence that the decks be washed down with freshwater instead of saltwater, the practice on most ships. Obviously, a ship's freshwater supply was limited (we produced freshwater with evaporators, a slow process), while saltwater was plentiful (all you had to do was pump it out of the ocean and wash down the deck). Captain Pendleton didn't care. He wanted those decks scrubbed down with freshwater.

One afternoon some garbage spilled onto the ship's fantail, and I had the men wash it down with saltwater. The skipper happened by and discovered what we were up to. "Cut out the saltwater," he barked. "I want those decks washed down with freshwater."

"But Captain," I responded, "we were taking spray over. Since saltwater was already on the deck, I didn't think it would hurt to use it." "Williamson," he said, in his inimitable way, "I don't know how to stop saltwater spray from coming over these decks, but I do know how to keep hoses from spraying saltwater on the decks."

Once, we were anchored at a little island called Emirau to have our firesides and watersides cleaned. Captain Pendleton asked if anyone played bridge. "Bob Webb was a tournament bridge player back in the States," I replied. I told him I played, as did our gunnery officer, George Brines, though neither of us very well.

So the four of us got together in the wardroom for a game. Pendleton announced, "Webb and I will play you and Brines." That sure was a match between giants and midgets. It cost me $58 to brush up on my bridge game. After that I always made excuses when Pendleton went casting about for bridge players. Practically every time I passed through the wardroom, there would be the skipper saying, "Williamson, let's get a bridge game going."

Despite all his leadership quirks, Captain Pendleton remained dear to our hearts, as we did to his. Later, after the *England*'s accomplishments would make her a household name in the fleet, Pendleton was promoted to commander and transferred to take command of a division of destroyer escorts. After the war I got to know a skipper from one of the ships in that division. Commander Pendleton often rode on his ship. He said all Pendleton could talk about was the *England*—"the *England* this" and "the *England* that." He and his officers got damn tired of hearing about the *England*.

———

Getting back to our cruise to Funafuti, at 2124 on February 25, we crossed the equator. Because we crossed at night, we had to wait until the next day to initiate all the pollywogs for whom this was a first, which was most of us. Captain Pendleton, if I recall, was the only commissioned officer who had crossed the equator, and only twenty or so senior petty officers had crossed. It was up to those few to initiate us into the "Ancient Order of the Deep." Boatswain's Mate First Class Frank Manlove, selected to be Davy Jones, was in charge of the ritual.

Those few guys played various diabolical tricks on the remaining two hundred of us. I was one of their prime victims. They handcuffed me to the stanchions supporting a 20-millimeter gun and hosed me down with saltwater until I thought I was going to drown. When they finally relented, I was ordered to get dressed and don a topcoat, not a prospect I relished in the equatorial heat. Then they hung a sign around my neck and made me stand over the garbage so that the Japanese would not steal it.

All of us pollywogs had to crawl through a twenty-foot aircraft-towed sleeve that had been sprayed full of fuel oil. We emerged covered with the gunk from head to foot, and even though it would take a long time to get all that stuff off, we had a good laugh. When our tribulations ended we were issued cards qualifying us as proud members of the Ancient Order of the Deep.

That same day, February 26, we crossed the 180th meridian, the international date line, and set our clocks ahead twenty-four hours, which took us from Saturday straight to Monday. You could set the clocks ahead either at 2400 on February 26 or at 0000 on February 27. However you looked at it, we missed a day and ended up with February 28 as our next log date.

That day, we arrived at Funafuti, refueled, and loaded up with provisions. By March 2 we were under way once again, this time to escort the troop ship *Torrens* to Guadalcanal in the Solomon Islands. We took our station fifteen hundred yards ahead to patrol and to protect her from submarine attack. During daylight hours the *Torrens* would follow a zigzagging course, and we had to stay alert in order to anticipate her turns. Soon we were joined by the destroyer escort *Forman*. This was the first of the ships to be commissioned in our division, Destroyer Escort Division 40. The officer in charge of the screen, the commander of Escort Division 40, who was on the *Forman*, put us on the port bow of the *Torrens* while his ship took the starboard bow. After dropping the *Torrens* off at Guadalcanal, we proceeded to Tulagi Harbor, Florida Island, also in the Solomons, and moored alongside the destroyer escort USS *George*. The *George* was a part of Escort Division 39, and we would later see much more of her.

By this time the United States had control of the Solomons, which had been secured after much fierce fighting and many lives lost. The Solomons were a thousand miles northeast of Australia, and the main island, Guadalcanal, was the first Pacific island on which the U.S. Marines and Army had landed in force. Guadalcanal was a strategic spot because it lay in the shipping lane used by the United States to ferry men and matériel for the Pacific offensive.

Several naval battles had been fought in the strait between Florida Island and Guadalcanal, and Tulagi Harbor, or Purvis Bay, was known as Iron Bottom Bay for the many ships sunk there. Being a secluded bay, Iron Bottom was also cluttered with ships afloat, everything from small minesweepers and destroyer escorts to larger destroyers, cruisers, battleships, and aircraft carriers. The senior officer present afloat was in the cruiser *Honolulu*. Comparatively small fry, we on the *England* had been told to anchor near the harbor entrance.

Gone from the States for three weeks, we were feeling pretty confident. During that time we had performed numerous drills successfully and crossed the equator and the international date line. None of our crew was seasick any more. After our long crossing (its duration brought home just how big the Pacific was), we were finally near the area of combat, and we were ready for it. Japanese aircraft and submarines were still lingering in and around the Solomons. But we had yet to be put to the test.

Tulagi Harbor, surrounded by hills on all sides, never had strong winds. There was a shack on the beach that served as an officers club, and there were spots on the beach for the enlisted men to drink beer and to play softball or horseshoes. Since alcoholic beverages were not allowed on ships, we carried beer on the ship, and whenever there was a chance we sent the guys ashore with some cold beer. It wasn't ideal, but at least it gave the men some time off and let them feel solid ground under their feet.

Mid-March was taken up with screening duty and further training in the southwest Pacific area. On March 12 we arrived with our convoy at Espíritu Santo for minor repairs and to take on supplies and men transferring to other ships. Espíritu Santo was a large base and a good supply point for ships of the U.S. Fleet.

Navy enlisted men wore black-shined shoes and white navy caps. While in Espíritu Santo I noticed that the enlisted men from several other ships were wearing high-top shoes and baseball caps instead. These struck me as much more practical on board ship in combat areas, so I sent our supply people over to the base to see if they could get their hands on some. We ended up with several hundred pairs of marine combat boots and several hundred baseball caps. The combat boots did prove more useful for all the rough work the sailors did in wartime, and the caps were an improvement as well. They didn't blow off as easily as navy caps; they cut down on glare, allowing gun crews to see better; and they were much more comfortable. In fact, these uniform accessories were such a hit that Captain Pendleton and the other officers took to wearing combat boots and baseball caps. I stuck to my regulation cap.

On March 18 we got under way for Guadalcanal. The two anchorages off Guadalcanal were Lunga Point and Koli Point, neither of which was safe from submarine attack, so off and on over the next few days we performed screening duty to protect ships anchored there.

To create the steam for the turbines that ran the *England*'s turbo-electric engineering plant, we had to have boilers, which needed to be cleaned frequently—every five hundred hours for the firesides. Toward the end of the month, it being time to clean the firesides, Captain Pendleton requested a limited availability in Noumea, New Caledonia, well to the south of Guadalcanal. We escorted the *Crescent City* there. All the officers and crew were looking forward to Noumea, because it was something none of us had seen in months—a bona fide city—and because Noumea, a French possession, had French-speaking girls, or so we thought. We arrived with our hearts full of anticipation, only to find nothing much of interest, and no beautiful French girls.

In early April we continued our work of escort and screening duty in the area. The troop ships and supply ships we escorted were carrying precious cargo, including wounded men whom the hospital ship USS *Pinkney* was transporting from Guadalcanal to Noumea. On April 13, while escorting the *Pinkney* on this mission, we picked up a suspicious sound contact and immediately made for the location where it had originated.

While the *Pinkney* proceeded independently, we dropped five depth charges and continued to search for what we thought might be a submarine. After another attack with a single hedgehog, we lost contact, conducted a retiring search curve, and concluded that it was probably just a large fish. Poor fish—it must have been quite shaken up by our attacks. No doubt the native inhabitants of the Pacific were glad when the war ended.

Three days later we received orders from the commanding officer of the Utan Naval Air Base on Espíritu Santo to investigate another sound contact. At 1510 we arrived at the point where the submarine was supposed to be and relieved the destroyer escort *Levy,* which had received the original contact. Accompanied by our sister ship, the *Spangler,* we conducted a retiring search curve from the point of last contact but again found nothing. It was true: enemy subs were tough to locate in the vast battleground of the Pacific.

By April 21 we were back in Tulagi for refueling, with the *Spangler* tied up to our port side. We had never seen our division commander. That day he transferred his command ship from the *Spangler* to the *England* and came on board with his staff. Commander C. A. Thorwall was in his forties, about the same age as Captain Pendleton. I didn't realize that the day Commander Thorwall came aboard with his staff, my troubles would begin.

Thorwall had received his commission through the merchant marines. When a person graduated from the Merchant Marine Academy and received a commission as a third mate, he could also receive a commission as a navy ensign. As he worked his way up the line and qualified for second mate, first mate, chief mate, and then master of a ship, he got equivalent navy promotions. Commander Thorwall had risen through the ranks this way, becoming master of a merchant ship and navy lieutenant commander. After coming on active duty in the navy, he was appointed commanding officer of a destroyer escort and later promoted to commander of our six-ship Destroyer Escort Division 40.

The same day Commander Thorwall came aboard, Commander Hamilton Haines, in command of Destroyer Escort Division 39, transferred to the *England* with his staff. They were to ride with us until we rendezvoused with the destroyer escort *Raby* a few days later. We were going to be seeing a lot of the USS *Raby* and the commander of Escort Division 39.

Over the next few weeks, the *England* hustled all over the southwest and central Pacific escorting ships hither and thither, often with the *Spangler* and the *Raby* in our screen. During some of these voyages we escorted CVEs (small, somewhat crude carriers built out of merchant ship hulls). They were much smaller than fleet carriers, but they could be built much more quickly and in greater numbers.

One of our many destinations was Seeadler Harbor on Manus Island in the Admiralties, northwest of New Guinea. At the time, Manus Island was the farthest point of the U.S. advance on Japan, and it was still being contested as General MacArthur's troops made their way up the islands of the southwest Pacific toward Japan. I was a little concerned about entering Seeadler Harbor because the only navigational chart I had was a 1790 chart made by Dutch explorers, the first Western explorers in this part of the Pacific. At every port we had been to, I tried to obtain a more modern chart of Manus Island, and though modern charts existed, every place that stocked them had run out. So I had to rely on this 1790 Dutch chart, which, amazingly, guided us in safely. After we anchored, we could hear artillery and small-arms fire as the two sides fought over this faraway island.

No sooner had we arrived at Manus than we refueled and reversed course, helping escort the CVEs *Petrof Bay* and *Barnes* to the central Pacific island of Majuro in the Marshalls. Finally on May 11, after several additional voyages between Guadalcanal and the Marshalls, we anchored at Tulagi Harbor for a five-day availability to clean firesides.

Late one afternoon while we were anchored there, I happened to be on the bridge when all of a sudden three Japanese planes came over the hill from the west in search of targets in the harbor. This was the first time I had seen enemy aircraft, and it came as a complete surprise—there had been no warning of Japanese planes in the area. That's because the planes, flying low, were screened from radar by the hillsides surrounding the harbor. But we were just small fry. They flew right past us in search of larger targets in the inner harbor.

Ever since April 21, Commander Thorwall and his staff had been on the *England.* With all the other ships in his division operating elsewhere or only sporadically with us, the commodore and his staff had little to do. He would wander the decks and come and go on the bridge as he pleased. No one liked him—not Captain Pendleton, not the officers, and certainly not the enlisted men.

Thorwall grouched about everything being wrong on the ship. When he was on the bridge he could always find something wrong. When he walked about the decks he didn't speak to the enlisted men unless he found something he thought was nonregulation. He had been on the ship only two or three days when he called me aside and said, "Williamson, your men are out of uniform."

"What do you mean, Commodore?"

"They're wearing nonregulation shoes and caps. I want your men in regulation black shoes and white caps. Get rid of those combat boots and baseball caps."

"But sir, the marine combat boots are much more advantageous to our crew when they're working around the ship, and especially if they go into combat. And the baseball caps cut down glare—the gunners and everyone topside can see much better." I enumerated all the other benefits introduced by our nonreg uniform and told him that this garb was being worn on other ships as well. "Some admirals have even taken to wearing baseball caps," I added.

"Williamson, I don't care if other ships are wearing this stuff or if you think it's better; I want your crew in uniform *now*."

"But sir, Captain Pendleton has given the men permission to wear these boots and the baseball caps. I respond to orders from the captain since I'm subordinate to him. If you want me to order our men to put on the black shoes and the white caps, please get the captain to give me those orders. I can't change his orders without his permission."

Commander Thorwall was all steamed up by now.

"Williamson," he said, "Captain Pendleton is too old and has been in the navy too long for me to tell him anything. I doubt he'll do it."

"I'm sorry, sir," I persisted, "but I can't do it without his permission."

To be honest, I didn't think Captain Pendleton gave a damn whether the men wore black shoes and white caps or marine combat boots and baseball caps, but he did agree that the nonregulation items were far more practical for combat. At any rate, Thorwall didn't approach him, which was odd considering his passion about the matter. The commodore continued to nag me and I continued to resist, saying that I had to have orders from my skipper.

It was obvious to me and no doubt it was obvious to Commander Thorwall that he and I were never going to get along. I sensed that this was just the beginning, and that it would only get worse.

Destroyer Escort DE635: Bow view 45° off centerline.

John A. Williamson photo taken by the navy shortly after the Battle of Okinawa.
(United States Navy photo)

Three Top Soundmen. L–R, Paul Ayers, Third Class; Roger Bernhardt, Second Class; John Prock, First Class, Lead Soundman. All three guys were instrumental in keeping our sound gear going.

The USS *England* entering the water after Mrs. England had christened it. (National Archives)

The overhead between the bridge and the number 2 gun after we were hit by a five hundred-pound bomb carried by a suicide plane. The bomb exploded in the forward part of the wardroom just above the main deck. (National Archives)

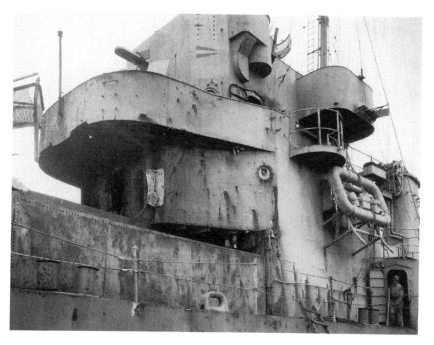

The damaged part of the ship. The section of the hull just to the left and above the ladder is a long section of 7/8-inch steel that was cut from a captured Japanese ship and welded into place from the beginning of the picture to the end, just to the left of the ladder. Since our main deck was blown out just behind this plate, it helped in preventing the waves from washing over our main deck and going in to the sections below. Other damage to the ship is also visible. (National Archives)

Damage done in the part of the ship control section called the "Pilot House." It was on Pilot House deck that we found water about five inches deep boiling from the fires raging below it. In the forward part of the Pilot House, the portholes were so darkened that one could hardly see out of them. (National Archives)

9

The Twelve Days of USS *England*

Up to this point in the war, the USS *England* had busied herself with a seemingly endless string of duties that had little to do with combat. We drilled; we escorted ships; we refueled and took on supplies; we ferried men around the southwest and central Pacific; we pursued a handful of suspicious sound contacts to no avail; and all the while the war raged around us. We were anxious to test the antisubmarine skills we had worked so hard to hone. Now our time was about to come. Over a period of twelve days in May 1944, the *England* was to rack up a series of tactical successes that would make her one of the most famed ships in the annals of antisubmarine warfare.

In February 1944, with the Marshall Islands secured, the question for an increasingly powerful and confident U.S. Pacific Fleet became, What is our next stepping-stone as we go island-hopping across the Pacific? The same question was being asked from a different perspective in Tokyo. Japanese naval leaders knew that after the U.S. Navy's victory in the Marshalls, it would again be on the move, edging ever closer to the Japanese homeland. The Imperial Navy's senior commanders dreamed of a decisive fleet action, the triumphant "big battle" that would deliver a death blow to the U.S. Fleet. This was the sacrosanct foundation of Japanese strategy, laid down before the war when the emperor's strategists had debated and planned for a possible Pacific conflict with the United States. In fact, Japan's attack on Pearl Harbor had been intended to deliver the death blow. That was a fatal miscalculation, for the shock to the United States of having fourteen ships either sunk or seriously damaged there immediately activated the huge American military-industrial machine, which began building the aircraft carriers that would eventually ensure U.S. air superiority in the Pacific. Despite the Imperial Navy's setback at the Battle of Midway, where the loss of four aircraft carriers left it badly shaken, Japanese commanders remained in the grip of this dream about a decisive battle. Now viewing the U.S. Navy's voyage across the Pacific as a ripe opportunity, they decided to regain the initiative.

Their idea was to lure U.S. forces within the reach of the Japanese Combined Fleet's aircraft carriers and Japanese land-based air power. Air attacks, together with assaults from an advanced line of submarines, would destroy a third of the American ships. The Imperial Navy's main striking force would then sally forth and polish off the remainder. That was the Japanese hope.

On March 12, while Tokyo pondered exactly where the Americans were headed—westward toward the Palaus in the Caroline Islands or northwest toward the Mariana Islands—the Joint Chiefs of Staff designated the Marianas as the next stepping-stone. Invasions were planned for Saipan, Tinian, and Guam, which would provide air bases for B-29 bombers to launch strikes against the Japanese home islands. D-day on Saipan was set for June 15.

Unaware of this decision, Admiral Mineichi Koga, commander in chief of the Combined Fleet, reached his own conclusion. On March 15 he issued his directive for the operation, calling for units of the Combined Fleet, at that time scattered in various places from Singapore to Truk to the Inland Sea, to come together and get positioned to spring the trap. The point of concentration chosen—Tawitawi in the Philippines' Sulu Archipelago—indicated that Koga was anticipating an American line of advance in the direction of the Palaus in the western Caroline Islands, along a path that Admiral Bull Halsey's carriers had taken on two previous raids into the western Pacific. Allowing himself some leeway, Admiral Koga stated more broadly that the signal for action would be given when U.S. forces entered the Philippine Sea.

Admiral Koga disappeared on March 31 in a plane shot down by U.S. aircraft that had been tipped off as to the admiral's whereabouts. Koga's successor, Admiral Soemu Toyoda, clearly shared Koga's dream and his estimate of enemy intentions. Toyoda issued a barely revamped plan, Operation A-Go, on May 3. Among the recipients of the A-Go plan was Rear Admiral Naburo Owada, commander of the Japanese submarine force.

Squadron 7 was headquartered at Saipan. Owada wrote in his war diary: "In the A-Go operation, the greater part of Submarine Squadron 7 will be concentrated in the area south of the Caroline Islands and will engage in patrols, reconnaissance, and surprise attack against enemy task forces and invasion forces. At the same time, an element will be employed to continue operational transport for the southeast area and northern New Guinea."

The southeast area and northern New Guinea happened to be the area where the *England* had been performing so many escort screens. It also happened to be the area through which Imperial Japanese submarine I-16, commanded by one Yoshitaka Takeuchi, would soon be headed.

The I-16 had been a part of the Japanese group that attacked Pearl Harbor. He had a tunnel-like structure on her forward deck that was designed to carry a retractable-wing floatplane or a miniature submarine. At Pearl, the I-16's mini-sub had made an attempt to penetrate the harbor and sink American ships. Whether that mini-sub was the one sunk inside Pearl Harbor or was damaged and beached near the harbor is not known. At any rate, the I-16 never retrieved his baby.

I can imagine that on the evening of May 13, 1944, in Truk Harbor in the central Carolines, Commander Takeuchi was watching as a file of seamen struggled up the gangway of the I-16, each sweating under the load of a seventy-five-pound bag of rice in a sealed rubber container. He must have viewed this procession with some chagrin. The I-16, one of the largest submarines Japan ever built (348 feet long, with a 30-foot beam), provided ample stowage space, both below decks and in that tunnel-like structure designed to accommodate a mini-sub or floatplane. But right now she was being used to transport cargo. With decisive action looming and eight torpedo tubes loaded and ready, his role as cargo vessel must have been a grave disappointment.

Disappointed or not, Takeuchi had his orders, and he carried them out to the letter. On May 14, at 0800 on the dot, the I-16 got under way for Buin, on the southeastern tip of Bougainville in the Solomon Islands. His mission: to supply a battered garrison on the verge of starvation. He estimated his time of arrival at Buin as 2000 on May 22.

These orders, addressed and radioed to "Commander, Submarine Squadron 7" on Saipan and to the I-16, received wider distribution than the sender intended or could ever have imagined. Intercepted and decoded by

American intelligence and promptly forwarded to Admiral Halsey, they resulted in a priority dispatch from the commander of the South Pacific Area to the commander of Escort Division 39 in Tulagi Harbor, Commander Hamilton Haines, who was designated tactical commander of a mission to go after I-16. The same message came to the *England,* indicating that the tactical commander would be Commander Haines in the USS *George.*

Usually, a division of destroyer escorts consisted of six ships, but at the time Commander Haines only had two of his ships—the *George* and the *Raby*—at his disposal, so Admiral Halsey issued the following specific order to Captain Pendleton on the *England:* "On or about 1700, 18 May, get under way in company with USS *George* (DE 697) and USS *Raby* (DE 698) with OTC to be Com Cort Div 39 embarked in *George.* Proceed to position 15°10'S and 158°10'E. Japanese submarine believed heading to supply beleaguered forces at Buin. He is believed to be approaching this point from the north and should arrive that area by about 1400, 20 May. Good hunting."

You can imagine our reaction on board the *England.* The news was received with a heady mixture of excitement, eagerness, and trepidation appropriate to new boys on the block. We thought we were ready; we knew we were about to find out. One way or another, we were in it at last.

As each of us wrestled with his own private thoughts, our three little ships sortied right on schedule, passed west of Florida Island, and threaded through Indispensable Strait, between Guadalcanal and Malaita Island. We were steaming in column. Shortly after midnight, as we entered the dark open sea that seemed to await us with silent menace, Commander Haines ordered a scouting line, with the *George* in center as guide, the *Raby* four thousand yards abeam to port, and the *England* the same distance to starboard.

At 0800 on May 19, Haines changed course and speed so that we would arrive at the designated point by 1400. He wanted to reach the estimated track twenty-four hours ahead of the submarine and run up the track. As the morning wore on, we looked at the world around us with fresh eyes—it was one of those incomparable days that the South Pacific occasionally puts on exhibit to satisfy the fondest illusions. The sky was clear, the wind was blowing gently from the east, and the sea, which only a few hours ago

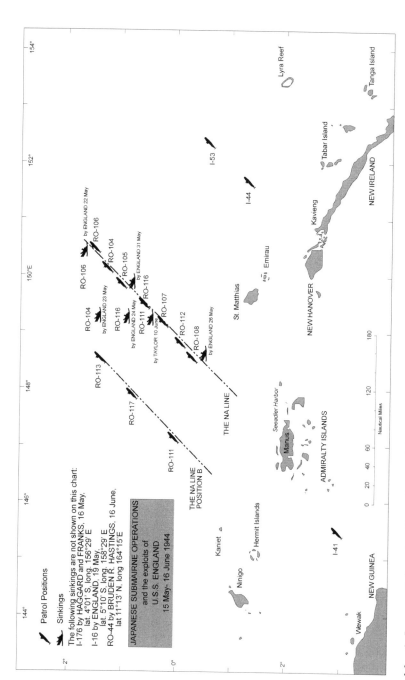

Map 2: Japanese Submarine Operations and the Exploits of the USS *England*, May 15–June 16, 1944

had seemed so hostile, now seemed almost benign. So composed and remote, it was not to be disturbed.

In the other world inhabited by quarrelsome humans, that dream of peace was shattered in an instant. At 1325, as we were steering 297 degrees and preparing to enter the search area, Soundman Roger Bernhardt suddenly announced, in a voice louder than intended, "Contact! Bearing 305 degrees, range 1,800 yards." We weren't expecting to encounter a submarine so soon.

"The echoes must be coming from fish," said the officer of the deck, R. D. "Bob" Webb.

But Burnhardt was certain. "Echoes sharp and clear, sir!" he said from the sound shack. "Sound is good—range now one-four-double-0," which meant 1,400 yards.

Bob Webb reacted promptly. "Call the captain and the exec! Prepare for hedgehog attack. Tell the OTC that we have possible submarine on the starboard bow. We're investigating."

I scrambled into the combat information center (CIC) to set up the dead-reckoning tracer (DRT) plot and then headed for the open bridge. My assignment as executive officer should have been in the CIC, where radars, plotting boards, and communication and other equipment were used to relay vital information to the captain on the bridge one deck above. But you'll recall that because I was experienced in antisubmarine operations, Captain Pendleton and I had agreed to share the conn on the bridge during attacks. That is, Captain Pendleton would take the conn and I would stand by his side, translating information to him as he launched attacks. Our division commander, Thorwall, who was still on the *England* at this time, wasn't very happy about my presence on the bridge, but there was nothing he could do about it—Commander Haines on the *George* was officer in tactical command, relegating Thorwall to the status of a supernumerary. When our team took over, Ensign A. D. "Gus" Dailey took over as recorder operator in the sound shack.

The sound shack is located in a weatherproof compartment on the front part of the flying bridge where the officer of the deck controls the ship. It houses the operational part of the sound gear, controls the pings, and receives echoes from underwater objects. It also houses the recorder, which shows submarine relative speed and distance to the submarine. The recorder also indicates firing time. The opening to the sound shack is near the officer conning the submarine attacks. He can hear the pings and echoes and reports from the officer operating the recorder.

By the time I got to the bridge, the range to contact was seven hundred yards.

"Hedgehogs ready to fire!" came the report from the forecastle, the forward part of the ship.

"Echoes sharp and clear," Bernhardt reported confidently from the sound shack. "Believe target is submarine."

It certainly seemed so, and we wanted to believe it, but as with all initiations to combat, belief comes hard. After all the endless drills, *could* this, in actual fact, be the real thing? I could almost hear Pendleton thinking, Stay calm, hang loose, and make sure. And because I was thinking the same thing, I suggested that this be a nonfiring run. We would keep a sharp eye on him to be certain it was a sub.

The *England* surged ahead, and at four hundred yards the target turned hard left and kicked his screws. Now we were sure. We opened out and notified Commander Haines that this was a solid contact, definitely a sub. He had directed the *Raby* and the *George* to circle us at a distance of two thousand yards so that the sub wouldn't slip out of our contact range and so that they would be ready to assist us if necessary. Because the sound gear on all three destroyer escorts was about the same frequency, the echo-ranging of the other two ships interfered with our own, and we requested that they cease while we had contact.

So that all three ships might keep track of the submarine, we decided that the attacking ship (us, at this point) would pass on range and bearing to the sub by voice radio. The two other ships could get a radar range and bearing to the attacking ship and thus plot its position and track accurately.

The time was now 1337. We headed in for a firing run, the *England*'s first against a live enemy target. Bearing to the sub was 173 degrees, our course 183 degrees coming left, and the range thirteen hundred yards, echoes clear.

The target drew right. Slight-down Doppler indicated that the sub was going away from us. The traces on the tape recorder signaled a stern chase.

By 1339 we were bearing 176 degrees at a range of 770 yards. At 1340 the range had closed to 460 yards. I gave the firing course and told Gus Dailey to fire when ready. Then at 1341: "*Fire!*" he yelled from the recorder.

The first salvo of hedgehogs arched away and dove into the sea. We waited and listened, our hearts pounding in our ribcages. No sound, no hits. How could that be? Since the target was moving hard right, we figured we had failed to give him enough lead and missed to the left.

And so we tried again, opening, regaining contact, and turning for another attack. This time the target was moving left, and it looked like a quarter attack. Then suddenly he showed us his stern and kicked his rudder from right to left to throw up knuckles, or disturbances in the water that often gave false echoes. We anticipated his movement and fired on a center bearing of 210 degrees, with slight-down Doppler and an estimated target speed of 3 knots. One hedgehog hit and exploded at 130 feet.

We had made the first two attacks from our war-cruising condition, but now, certain that we had real live submarine action, we went to general quarters, and Soundman John Prock took over sound gear operation from Roger Bernhardt. Bob Webb was relieved and went to his battle station. Even after the hit, however, there was no evidence of damage, and quickly we realized that we still had a lively enemy on our hands. Apparently the hedgehog had hit a nonvital area of the sub.

Down below, Commander Takeuchi may well have been taken by surprise, since the hedgehog was still fairly new in the Pacific. But whatever confusion he experienced, it wasn't enough to fog his mind. Hastily he followed up our course and attempted to hide in our wake. For a few minutes he succeeded. Then at 1410 we regained contact, bearing 218 degrees, range 740 yards.

Guessing that the sub had gone deeper, we fired on a center bearing with an estimated depth of 200 feet. As we passed over the target, the Fathometer showed 325 feet. We had missed astern.

Our fourth run was a bow attack. The enemy sub was making about 3 knots and throwing his rudder erratically from side to side to avoid getting hit. Our last best information indicated that he was turning right, and we led him in this direction. But he fooled us, turning hard left. We fired late and missed right.

The conning arrangement, with me translating information to Captain Pendleton as he launched attacks, was frustrating for both of us. It was a slow process, and because a successful hedgehog attack required dead accuracy and quick decision making, after the fourth run the skipper turned to me and said, "OK, Williamson, it's your turn. You take over the conn. I can't tell what's happening while I'm doing this." Then he repaired to the starboard side of the bridge and sat in his chair.

My heart was racing. I was elated, and yet calm, confident that we could sink this sub on the next run. And I was grateful to Captain Pendleton for having the humility and generosity of mind to give up control when the *England's* reputation was finally at stake, and when so many lives hung in the balance.

One thing that all those previous runs had given us was vital information about the enemy. Now it was time to put that information to use and end this game. We opened out, turned, and went in for the kill. The run started as a shallow quarter attack, with the target drawing left. As we closed, the sub kept moving left, the Doppler going from slight down to none at a range rate of 9 knots. Our information looked perfect.

At 1433 salvo five was up and away. All I could hear over the next few seconds was the sound of waves beating against the *England's* hull. No one said a word. All eyes were fixed on the water's surface, everyone imagining the huge steel fish below. Then the sound erupted: *V-r-r-oom!* We heard it again and again, in rapid-fire succession, four to six hits coming so fast on top of one another as to seem almost simultaneous. Bull's-eye!

The *England* broke out in cheers, everyone jumping and slapping one another on the back like a team that had just won a tournament game. Two minutes later the cheering was just beginning to die down when all of a sudden we heard a giant *wham!* Our little ship shuddered violently and started rocking and reeling. The fantail, lifted as much as a foot, plopped heavily back into the water, while men throughout the ship were knocked off their feet and deck plates sheered loose in the engine room.

My first thought was, We've been torpedoed! Then, when a quick check showed no damage, we thought that maybe this was the concussion from the submarine's hull crashing or that the Japanese commander had detonated his torpedoes in an act of suicide. In any event, that concussion was cataclysmic certainty that we had heard the last of the Japanese submarine. Later, we would find out that the explosion was felt almost as sharply on the *George* and the *Raby* a mile away. That final blast left us sobered and subdued.

Though we no longer felt like cheering, we did stand a little straighter. The *England* had made her mark; the new boys had had their baptism. We had sunk a Japanese submarine! Before, we had merely joined the Pacific Fleet—now we had arrived.

These premature self-congratulations were interrupted by a reminder that despite the confirmation of a giant concussion, we needed tangible evidence. Commander Haines ordered the *George* and the *Raby* to make a thorough search of the area. While they were searching, we remained in place, keeping a sharp lookout. Twenty minutes later, shreds of cork used for insulation began bobbing up, then some deck planking and pieces of wood that appeared to be the remnants of cabinets. The tremendous underwater explosion must have occurred at something under five hundred feet, we figured, since it took so long for this first debris to appear. It was followed by a prayer mat with Japanese characters, a chopstick, and some bits of wood with grains of rice imbedded, along with traces of blood. Finally, and most conclusively, a sealed rubber container rose to view with a seventy-five-pound bag of rice.

Soon a dozen or so well-fed-looking sharks were milling around the vicinity, and almost an hour later a small oil slick appeared, mute evidence of an enemy sub's fate. The slick grew steadily in size until profuse amounts of oil were bubbling to the surface, along with more debris.

We had to collect enough evidence to prove our kill to the navy. This was a grisly and dangerous task. The whaleboat was launched with a boat engineer, a coxswain, and couple of other men. There were a dozen or more huge sharks swimming excitedly through the floating debris, looking for blood and shredded limbs. If one of our men had fallen overboard he wouldn't have lasted five seconds. Glenn Wagner, the boat engineer, told me later that the men in that boat were genuinely frightened—they thought the sharks would sink the whaleboat and eat them alive.

The oil slick continued to spread until sunset. I was able to get a four-star fix at the center of the flow: 05°10′S, 158°18.2′E. It wasn't precisely the fix indicated in the message that American intelligence had intercepted, but it was close enough to make us believe that the sub we sank was the I-16.

When the *George* and the *Raby* returned to us at sunset, Commander Haines, although satisfied that our target had been destroyed, had to consider the slight possibility that this may have been a submarine other than the one we were expecting. After all, according to naval intelligence, the submarine we were looking for shouldn't have been at this location until twenty-four hours later. Could the I-16 have been a full day ahead of schedule?

Though it was unlikely that a submarine other than the one we were seeking would have been in the area, it seemed prudent to search the track we had expected him to follow. This we did, returning to the attack area about daylight. After arriving at the point of sinking, I got another good star fix in almost the same position as the previous night. The three destroyer escorts moved to the center of the slick and found oil still bubbling from the watery grave of the I-16, which, as we would discover later, had indeed been commanded by the ill-fated Lieutenant Commander Yoshitaka Takeuchi.

By this time the oil slick was three miles wide and six miles long, with debris scattered over the entire area. Clearly, it was mission accomplished. We remained in the area, searching on various courses and awaiting further orders. Somewhere far below, whatever remained of the I-16 had drifted down to the ocean floor.

We felt that our team had worked pretty well. We had used two different soundmen on the attacks and each one had obtained a hit. The antisubmarine warfare officer had been on the recorder for all the runs. Our hedgehog gunnery team had performed admirably. We had used all our ready ammunition, and in the nine minutes between two of the runs, the gunners had brought up ammunition from storage below and completely readied a load of hedgehogs. Our gunner's mates and the gun captain on our number 1 gun had also done an outstanding job. We had had no personnel or matériel failures. These were the sorts of requirements that had to be met by ships facing the enemy, and we had fulfilled them.

Now what do we do? we were wondering. The Japanese soon made that decision for us.

On May 20, 1944, Admiral Toyoda issued the order to prepare for Operation A-Go. Admiral Owada, commander of Submarine Squadron 7, had already made his preparations. He had ordered Captain Ryonosuka Kato, commander of Submarine Division 51, to sortie from Saipan on May 17 in RO-105, with RO-104, -109, -112, and -116 in company. By separate dispatches, Owada had also ordered the RO-108 to sortie from Truk on May 15 and the RO-106 to sortie from Truk the next day. Both submarines were to arrive on the designated scouting line between Manus and Truk no later than 0000 on May 21.

The seven units thus deployed were all the latest type of Japanese fleet submarines, built between 1942 and 1944. Slightly more than two hundred feet in length, with twenty-foot beams and displacing 525 tons, they carried a crew of forty and were armed with four 21-inch torpedo tubes and two paired 25-millimeter antiaircraft guns. They had no radar, but they did have a useful radar-detection device.

Captain Kato's Submarine Division 51 represented the greater part of Admiral Owada's Submarine Squadron 7. Submarine Squadron 7, in turn, represented the greater part of the offensive strength of Japan's modern advance submarine force, the Sixth Fleet. Thus when Admiral Owada executed his plan for Operation A-Go, he was making a major strategic commitment, with major consequences.

On May 21, Admiral Owada issued a top-secret operational order: "Submarines at Saipan will take station (time of arrival to be ordered later) in the NA scouting line from position 01°30′N, 150°30′E, to position 00°30′S, 148°30′E, and submarines at Truk will do likewise but in accordance with separate orders. Orders of deployment starting from north: RO-106, -104, -105, -116, -109, -112, and -108. Deployment distance 30 miles. Direction of search for enemy 135°."

Once again, the Japanese dispatches were intercepted by American intelligence people. They forwarded the information to the commander in chief of the Pacific, who sent it to the commander in chief of the South Pacific (Admiral Bull Halsey), who passed it on to the commander of Escort Division 39. Thus the information made its way by twists and turns until, late in the afternoon of May 20, the *England* received what must be one of the most detailed and most exhilarating communications ever addressed to an antisubmarine group: "Seven Japanese submarines are believed to be preparing to form a scouting line in a position between Manus and Truk. Line believed to run from position 02°00′N, 150°22′E southwest on a line of bearing 216° true. Subs thirty miles apart on line. Seek out—attack—and destroy the five submarines in our territory. Do not cross line unless in hot pursuit of sure contact. Make no report until entering port."

The line we weren't supposed to cross was the one separating the Pacific Ocean Area under Admiral Nimitz from the Southwest Pacific Area under army general MacArthur. Odd as it may seem, the five submarines in "our" territory were fair game, while the two in "their" area, or as some would have it, "his" territory, were forbidden fruit—protected, in a fine irony the Polynesians would have appreciated, by a white man's jurisdictional dispute. Apparently General MacArthur, who had the territorial instincts of an alpha dog, wanted none of Admiral Halsey's ships in his water.

I simply couldn't understand it. This was war, and all Japanese submarines were enemy submarines. I was determined, if we had a chance, to disobey that order and go after those submarines. Was I wrong? As an executive officer on a destroyer escort, did I have the right to disobey an admiral's order? Fortunately or unfortunately, that was a decision I wouldn't have to make.

With five prospective birds in hand, Commander Haines wasn't disposed to quibble about two in the bush. He proposed quite simply that we start at the northeast end of the Japanese line and work our way down it toward the southwest—leaving it to be seen what might develop in the way of hot pursuit.

Shortly after dark on May 20, Haines had his ships moving northward to the happy hunting grounds. Our spirits were running high. After our success of the day before we felt we could sink anything the enemy had to offer, and we couldn't wait to tangle with the five submarines designated as ours.

The next afternoon we were spotted by a low-flying Japanese Betty, a bomber and torpedo plane, seven miles to the east of us. With every passing minute we were getting closer to the enemy base at Truk, well within range of land-based bombers and torpedo planes. But as the afternoon slowly waned, the skies remained clear, and with welcome suddenness darkness fell and our three ships passed under the veil of night. We crossed the equator and at about 1800, we headed north.

At 0350 on May 22, Commander Haines's small fleet was fifty minutes away from Point X-Ray, as we called the northeastern end of the Japanese line. Our three ships were following a base course of 321 degrees in line of bearing at four-thousand-yard intervals. One minute later the *George* reported a radar contact bearing 303 degrees, range eight miles. We raced to general quarters and within thirty seconds had the contact on the *England*'s screen. It looked like a surfaced submarine.

The *George* pressed in, leading the *Raby,* and at a range of fifteen thousand yards accelerated to 20 knots. Keeping the target slightly on her port bow, she readied her searchlight, torpedo tubes, and main battery for action to port. At four thousand yards she turned to starboard and turned on her searchlight.

The men on the *George*'s bridge saw the bridge of an enemy submarine. Reacting quickly, the sub's skipper ordered a crash dive before the beam had barely touched him. After one fleeting glimpse of a conning tower on its way under the surface, the *George* swung back to port, picked up sound contact, and went in to attack. At 0414 she fired a salvo of hedgehogs, missed, and, coming out of the run, lost contact.

At once, Commander Haines voice-radioed us on the *England.* "Do you know where the sub is?" We could hear the edginess in his voice.

"Affirmative," we replied, not completely honestly. Having tracked him submerging on a course of 120 degrees, we figured that he had continued on that course, since it was as good a course as any to clear the area.

The time was now 0425. Captain Pendleton was at the conn, giving it another try. After receiving search information from the CIC, we made a firm submarine contact bearing 193 degrees at a true range of 2,500 yards. We were ready for number two. As we closed in on the sub, we had good information. The Doppler went from almost none to down; the echoes were sharp and clear. We figured we had a beam attack at first, which would change to stern with the submarine making about 3 knots, and we guesstimated that he would be 150 feet deep. At 1443 we fired, but apparently the salvo headed too much to the left.

It was time to open for another attack. Once again, the skipper turned to me and said, "Williamson, take over, you make this next run."

I was jubilant. We opened and turned and were heading back in quickly when, unexpectedly, the enemy reversed course and came to meet us, bows on. Now the Doppler was up and so was the range rate. I guessed that the commander of this sub, like Takeuchi before him, had gone deeper— 250 feet.

"Set depth at 250 feet," I told Gus Dailey on the sound recorder. As the sub's bearing started to drift left and range rate dropped to 9 knots, I assumed he had put his rudder hard right and cut his engines. So at 0501 we led left and fired a full salvo, *v-r-r-r-oom!* Three or more hits at 275 feet.

We increased speed, opened out, and waited for another underwater explosion or for a damaged sub to surface. Five minutes dragged by. We heard nothing, saw nothing. Then as we regained contact and started on another run—*wham!* It wasn't as violent or as close aboard as the previous explosion, but it sure was strong enough to be felt on all three ships. At the time, 0505, we had a clear echo, a few more pings, and then the recorder traces elongated and dissolved. The sub appeared to be disintegrating.

For the next hour, we combed the area thoroughly. There were no contacts and in the darkness, no sighting, but the smell of diesel oil was strong. As day broke, weakly, with violent rainsqualls, we saw what our noses had told us: a heavy slick about six hundred yards in diameter, and oil bubbling to the surface in a steady flow. The *George* reported bits of cork and deck planking before the rain grew so heavy that the search had to be cut short. We had not yet launched our whaleboats—it was too dark and rainy.

The next day, May 23, a carrier plane on patrol sighted and reported a fresh oil slick at 1°36'N and 150°45'E, still bubbling. This was believed to be the oil slick from the submarine we had sunk, since no other attacks were reported in that area.

We found out later that the sub we had sent to Davy Jones's locker was likely the RO-106, commanded by one Lieutenant Shigehira Uda.

Our second kill, coming practically on the heels of the first, just days apart! You can imagine the confidence and excitement we felt. We didn't waste time feeling sorry for the crew of the *George* for not making the kills themselves. They had had their chance, fired, missed, and lost contact. But we were grateful to them for picking up the submarine by radar first.

The tremendous explosions following this attack and our earlier attack of May 19 were puzzling. We felt they could surely be acts of self-destruction. There must have been some way for the commanding officer, who was in the control room, to detonate his torpedoes when he saw there was no chance to save his submarine. This would certainly prevent us from taking prisoners and would bring a quick end to all hands. On the other hand, the Japanese might have developed a means of firing torpedoes to run deep and explode at a short distance as a ruse to persuade U.S. antisubmarine ships to abandon searches. In view of this possibility, Commander Haines ordered that should such an explosion occur again, the ship on the attack would go in and drop a thirteen-charge, deep-set pattern of depth charges on the last best-known position of the submarine. We had a chance to do this before long.

You'll recall that it was normal for submarines to surface at night and run their diesel engines in order to recharge batteries and fill tanks with fresh air. Assuming the submarines were doing this, I requested permission from Captain Pendleton to recommend to Commander Haines that we continue patrolling in the daytime at four-thousand-yard intervals, but that we open up at night to sixteen thousand yards between ships, giving ourselves a wider sweep to contact surfaced submarines by radar.

The skipper granted permission and we sent a message to Commander Haines, who concurred. Now at night we had sixteen thousand yards between ships. The two destroyer escorts on either flank would be able to contact submarines an additional eight thousand yards out on the far side, so that in fact we now covered a forty-eight-thousand-yard range. At dawn general quarters, we shifted back to sound search formation, with four-thousand-yard intervals.

Early in the morning of May 23, when I went to the bridge to take star sights, I was still flush with the victory of the day before. Shortly after 0600, I called Captain Pendleton to ask permission to go to general quarters. As he arrived to take the conn, we were steaming up the Japanese line on a base course of 036 degrees, with the *George* as guide eight miles away on our port beam and the *Raby* another eight miles beyond her.

It was still dark. Anticipating Haines's order from the *George* to go to day formation, we were ready to shift our helm at his word. But when the first sound crackled over the radio, it was the *Raby* speaking: "We have a radar contact bearing 085 degrees, range eight thousand yards."

Commander Haines ordered the *Raby* to attack; the *George* and the *England* were to close at best speed. With some sixteen thousand yards to cover, we rang up full speed and hoped for something better than the best.

As the *Raby* went boring in on the sub, his radar detector picked her up, and at range of six thousand yards he pulled the plug. Down the sub went, and as he did his commander must have wondered if it was for the last time.

Her screen gone blank, the *Raby* forged on and at 0610 made sound contact. Seven minutes later, she fired her first salvo of hedgehogs and missed. Three more runs, three more salvos, and three more misses.

Cocky as we now were on the *England,* some of us actually prayed that she would fail. "*Raby* keep missing; *Raby* keep missing!" Not that we wished her any bad luck, but we were dying to rack up another kill.

"He's maneuvering erratically," the *Raby* reported. The sub was performing like any good sub in a defensive position, alternately running away and fishtailing to create knuckles, then following up the *Raby*'s path to hide in her wake, all the while pinging on her frequency to cause interference.

We listened to these reports, cranked on more turns, held our breath, and crossed our fingers, while down below the Japanese commander was following his tormentor on his sound gear and planning his next evasive move. After almost an hour of patient observation, Commander Haines decided it was time for a change. He called off the *Raby* and sent in the *George.* At 0707 the *George* fired her first salvo and not only missed but lost contact.

At last the *England* arrived on the scene, while the *George* and the *Raby* were anxiously circling and echo-ranging. Two hundred feet beneath them, an alert commander had guessed what had happened, ceased pinging, and began making his quiet way out of there. Heading away at 5 knots, he almost succeeded.

Then, three minutes after we joined and took our place in the ring, the *George* regained contact. The target was bearing 310 degrees, range one thousand yards—already outside our circle and slipping off to the north-west. Again the *George* attacked, and again she fell short of the mark. Between 0730 and 0810 she made three more firing runs, and each time came up empty. Like the *Raby*, she was baffled by an elusive, and lucky, opponent.

As time passed we grew increasingly anxious on the *England*. What was Commander Haines waiting for? we wondered. If the *George* and the *Raby* couldn't sink that sub, why wouldn't he let us have a chance?

After two fruitless and frustrating hours, Commander Haines yielded to what was beginning to appear as the inevitable. "Sheer off," he ordered his crew, with a touch of exasperation. "Give way to the *England*."

And so at 0819, with a firm contact, we went in for a firing run. The sound stack gave a slight-down Doppler, and recorder traces indicated a quarter attack. Captain Pendleton had the conn on this run, and as before I was trying to feed him information for a more accurate attack. "Target's moving left, relative speed 8 knots," I told the captain.

On her final run, the *George* had obtained a Fathometer reading of thirty-nine, so we estimated target depth at 240 feet. Thus at 0832 we fired a full salvo and missed to starboard. After we missed, Pendleton turned to me, said, "Okay, Williamson, you make the next run," and repaired to his seat on the starboard wing of the bridge.

We opened out and the sub followed up our wake at 5 knots. This was probably how he had escaped before, but he had tried the dodge once too often. As we turned to bring him on our quarter and continued to open, he lagged behind, changed his mind, and cut power abruptly. At that, we promptly reversed course and headed in to attack. Meanwhile, the other ships were circling us at two thousand yards and echo-ranging, which they weren't supposed to do during an attack because it interfered with the echoes we were getting back from the target.

"Tell them to knock off the echo-ranging!" I barked to our voice radio operator.

As soon as the words were out of my mouth, Commander Thorwall turned to the voice radioman and said, "Don't you tell them to knock off echo-ranging—I want them to continue."

My head snapped around in the radioman's direction. "I said tell them to knock off echo-ranging!"

Well, the radioman obeyed me, which sent Thorwall into a lather. He turned to me and said, "I don't want them to knock off echo-ranging."

"Commodore," I replied, "I can't sink submarines and argue with you about this at the same time. We'll talk later."

I was so preoccupied that I didn't have time to consider the weight of my insubordination. Fortunately, Captain Pendleton had the courage and common sense to add his own voice to the debate. "Commodore, if you don't leave Williamson alone, we're going to send you below."

By now, Commander Thorwall was boiling. "I'm going to get you both a court-martial! I'm going to court-martial you for disobeying my order in combat!"

I had to swallow my own anger, and any thought of a court-martial, to focus on the task at hand. After all these months of training to sink subs, we couldn't let chances like this pass us by.

Unfortunately because of the distraction, our first run wasn't a firing run. We passed over the submarine and headed out, then turned to regain contact. Recorder traces suggested that we should launch a beam attack, but there was little bearing movement. The range rate was 9 knots, no Doppler. Guessing that the target was stationary, we fired at 0834 on a center bearing. The hedgehogs plunged resolutely into the sea, and, in a few seconds, we were rewarded with a *v-r-r-r-oom* of unprecedented and magnificent proportions. We estimated that there were ten to twelve hits at three hundred feet.

The first ripple of hits was followed, in the next half minute, by several more minor explosions. Then, three minutes later, the now-to-be expected *wham!* Once again, a crashing underwater explosion sent the *England* reeling.

On the chance that this after-explosion was a ruse to persuade us to abandon our search, at 0839 we went in at 15 knots and dropped depth charges, but with no discernable results. My guess was that by then, the remnants of our target were on their way to the bottom, far below our depth setting of 450 feet. This was confirmed when at 1045 the first debris began to bob to the surface, along with a steady flow of oil. The ever-present spirited sharks helped confirm the kill. We lowered a boat and collected the evidence—planking, bottle stoppers, a piece of interior wood with Japanese characters, and the usual shreds of insulating cork. Half an hour later we had sufficient evidence in the form of wreckage and oil samples, and I decided to go below for a much-needed cup of coffee.

We would find out later that this third sub we had sunk was the RO-104, commanded by one Lieutenant Susume Idebuchi. This time success produced a muted response, some grim satisfaction but little jubilation. It seemed as if we were beginning to take time for second thoughts. And when, on my way to the wardroom, I was intercepted by a young seaman, I sensed what was coming.

"Lieutenant Williamson," he said, "can I have a word with you?"

"Sure, son."

"Are we really sinking those submarines, sir?"

"Yes, we really are."

He paused. "When those hedgehogs explode, men are dying down there, aren't they?" I nodded. "How many men are on those submarines?"

"It depends on the type of sub," I replied. "Probably somewhere between forty and eighty."

Then he popped the question. "Sir, how do you feel about killing all those men?"

I had no good answer, but I didn't let him know that. "Son, war is killing. The more of the enemy we can kill, and the more of his ships we can sink, the sooner it will be over. This is our duty. Sinking these submarines may save untold numbers of our troops or ships. We can't go into it deeper than that. We cannot sit in judgment of our actions now. We are in a war that we must win, for to lose it would be far worse."

My young inquisitor seemed relieved. At least he thanked me. But somehow when I reached the wardroom, that cup of coffee didn't taste as good as I thought it would.

Our three destroyer escorts continued to search the area until dusk, then formed a night scouting line and resumed the sweep to the southwest. My cup of coffee was just a brief interlude in a hectic string of duties. Not only did I have the regular duties of an executive officer and a navigator—I was getting star sights mornings and evenings and sun lines during the day—but I had to keep the war diary of all our encounters with the enemy. As I've mentioned, this wasn't the normal log, which was kept by the quartermasters and the officer of the deck, but a confidential report of the ship's combat actions and movements. Sleep wasn't a luxury I could indulge in, but the unique situation in which the *England* found herself kept my adrenaline flowing, and I didn't miss my bunk one bit.

Though Commander Thorwall was still steaming, he was proud that one of the ships in his division had sunk three submarines in record time, and he wanted to send a dispatch to Admiral Halsey relaying the good news.

"Commodore," I said, "you remember our orders said, 'Seek out, attack, and destroy. Make no report until entering port.' We're in the range of Japanese planes based on Truk. If we break radio silence, they'll know exactly where we are and they'll attack. Please don't break radio silence."

Seeing that he was determined, I went and told the chief radioman what the commodore was up to. "I want you to make damn sure that when Thorwall breaks radio silence, the message he sends comes from him, Commander, Escort Division 40, and not from our ship!"

That very night, Commander Thorwall sent his message.

—◦◦◦—

At 0815 on May 23, about the time the *England* was launching her first attack on the RO-106, the commander of Submarine Squadron 7 received a report of an intercepted message from a U.S. patrol plane: "Submarine sighted in position 149°50′E, 01°25′N." Admiral Owada, concluding that this might be one of his subs, slightly off station, issued an order at 0852: "RO-106, -105, and -104 will secretly shift to line of bearing 135 degrees, deployment distance 60 miles." Little did Owada know that only twenty minutes earlier the RO-104 had been sunk, and the RO-106 was already lying on the bottom of the sea, a soon-to-be rusting hulk. As for the RO-105, if she received this order, she delayed too long in executing it.

The day before this Japanese order went out, the escort carrier *Hoggatt Bay* and the destroyers *McCord, Hazelwood, Herman,* and *Hoel* had been ordered to come assist us with the submarine searches. The *Hoggatt Bay's* commanding officer, Captain W. V. Saunders, was to be officer in tactical command of the entire operation. The group wouldn't arrive until the morning of May 26, and as it turned out, Saunders would permit us to operate independently. The carrier and her covering destroyers remained in the area but not near the sub scouting line. Carrier planes would make sweeps during the day, while at night we had Black Cat patrols. (Black Cats were antisubmarine patrol seaplanes.)

At 0120 on the morning of May 24, the *George, Raby,* and *England* were still steaming to the southwest along the sub line when the *George* reported a radar contact dead ahead at a range of fourteen thousand yards. All three ships went to 20 knots and began to close on the target. When the *George* was within nine thousand yards of the enemy sub, he went into a crash dive.

At this point, the *England* was eight and a half miles away to the east, with the target bearing 274 degrees. At 0147 we joined the *George* and the *Raby.* Neither had been able to make sound contact, so we reduced speed and joined in the sound search. At 0150 we gained a contact bearing 307 degrees, range 1,750 yards. Immediately, the target started evasive tactics.

Since we had the contact, we proceeded to attack. Captain Pendleton was sitting in his seat on the wing of the bridge, letting me conn the ship on the first run this time. As we entered the run, the sub took a sharp turn away and kicked up so much wake that we got echoes from the disturbance and couldn't obtain enough information to fire accurately. The traces from the roiled water were so definite that we wondered if the submarine was towing something astern.

John Prock, our leading soundman at general quarters, was on the gear in the sound shack, crossing the target back and forth and reporting ranges and bearings to me. I had a bearing gear repeater in front of me on the open bridge, just outside the shack, and hearing the submarine echoes quite clearly, I told Prock to keep crossing the target but not to report the bearings to me. I did, however, want his continued feedback on the Doppler. With every enemy encounter, we were getting better as a team.

While we discussed this, the enemy, two hundred feet beneath us, continued to kick one screw and then the other, making frequent shifts of rudder. He heard us pass overhead without firing and followed up our wake. The submarine appeared to be on a center bearing, but I wasn't confident enough about our information to make an accurate firing run.

We opened out, regained contact, and went in again, only to encounter more false echoes and the submarine's counter-pinging. Once more we held fire, but as we passed over the target we managed to obtain a depth reading of twenty-eight fathoms. This useful information made up for the counter-pinging that interfered with recorder traces and gave inaccurate information about when Gus Daily's gunners should fire.

As we closed on the sub we decreased the time between pings, which gave us more information more quickly. But it also indicated to the sub that we were close and approaching firing time. His pinging was an effective countermeasure. This guy was bright. But we had something up our sleeve that we thought might get him.

As we came out of our second run, it seemed as if the sub was turning left. When we turned and headed for him, however, he swung around and came straight at us. We were steady on him, with Doppler up and a range rate of 10 knots. At seven hundred yards and closing fast, we continued pinging at the interval normally used for a one-thousand-yard range so that he couldn't tell we were approaching firing time.

The ruse worked—there was no counter-pinging and no last-minute maneuvering. When we fired, at 0214 on center bearing, the target appeared to have just about stopped. Three to five hedgehogs exploded at 180 feet. The initial *v-r-r-r-oom* was followed almost immediately by rumbling noises and several minor explosions, but as we hauled off and waited for the expected conclusion, nothing happened. After a five-minute pause we resumed searching, latched onto a mushy, doubtful contact, and at 0224, largely on a hunch, went in to fire an insurance salvo. No results.

We tried to regain contact without success, and then, with the *George* and the *Raby* joining in, proceeded on a wide hunt, thoroughly sifting the area. An hour later, still with no results, Commander Haines ordered the *George* and the *Raby* to make a retiring search and the *England* to stay on the spot until daylight. At sunrise, we saw the confirming evidence, but it was comparatively sparse—a few small patches of oil and some deck planking. Other evidence of a kill was the presence of hungry sharks in and around the area where there was debris.

We got under way at 0817, on orders to resume the patrol. We had launched our boats and picked up some debris—pieces of chronometer and sextant boxes and other bits of evidence suggesting that one of our hedgehogs had hit near the conning tower where the commanding officer would have been. Had we killed him, so that he couldn't blow up his ship? We'll never know, but we felt almost sure that the ill-fated skipper had joined two of his counterparts from the Japanese Imperial Navy's Submarine Division 51. It would be our fourth submarine kill.

At 0944, once more in company and about eighteen miles away from the point of the earlier attack, we picked up another sound contact, but a vague one. Making a dry run, trying for better information, we didn't get a clear echo, but we did get a depth reading of thirty-five fathoms. Our second approach started with a good echo and definite traces. As we closed, the echo faded and the traces blurred, and we fired a full salvo to no avail. Unwilling to dismiss the contact as non-sub, we regained weak contact, made several more dry runs and at 1108 fired another futile salvo.

Though the other ships were unable to obtain a contact, at 1115 Commander Haines decided to try a creeping depth-charge attack, with the *George* leading and the *England* conning her in. While this was proceeding, with the *George* about four hundred yards away from firing point, we heard noises that sounded like a submarine blowing tanks or firing torpedoes. The *George* picked up speed and dropped a thirteen-charge deep-set pattern. There was nothing to show for it but a lot of disturbed water.

Tantalizingly, we regained contact about five hundred yards from the *George's* drop point and added our contribution, another thirteen-charge pattern. More angry water, no discernible results.

The contacts were puzzling—good echoes that disappeared, clear recorder traces alternating with wobbly, definite Fathometer readings, but no results. Four days later, on May 28, a patrol plane reported an object in the water some twenty miles from the site of our encounter. On closer investigation, it proved to be a very innocent, very dead whale. The whale could have dodged the hedgehogs; maybe it was our depth charges that spelled his doom. As far as we knew, then, the *England* had destroyed four submarines and one whale—a blot on our stellar record. The ocean current in our area would have carried the whale the approximately twenty miles in the four days from our attack position.

At the time, of course, all we knew was that there might be a sub down there, and that we hadn't sunk it. Somewhat chagrined, we gave up on our phantom target and resumed patrolling.

By the morning of May 25, we had returned to the area where we thought we'd sunk a fourth submarine. All lingering doubts were now removed. The oil and debris covered an area of several square miles. We picked up oil samples and retrieved some deck planking with the bolts embedded, a chopstick, a piece of mahogany, some varnished wood with Japanese characters, and a pair of oil-soaked gloves. Later, we would find out that the sub in question was the RO-116, commanded by Lieutenant Takeshi Okabe.

———•/\/•———

On May 25, about the time the RO-116 was drifting down to the bottom of the ocean, Admiral Owada received a signal informing him that in view of the likelihood of discovery in the area of the NA line, the RO-109 was withdrawing sixty miles on a bearing of 360 degrees. This unauthorized but judicious departure probably saved the Imperial Navy one submarine.

As the RO-109 withdrew, a new U.S. force was making its entrance. Three days earlier, you'll recall, Admiral Halsey had formed a hunter-killer group composed of the escort carrier *Hoggatt Bay* and the destroyers *McCord, Hazelwood, Herman,* and *Hoel.* This group, with Captain Saunders of the *Hoggatt Bay* as officer in tactical command, was ordered to proceed to the vicinity of the NA line and, in conjunction with the *England, George,* and *Raby,* complete the mission of seek and destroy.

Because we were maintaining radio silence—with one exception, Commander Thorwall's message—Captain Saunders arrived on station early in the morning of May 26 with no knowledge of what had been transpiring. Commander Haines ordered the *England* to detach and rendezvous with the *Hoggatt Bay* to convey a full report of the operation to date.

After the rendezvous, Escort Division 39 was headed to Manus, in General MacArthur's Southwest Pacific Area, to replenish fuel and ammunition. It was the nearest friendly port, and Admiral Halsey had obtained permission from MacArthur for our "intrusion" into his bailiwick. We were to head for Seeadler Harbor to meet up with the *Spangler,* which was en route from Purvis Bay with a fresh supply of hedgehogs.

Presented with this opportunity to traverse the "do not cross" line legitimately, Commander Haines decided to make the most of it. Instead of heading directly for Manus, we would take a course that ran down the southwestern extremity of the NA line, then veer westward. Though this was a bit out of our way, we figured a little cheating with the hope of destroying another enemy submarine was well worth it. After all, a Japanese submarine was a Japanese submarine, regardless of whose territory it was in. We were only supposed to enter MacArthur's area if we were already in hot pursuit of the enemy. Was Haines right to disobey orders?

This exercise of initiative paid off. On the evening of May 26, the sub hunters formed a night scouting line on base course 220 degrees, eight miles apart. At 2303, the *Raby* reported a radar contact bearing 180 degrees, range fourteen thousand yards.

One minute later, the *England* had a contact bearing 243 degrees, range twelve thousand yards. We went to general quarters and made preparations for star-shell illumination, main-battery fire, and a torpedo attack. At the same time we discontinued echo-ranging, hoping to approach undetected. Ever since my days in the Atlantic, I had wanted to sink a sub with a torpedo—using a submarine weapon on a submarine. This might be my chance, I thought. I also wanted to beat the *Raby* to that submarine. Although she had contacted him first, he was about the same distance from both of us, so we had an equal chance of getting there first.

When the submarine was sighted by radar, the *Raby* went to general quarters. Normally at general quarters the captain would take the conn, which he did. He also gave the order "All ahead flank" to the engine room and "Left full rudder" to the helmsman, indicating that the ship should head for the sub. Just as the *Raby* was going to general quarters, her radar man said, "Captain, you ought to come see this image on the radar. It looks like a tanker!" The captain, forgetting his ship was on all ahead flank and left full rudder, went down one deck to the CIC to look at the radar screen. Meanwhile the *Raby* was going in circles. After she had made two circles, the gunnery officer brought it to the attention of the skipper, who returned to his station and gave orders to head straight for the enemy.

That gave the *England* a big head start. We had another advantage as well: as we changed course to head for the target, by a stroke of luck he changed course toward us. From his radar-detection device he probably knew he was detected, but he probably didn't know where we were. His course was 065 degrees, speed 11 knots. At 2312 we steered 180 degrees to get on the sub's starboard bow, in position to launch torpedoes. We planned to launch at three thousand yards, but the enemy must have finally become aware of our presence, because just as we approached to four thousand yards he pulled the plug and vanished.

We headed for the point of submergence, commenced echo-ranging, and at 2318 had a good sound contact, bearing 277 degrees at a range of seventeen hundred yards. In the CIC we shifted into our now-familiar routine, and I headed for the bridge. With Doppler moderate up and a good trace on the recorder, we launched a bow attack, changing to beam. As we closed, the Doppler and range rate both dropped and the bearing started drifting to the left. At 2323, we headed left and fired on a left-of-center bearing.

As the salvo of hedgehogs flew through the darkness, I waited with desperate hope. We were woefully low on ammunition—with this pattern gone, we had exactly one more shot of hedgehogs left in our locker.

Fortunately, it wasn't needed. Four to six of them exploded at 250 feet, and twenty seconds later we heard several more underwater explosions, followed by loud rumbling noises and then the grand finale that had become so familiar—*wham!*

The ship erupted in cheers. We had killed a submarine in MacArthur territory, and in record time! From first radar contact to final explosion was only nineteen and a half minutes. A frustrated *George* and *Raby* joined us for a thorough sweep of the area. The sea was quiet as the grave.

The long night passed, and at daybreak, we put a boat over to collect evidence. The water was afloat with shards of deck planking and polished wood, cork stoppers bobbing lightly, and scattered patches of oil. Among other items, we retrieved a piece of mahogany with a brass fitting that looked like part of a chronometer case. The debris was scattered over two square miles, near the center of which a fountain of oil bubbled to the surface, leaking from the crushed shell of what turned out to be the RO-108, commanded by Kanichi Kohari.

It was a sweet victory, and Commander Haines was never reprimanded for making an excursion into MacArthur's home turf.

—◦◦◦—

The excitement kept on coming. Shortly after daylight, one of our lookouts reported a mast on the distant horizon. The night before we had received a message from South Pacific Force headquarters that an enemy heavy cruiser had been spotted leaving Truk and heading south. We thought at the time that he might be looking for us, since we had been spotted by enemy patrol planes. As soon as the mast appeared, I felt sure it was the fore truck of a heavy cruiser.

Our whaleboat was still in the water collecting debris. Without losing any time, we snapped it up and went to general quarters. As to what to do then, we were in something of a quandary. Our antisubmarine experience wouldn't do us a lick of good now. It took some of the wind out of our sails. I thought of what a British officer had told me in Iceland shortly after the *Bismarck* sinking. He had been on a light cruiser that had sighted the German ship. "What did you do?" I asked him. "Rang up flank speed," he replied, meaning they had turned tail and made a dash for it. I didn't think this would do us much good, however, as a heavy cruiser's top speed would easily best ours.

As we were pondering our next move, the welcome sound of American voices crackled over the voice radio. We swallowed and returned our hearts to our chests, realizing this ship was the *Hoggatt Bay*, part of our own task force.

Woefully low on fuel and ammunition by now, we headed for Seeadler Harbor in a state of subdued elation. The *England* had sunk five subs in a matter of days. I didn't know what the historic record was for sinking enemy ships, but I knew we must be somewhere close to the top, and I was proud of that ship and our men.

—————

Back in Saipan, Admiral Owada was unaware of the fate of his five subs. On May 26 he received an intercept of a plain-language transmission from a U.S. plane: "Successfully attacked enemy sub at 1753, approximate position 01°30′N, 151°05′E." For whatever reason, the message was wrong—in fact, no Japanese submarine had been lost to air action on May 26. But as a result of this report Admiral Owada decided to make a major change. At 1457 on May 28 he issued his order: "Submarine Force A will station itself along scouting line B from position 01°30′N, 148°50′E, to position 00°35′S, 146°50′E, starting from the north in the order of RO-106, -104, -105, -116, -109, -112, and -108. The transfer direction of patrols in scouting line B will be east to west."

In effect, Owada was shifting his entire line sixty miles westward. But of the seven submarines addressed, four were no longer around to receive the order, and one, RO-105, either did not receive the message or chose to ignore it. The only boats to report on the new station were RO-109, which arrived on the thirtieth, and RO-112, which came the next day.

As for us three destroyer escorts, after a twenty-four-hour layover at Seeadler Harbor, we got under way for the NA line at 1800 on May 28, this time in company with another destroyer escort from Division 39, the *Spangler*. It was time to resume the hunt.

The twenty-ninth passed without incident, but in the early morning hours of the thirtieth, the pace began to quicken. In Captain Saunders' hunter-killer group, the *Hazelwood*, screening the *Hoggatt Bay*, picked up a radar contact at 0156 bearing 230 degrees at a range of ten thousand yards.

The *Hazelwood* had just started to pick up speed when the radar blip disappeared. A few minutes later, she gained a sound contact. At that time destroyers, unlike destroyer escorts, didn't have hedgehogs; they had only antiquated depth charges, and the *Hazelwood*'s only option was to proceed with a depth-charge attack. No results.

Our group of destroyer escorts was in the general area but outside of radar range. The *Hazelwood* asked for our position, and Commander Haines offered assistance. Since the *George* and *Raby* were closer to the locus of action, he ordered them to close on the *Hazelwood*, while the *England* and the *Spangler* continued to patrol down the line. On the *England* we were sorely disappointed, having no idea that in the coming hours we would be pitted against one of the most experienced and clever submariners in the entire Japanese Imperial Navy.

At 0400 the *Raby* joined the *Hazelwood*, which had made several more depth-charge attacks and at this point had lost contact. At 0405 the *Raby* got a radar blip just astern of the *Hazelwood*, but it faded quickly. The two ships groped for a sound contact without success. Within half an hour the *George* arrived and the *Hazelwood* departed to resume her place in the *Hoggatt Bay*'s screen. Simultaneously, the *Raby* reported another fleeting radar contact. Commander Haines then ordered the *George* to proceed to the point of the last sure contact reported by the *Hazelwood* and make a retiring search to the west, covering the most likely route of escape.

At 0528, with the *George* seven miles on her way, the *Raby* obtained another sound contact, range twelve hundred yards. Commander Haines ordered the *Raby* to attack and the *George* to withdraw. On the *Raby*'s run, at range four hundred yards, her recorder malfunctioned, and, forced to fire on stopwatch timing, she missed. Minutes later she regained contact, but with her recorder still out she notified Commander Haines that she would hold the contact and await the *George*. At 0600 that ship arrived, picked up an echo, and fired hedgehogs on her first run. She got no hits but obtained a depth reading of thirty fathoms.

Twenty minutes later, the *George* fired her second salvo, but again the only result was an updated Fathometer reading, twenty-five fathoms. At 0630 the *George* unleashed salvo three and reported several hits at 160 feet, but these did not show on her recorder traces. The *George* made a dry run to check the sub's movements, and at 0703 she fired a fourth salvo of hedgehogs that failed to hit their mark.

When hedgehogs exploded they always made definite, identifiable traces on the sound recorder. Later the navy submarine analysis section would evaluate this action and determine that the *George* hadn't inflicted any damage to the submarine. As sorely disappointed as the men of the *George* must have been at the post-action analysis, they could be extremely proud of the role they played in this encounter. They made radar and sound contacts, and more important, along with the *Raby*'s, their repeated runs wore down the enemy before the *England* took her own stab at bringing about his demise.

At this point the *Raby*, her sound recorder back in commission, took over from the *George*, obtained contact, and fired her second pattern of hedgehogs, followed by two more firing runs. On a fourth attack she heard sounds resembling the noise of a submarine blowing tanks. After a fifth fruitless attack, Commander Haines decided to hold off for a while and let the water settle. In view of the lack of results from hedgehogs, he also directed the two ships to prepare for depth-charge attacks.

At 0940, the *George* forged in and laid a thirteen-charge pattern. Then, coming about, she swept down one side of the attack line while the *Raby* swept down the other. There were no contacts, so the ships opened out for a circular search around the area. At 1000 a seaman on the *George* reported a possible periscope on the other side of the circle. The *George* headed for the spot, about three-quarters of a mile from the site of the depth-charge attack, and at 1034 regained contact at a range of thirteen hundred yards.

As she entered on a firing run she lost steerage control, and Haines ordered the *Raby* to take over. The *Raby* obtained contact at 1046, but the echo was indistinct and faded before she reached her firing point. Her steering gear repaired by now, the *George* rejoined, and the two ships continued to search, alternately gaining and losing possible contacts. It seemed that no matter the direction from which the search was made, the contact was always behind a wake. If the contacts were genuine, this was one slippery customer.

Shortly before noon, Commander Haines decided to adopt some devious tactics of his own. Either ship, on obtaining contact, would open to twelve hundred yards and then close exactly as though she were making a firing run. At five hundred yards she would break left or right and open out, maintaining contact. On every third run she would keep on, cross directly over the target, and obtain a Fathometer reading. This maneuver, it was hoped, would wear the submarine down and eventually exhaust her batteries. After an hour of this cat-and-mouse game, the *Raby* got too good a target to pass up and, at 1245, fired her sixth salvo of hedgehogs. Again no luck. Subsequently, the *George* got a clear echo and launched her fifth flight of missiles, and though she claimed several hits, there was no confirmation from the sound recorder.

Contact was maintained while the game continued, but some men were beginning to have their doubts about the nature of the target. The submarine had been contacted about 0200 and by this time would have used a lot of battery power. If the target was truly a sub, he was almost motionless, going just fast enough to maintain depth control, trying to save as much power as possible. Could it be that we had lost the sub and picked up an inversion layer, or perhaps even an uncharted reef?

The *George* proposed to answer the question in the most direct way possible. Where the phantom target had last been contacted, the ocean was 2,700 fathoms deep. The ship made a very slow approach and at the appropriate spot dropped a lead line—and got a solid sounding at 50 fathoms. So it *was* a submarine. That must have been the first and last time a navy ship got a lead line sounding on an enemy submarine!

A lead line is a heavy piece of lead tied to a line marked to show water depth when the lead hits the ocean bottom, or, in this rare case, the top of the submarine. We could only imagine the consternation in the submarine when the Japanese crew heard the *tap, tap, tap* of that lead chunk bouncing off his hull. Without doubt, the *George*'s was a new and unique approach to locating underwater targets—too bad there wasn't a hedgehog tied to the lead line.

Certain that she had a real submarine under her keel, the *George* still couldn't hold contact throughout a firing run. Nor could the *Raby*. The two ships hung on grimly, knowing that the sub had to surface sooner or later. Sure enough, shortly after sunset the *George* obtained a radar contact bearing 225 degrees at a range of ten thousand yards. But as soon as she set out to investigate, the blip faded.

Then, at 1950, the men of the *George* and the *Raby* heard a loud *boom*— and then another and another, a whole series of explosions over a nine-minute period. It was believed that these were torpedoes fired at long range on a sound bearing on the *Raby*. Japanese torpedoes that missed their targets were thought to explode at the end of their runs.

This was the first time any Japanese subs had taken aggressive action against one of the three destroyer escorts in our group. We couldn't understand why they hadn't attacked up to this point. We weren't a huge fleet— maybe they felt they should evade, continue their scouting, and save their torpedoes for the U.S. naval armada that Japanese leaders expected in the area. Still, it seemed to us that any submarine commander worth his salt would order an attack if he ran across an enemy ship.

At 2035 the *George* closed the *Raby*, obtained a sound contact, and held it for most of the night.

While their long cat-and-mouse game was being played out, we on the *England* had a routine time of it, sweeping the scouting line with the *Spangler*, oblivious to what was going on—I only heard the details later from officers on our sister ships. We had run to the southern end of the scouting line and were returning when, at about 0300 on May 31, as we approached the point where the *George* and the *Raby* had left us, we began to hear voices on the radio. We gleaned from the snatches of conversation that the two destroyer escorts had a submarine contact and were actively stalking.

We called in to offer our help and ask for a position. "We can hear but don't have radar contact," I said. "Where are you?"

This provoked an irritable, no doubt unauthorized, response. "We're not telling you where we are!" the voice snapped. "We have a damaged sub, and *we're* going to sink him. Don't come near us."

Rebuffed, we gave up any idea of crashing the party and returned to patrolling. Then fate, acting through a desperate Japanese commander, took a hand. After almost twenty-six hours of deep submergence, with little air and low batteries, the Japanese sub had to surface. His position calculated to a nicety, the submarine suddenly appeared midway between the *George* and the *Raby*.

Both ships immediately obtained radar contact at fifteen hundred to two thousand yards. The alert enemy maneuvered so as to remain between the two destroyer escorts, keeping them in each other's line of fire. Commander Haines ordered the escorts to clear the line of fire, illuminate, and open fire. What unfolded next led the *England* to the scene. As a seaman on the *Raby* illuminated a 24-inch searchlight and started to train it, his hand slipped and the light tilted upward. Thirty miles to the northwest, we saw this pencil beam of light piercing the night sky and started closing at top speed. If Admiral Nelson could turn a blind eye at the Battle of Copenhagen, we figured we were entitled to turn a deaf ear to the message we'd just received from the *George*.

While the *George* and the *Raby* maneuvered to clear their line of fire, the enemy sub remained on the surface for some twenty minutes more and then submerged again, unscathed, with fresh air and what must have been—considering the short time on the surface—barely recharged batteries. At 0315 the *Raby* regained sound contact and made two dry runs and one hedgehog attack, with no success. At this point, Commander Haines decided to hold off, retain contact, and resume attacking at dawn.

In company with the *Spangler*, the *England* bore down at flank speed and met with another, albeit gentler rebuff. "Stand off at five thousand yards and wait for orders," said Haines.

At first light Commander Haines went back on the offensive, with his ship the *George* making the first run. She fired at 0649, estimating the target to be at a depth of 180 feet. No hits. Ten minutes later the *Raby* fired and also missed.

Commander Haines keyed the mike. "It's your turn, *Spangler*," he said, calling in that ship for her debut. The *Spangler* gave it her best, but her salvo of hedgehogs disappeared below the Pacific, just shots in the dark. The ocean was silent.

By now on the *England* we were champing at the bit, praying desperately to be let in on the action. Finally at 0729—after more than thirty hours of chasing—Commander Haines picked up the mike and said resignedly, "OK, *England*, it's your turn."

Just the order we were waiting for. When the signal came, we had already edged to within two thousand yards of the target and had a good contact. Almost as soon as the words were out of Haines's mouth, we set out on a stern chase, pinging through the sub's wake. Down Doppler and a range rate of 8 knots indicated a slow target. At 0736 our salvo was on its way, and a few seconds later—*v-r-r-oom!* Six to ten charges exploded at two hundred feet.

On the bridge of the *George*, Commander Haines also exploded. "Goddamn it, how do you *do* it?" he barked over the voice radio.

Off the record, Captain Pendleton said, "Tell him we take out our pins."

Pendleton was referring to the pin that was pulled from the nose of a hedgehog just before it was fired. Removing the pin allowed the propeller to turn, which armed the missile after it had submerged about seven feet. To say "we take out our pins" would be to insult the *George*. Fortunately that message wasn't relayed.

Five minutes later—*wham!* Though the explosion was violent, it was so deep that at first the water wasn't even roiled. As we continued to comb the area, however, the now-familiar fountain of oil came bubbling up five hundred yards from the point of attack. Little by little, bits of debris bobbed to the surface. Once again we lowered a whaleboat and recovered oil samples, pieces of deck planking, shreds of insulating cork, a fragment of interior wood painted red, bottle stoppers, and a bar of soap. And once again the sharks came racing in, dozens of hungry opportunists zigzagging around, nosing through the flotsam. The men in the whaleboat used boathooks to retrieve their samples for fear that sharks might lop off their limbs.

Over a period of thirty agonizing hours the enemy had withstood twenty-one separate attacks, managing to outwit two destroyer escorts and a destroyer. It didn't surprise me later to discover that our foe had been none other than Captain Ryonosuka Kato, commander of Submarine Division 51, one of the Japanese navy's most senior and most experienced submariners. Riding aboard the RO-105, commanded by Lieutenant Junichi Knoue, Kato had used every bit of his experience and cunning to the bitter end. The RO-105 had gone to its final port of call defiant to the last.

It was fitting that the submarine in which Captain Kato rode was the last in the caravan of shattered submarines that the USS *England,* with the help of the *George* and the *Raby,* sent to the bottom. And it was easy to imagine that somewhere, three thousand fathoms down, Captain Kato had been piped aboard with honors to reassume command of his ghostly Submarine Division 51.

I couldn't but admire the enemy. Looking back on it all, there's only one thing I would criticize him for—lack of aggressiveness. He had had ample opportunity to unleash torpedoes against the *George* and the *Raby,* which were sitting ducks during the hours they spent holding contact between attack runs. Granted, the enemy did fire at the *Raby,* perhaps three torpedoes, but still he must have had several more torpedoes available.

Departing the scene late in the afternoon of May 31, our four destroyer escorts—the *George, Raby, England,* and *Spangler*—resumed their patrol. Although we remained in the area of the scouting line for the next two or three days, no more contacts were made. With six submarines destroyed, and two beyond reach (the RO-109, for unknown reasons, left station and departed for Truk on May 31, and the RO-112 was safely in MacArthur's sanctuary across the line), the remainder of the cruise was uneventful.

—⁂—

The *England* had sunk six submarines in twelve days. In a total of eleven firing runs, she had scored hits during seven; of the six targets she attacked, six were destroyed. A record that any antisubmariner would be proud of, it was the result of good fortune, good intelligence, and above all teamwork. The *George* and the *Raby* are to be commended for the work they did picking up targets. Had they not done so, the *England* might not have had her attack opportunities. And Commander Haines, the officer in tactical command, deserves high praise for the way he handled his ships during this operation. He was always alert to every opportunity, always on the *George's* bridge during contact and whenever contact was likely. His devotion to duty and his enthusiasm were an inspiration to all of us; his judgment and his commands earned our most profound admiration.

On the *England,* our antisubmarine warfare officer Gus Daily deserved recognition for his outstanding job as sound recorder operator. He was on the recorder during every run made by the *England,* and his accuracy in firing time was reflected in the number of hits we scored. Furthermore, Daily's interpretation of recorder traces was invaluable to me as I tried to figure out what each enemy submarine was doing.

We had three soundmen on the sound stack at different times when hits were made. Our leading soundman was John Prock, a quiet, sincere young man whose devotion to duty was one of the main factors contributing to the *England's* success. Prock was sonar operator during four of the hits we made. Soundman Second Class Roger Bernhardt, on the sound stack for two of the hits, was also deserving of praise for his performance in combat. And Soundman Third Class Paul Ayers, on the stack for one hit, gave an outstanding performance. These three men kept our sound gear in such mint condition that the *England* didn't suffer a single sound failure during the entire operation. Not only that, they were trained to perfection, so that once a contact was gained it was never lost. The information the soundmen fed me during combat was of pinpoint accuracy. I had thorough confidence in their judgment when they reported Doppler up or down or none.

The rest of the team was just as vital. The gunners played a critical role by having the hedgehogs up and ready every time we were prepared to fire. And our engine room gang was outstanding; they kept the *England's* speed at a steady 10 knots, which gave us a reliable point of comparison when the recorder showed a range rate of 9 or 11 knots. We knew the range rate was in relation to our 10 knots—we didn't have to guess whether we were going 9 knots, 10 knots, or 11 knots. Knowing that our speed was accurate helped us on the recorder.

The work performed by our soundmen, our gunners, and our engineering gang was a vast help. I had to digest the information they fed me to steer the ship and to aim the hedgehogs accurately. The trick was to get the hedgehogs to lift off and arrive at a spot directly above and ahead of the submarine, so that when they sank to the proper depth, they found their target and exploded. It was a tricky business, made easier by the various teams' undying devotion to accuracy.

One of Commander Haines's action reports following the operation stated that "an amazing series of peculiar circumstances always seemed to place the *England* in a position to attack." His comment suggests that the *England*'s record consisted of always being in position to attack. This is misleading. In my opinion, the main reason the *England* scored six hits was that our men appreciated the fine precision required to fire a hedgehog at a moving submarine and make it hit. We did always try to be in a position to make the attack.

More generally, we believed in ourselves. Unless you believe you're the best, you won't be. We enjoyed a special esprit de corps, the "*England* spirit," which was born way back in the wooden barracks in Norfolk, Virginia. Our officers and men not only trained and worked hard, they also developed a fine instinct—a knack—for being in the right place at the right time and for seizing opportunity by doing the right thing. Moreover, our skipper, Captain Pendleton, had an unwavering conviction that equipment should work and went to great lengths to make sure that that was the case. As a result, when the *England* was put to the ultimate test, all our shipboard systems operated as they were meant to.

Yes, the men of the *England* had reason to be proud of their success. But there was no gloating. We had killed men, and killing sobered our view of what had happened. Later, when we discovered which submarines we had sunk and the names of the officers who manned them, we also found out how many men each sub carried: some ninety-five on the I-16, and between forty and forty-five on the other subs. I regret that we had to kill those people in order to win. Unfortunately, war is killing. Let us hope that the future will lead to peaceful rather than warlike solutions to the problems between nations.

There was another good reason not to dwell over our success. This submarine operation did not end the war for the *England*. We knew there was more to come, and—though we didn't know it then—the Japanese would have their time for revenge.

In the United States, the feat of the *England* went almost unnoticed at the time, save for a message from Admiral Ernest King, commander in chief of the U.S. Fleet. With unaccustomed flair, King announced in a secret message of congratulations, "There will always be an *England* in the United States Navy." That promise was kept with the commissioning two decades later of the guided-missile frigate USS *England,* which was later redesigned as a guided-missile cruiser.

—◊◊◊—

Their initial reaction to the sinkings suggests that Japanese naval leaders felt their submariners should be more aggressive. On June 3, the supreme commander of the Combined Fleet sent this message to the Advanced Expeditionary Force: "The hardships of the advance forces engaged in patrol, transport, and reconnaissance of strategic areas under the enemy's vigilant anti-sub patrol for long periods are beyond imagination. Greater combat opportunities arise as the hardships increase, and the success or failure of Operation A-Go depends on the submarine's daring insight into various situations. Whether it be during combat or maintenance, submariners should endeavor to comply with their missions and devise schemes so as not to lose any combat opportunity."

Unbeknownst to Toyoda, there weren't enough submarines left to pursue combat opportunities. While the Imperial fleet anxiously awaited the return of Submarine Division 51—which, you'll recall, comprised the bulk of Submarine Squadron 7—its epitaph was being written.

By now, the Japanese were well aware that the U.S. advance was northwest toward the Mariana Islands, not westward toward the Palaus in the Caroline Islands. On June 13, 1944, as U.S. forces moved in for the invasion of Saipan, Admiral Toyoda ordered Operation A-GO to begin. "The fate of the empire rests on this one battle," he said. "Everyone must give all he has." That same day Vice Admiral Takeo Takagi sent an urgent appeal to Admiral Owada: "All the available strength of Submarine Squadron 7 is to be immediately stationed east of Saipan, to intercept and destroy American carriers and transports, at any cost." Admiral Owada replied succinctly but eloquently: "This squadron has no submarines to station east of Saipan."

On June 25, the missing vessels were officially declared sunk and their crews dead. Captain Ryonosuko Kato was posthumously promoted to rear admiral.

In a summary of Japanese submarine operations prepared by the Japanese Navy Ministry after the Marianas operation, this forlorn paragraph appeared: "Before the opening of this operation, SubRon 7 was assigned to the southern sector of the Carolinas where the small-type submarines took the full brunt of the enemy's force and, in an engagement lasting approximately ten days, lost most of its submarines. Inasmuch as only two or three destroyers were sighted, our battle gains were nil."

As for Operation A-Go, Japan's hope for vanquishing the U.S. Fleet in a single blow, it turned out to be a dismal failure. The plans had fallen into American hands, and when Vice Admiral Ozawa, commander of Japan's First Mobile Fleet, tried to lure Admiral Raymond Spruance's Fifth Fleet away from Saipan, where it was tasked with protecting the amphibious landings, Spruance refused to rise to the bait. Instead, the Fifth Fleet would conserve its fighter strength, waiting for Ozawa to come to it. On June 19, Ozawa dispatched 373 aircraft against the Fifth Fleet, of which only 130 returned. Fifty more Japanese planes were lost in the skies over Guam. While this encounter, known as the Great Marianas Turkey Shoot, was taking place, U.S. submarines torpedoed Ozawa's flagship, the carrier *Taiho,* and the fleet carrier *Shokaku.* That night the Fifth Fleet's Task Force 58, commanded by Vice Admiral Marc Mitscher, launched 216 aircraft against Ozawa's force, sinking the carrier *Hiyu,* damaging two others, and leaving the Japanese commander with a paltry total of thirty-five carrier aircraft. Japan's hopes for a decisive blow would have to be postponed.

10

The Aftermath

AMERICAN INTELLIGENCE KNEW THAT seven submarines had been assigned to the scouting line we were patrolling, and since the *England* had sunk five of these ships, that meant two subs could still be at large. We'd been in the area since May 19 and the Japanese had patrol planes that should have spotted us at some point, so on the *England* we doubted that either of these two subs was nearby. It was with much dampened enthusiasm, then, that we followed orders from Admiral Halsey to continue patrolling the area with the carrier *Hoggatt Bay*, which was being screened by Destroyer Division 42.

Except for a refueling and provisioning stop at Seeadler Harbor, we remained with the carrier until June 7, at which point our destroyer escort group split off and conducted an independent patrol for the submarines we sensed were not there. The next day Admiral Halsey sent us a message: "Bettys are looking for the task group. If you are spotted you can expect air attacks at dawn on 9 June." Captain Saunders of the *Hoggatt Bay* ordered us to rejoin his formation as part of an antiaircraft screen around the carrier.

Fortunately, heavy wind and rain began around dawn and lasted into the afternoon, and we weren't attacked. Visibility varied between two hundred yards and two miles—perhaps the Bettys didn't even spot us. At 1400 on June 10, the USS *Taylor*, on antisubmarine patrol, reported a contact. More than seven hours later she rejoined the formation and radioed Captain Saunders to report the probable destruction of a Japanese submarine. Now that the *Taylor* had sunk the sixth submarine, there was only one left, and that one, we suspected, might be patrolling outside our hunting grounds. As we would find out later, the RO-112 was indeed across the line in MacArthur's sanctuary.

On June 11, we were ordered to leave the task group and set course for Blanche Harbor on Treasury Island in the Solomons, where we would report to Admiral Thomas Kinkaid, commander of the Seventh Fleet, for temporary duty. The Seventh Fleet was in MacArthur's domain, so Admiral Kinkaid reported to the general. The two other U.S. fleets in the Pacific, the Third under Admiral Halsey and the Fifth under Admiral Raymond Spruance, reported to Admiral Nimitz. In fact, the Third and the Fifth were one and the same fleet. The designation changed depending on who was in charge at any given time; Admiral Halsey or Admiral Spruance decided to deceive the Japanese into thinking they were up against three fleets.

This command setup reinforced the rift between the navy and the army in the Pacific, which was felt even on lowly destroyer escorts, and in the most tangible of ways. I've already mentioned that MacArthur forbade us to operate across the line separating his command from the Third/Fifth Fleet's unless we were already in hot pursuit of an enemy sub. But we experienced the rift in more trivial ways as well—for example, in the matter of food. As long as we operated with the Third/Fifth Fleet, we received reasonably good, fresh provisions, especially when we were in or close to combat areas. But whenever we ventured across the line of demarcation and operated with the Seventh Fleet, the quality of the food deteriorated. There we ate so many dehydrated spuds and eggs that it made us long to get back into our own territory. Biting into that reconstituted gruel night after night, I actually felt sorry for Admiral Kinkaid, having to work under MacArthur.

The service rivalry generated by MacArthur may have been the source of bad feeling among navy men, but it was also the cause of much humor. The following is a poem I picked up in the Pacific in 1944, and it suggests that at least some men regarded MacArthur as a megalomaniac:

Doug's Communiqué
    —Anonymous (Found in a Floating Bottle)

For two years, since blood and tears
Have been so very rife,
Confusion in our war burdens most a

Sailor's life.
But from this chaos, daily, like a hospice
On the way,
Like a shining light to guide us, rises
Doug's Communiqué.

For should we fail to get the mail,
If prisoner won't talk,
If radios are indisposed and carrier
Pigeons walk,
We have no fear because we'll hear
Tomorrow's news today
And see our operations plan in
Doug's Communiqué.

Here, too, is told the saga bold
Of virile deathless youth
In stories seldom tarnished with
The plain unvarnished truth.
It's quite a rag, it waves the flag,
Its motif is the fray,
And modesty is plain to see, in
Doug's Communiqué.

"My battleships bombard the Nips from
Maine to Singapore.
My subs have sunk a million tons,
They'll sink a billion more.
My aircraft bombed Berlin last night."
In Italy they say,
"Our turn's tonight, because it's right in
Doug's Communiqué."

"My armored tanks have mowed his ranks,
So Rommel's gone to hide.
And the frozen steppes of Russia see

My wild D on Cossacks ride.
My brave beleaguered Chetniks make
The Axis sweat and pay."
It's got to be, it's what we see in
Doug's Communiqué.

His area is quite cosmic and
Capricious as a breeze;
Ninety times as big as Texas,
Bigger than Los Angeles,
It springs from lost Atlantis
Up to where the angels play,
And no sparrow falls unheeded, it's in
Doug's Communiqué.

He used to say, "and with God's help,"
But lately it has seemed
That his patience is exhausted,
And God's on his second team.
And the Cabots and the Lodges, too, have
Long ceased to pray
That they'll even squeeze a byline into
Doug's Communiqué.

And while possibly a rumor now,
Someday it will be a fact
That the Lord will hear a deep voice say,
"Move over God, it's Mac."
So bet your shoes that all the news
That last great Judgment Day,
Will go to press in nothing less than
Doug's Communiqué.

To put it mildly, MacArthur did exert his influence.
There was one odd difference that we couldn't help but notice when we

were with the Seventh Fleet. Nearly all operational-priority messages sent by the commander of our task group arrived by way of "bells" radio four to five hours after they had originated. In one instance we were unable to carry out our orders because the dispatch was received too late. Normally when we were with the Third/Fifth Fleet, dispatches arrived over selected radio channels shortly after they were sent. Why Seventh Fleet communications lagged so far behind we never understood.

On June 13 we arrived at Blanche Harbor and were smitten by its beauty. It was an atoll southwest of Treasury, attached to that island by a reef. A small island just to the south of the reef made up the harbor. We felt safe because of the surrounding reefs that protected the harbor and the antisubmarine nets guarding its entrance. There was a shack on the beach that served as an officers club as well as a place where the enlisted men could take their own beer and play ball.

Treasury was a small, almost perfectly circular island that rose uniformly from the waterline at the beach to a point about five hundred or six hundred feet high at the center. It wasn't populated, and I imagined it built with stately, circular rows of homes, each of which would command a stunning view of the Pacific and have a little path leading down to the water. Treasury lay some 8 degrees south of the equator; the water was always warm enough to swim in.

Alas, our stay there was woefully short. On the fourteenth we departed for Purvis Bay, Florida Island, to have some sound gear repaired and our boilers cleaned. We returned to Blanche Harbor for only a couple more nights before getting under way, on July 6, for Emirau Island in company with the destroyer escort USS *Forman*.

On the seventh, we thought we made a sound contact at 2°51.8′S, 152°14.7′E. At first it seemed to be a good contact and we launched two hedgehog attacks, but without success. During these runs the contact was fading in and out. We never had any Doppler reading and at no time was there target movement, so we concluded that it must have been a fish, abandoned the search, and proceeded on our way to Emirau.

Shortly after midnight on July 8 we received a dispatch from Commodore E. J. Moran, commander of the navy in the Northern Solomons, to proceed to position 2°28'S, 150°35'E and to patrol off the coast of New Hanover in the Bismarck Archipelago. The day before, aircraft had spotted two submarines crash-diving off the northwest coast of that island. An hour later one of the subs was again spotted two miles to the west of the original sighting by a fighter plane that strafed him as he submerged. PT boats were to block Ysabel Channel, and the USS *Duffey* was to set out on a patrol from Emirau. We arrived at our designated initial search point at 0700 on the eighth, then, finding nothing, resumed our voyage to Emirau.

Like Treasury, Emirau was a small, beautiful island, and like Blanche Harbor, Humboldt Bay was secure enough from enemy aircraft that we didn't feel the need to keep round-the-clock gun watches. Because there were no recreational facilities on the beach, we had swim call just about every day. At swim call anywhere from thirty to fifty of the guys would go swimming, myself included. We were intrepid souls, plowing through the water even though there was some risk of sharks. To reduce the risk, we would have a whaleboat patrol the area with two armed men ready to shoot any sharks that might venture into the area looking for lunch.

Being anchored in serene security didn't stop our drive for continued excellence. When we weren't swimming, we would be instructing, training, and conducting drills. Petty officers taught the younger men, and we would give tests to advance our people in ratings as fast as possible. This was important both for morale and from the standpoint of the ship's effectiveness and combat readiness.

So we swam and we trained, and we wrote letters home. I'm sure my mother, along with many other mothers, prayed every night for her son off at war. No doubt my family always imagined that I was in constant danger in the Pacific, but clearly this wasn't the case. In fact, most of the time we weren't in danger at all, though when we were, it was extreme danger. Too bad there wasn't some means of letting the folks back home know when we were safe, so they wouldn't worry all the time.

At the end of July we received orders to return to Seeadler Harbor for fuel and provisions. I still hadn't gotten my hands on an updated map of the harbor; the 1790 Dutch chart would have to do. As we came into the harbor early that morning heading at 5 knots for the fuel dock, Captain Pendleton was on the bridge, I was at the conn, and the quartermasters were doing their best to navigate the ship. The sun shone in our eyes and its bright path across the water obscured the course ahead. Unsure of our Dutch chart and unable to spot possible dangers, I sent a query to the fuel dock signal tower: "How much water is there between our ship and the dock?" The message came back: "Forty feet of water between you and the dock."

No sooner had we received this message than my heart sank; with a shuddering groan, the *England* hit a shoal and ran aground. The shoal was marked by three oil drums, but we hadn't seen them on account of the sun's glare. Uncertain whether the propellers were damaged, we immediately secured our engines and then sent a diver down to inspect.

He surfaced with the bad news that indeed the propellers were damaged. We didn't dare try to back off, which might have aggravated the problem. Meanwhile, slight waves in the harbor made the *England* rock back and forth on the shoal, which pushed in one of the struts housing the starboard shaft and nudged our twelve-inch propeller shaft out of line.

We immediately reported the grounding and started taking measures to ease the *England* off the reef. Another ship gave us an eight-inch manila line and tried to tow us off the reef, but the line parted. Then a shallow-draft barge ship came alongside and removed our depth charges in order to lighten the ship. In the end, a ship gave us a tow cable that cleared us from the shoal.

The next day, with great trepidation, we got under way to determine how much speed could be made on the damaged port propeller and the slightly bent starboard propeller shaft—10 knots, without much vibration. After fueling, we anchored to await our orders. Captain Pendleton was worried to death, as was I. I felt partly responsible and was heartbroken that our beloved ship had been damaged.

Whenever a ship runs aground, the navy orders an investigation and the captain and other officers face a possible court-martial. Shortly after this happened, then, the navy convened a board of investigation on the *England* and thoroughly looked into the circumstances leading up to the grounding. Fortunately for both the skipper and me, the board exonerated us. We were ordered to go to Milne Bay, New Guinea, for repairs and to get new propellers.

It was with a huge sigh of relief that we departed for Milne Bay, crawling along at 8 knots. There, the engineers put the *England* in dry dock and replaced the starboard propeller, repaired the port propeller, and replaced the tail shaft leading to the propeller. Finally on August 9 we got under way for trials at full power. The only remaining problem was minor vibration from the starboard propeller shaft, which was still slightly out of line. We remained at anchor until September 14, at which point we returned to full service and embarked on a busy schedule.

While in Milne Bay, which in addition to having navy repair facilities was also a fairly large U.S. Army base, we sought out female companionship. The base had a Red Cross unit staffed by five attractive young ladies, and one day I invited them out to the ship, where we held a dance on the fantail for the enlisted men. I don't remember what we used for music, but we did have some, and the guys and gals had a great time swinging around. After the dance we invited the women to dine with the officers.

At this point Captain Pendleton had been in the South Pacific for several years, and naturally, being in the South Pacific, he had seen many palm trees. It is from this tree that hearts of palm come. Captain Pendleton loved hearts of palm salad, and he especially loved his recipe for hearts of palm salad dressing. He was so proud of it, in fact, that any time visitors came on board he would ask them if they had ever had hearts of palm salad, and whether or not they had, he would tell them all about his favorite dressing. We got so tired of hearing about hearts of palm salad that we decided to enlist one of the Red Cross workers to play a trick on him.

I knew that at dinner the skipper would seat the prettiest woman to his right, the place of honor, and so beforehand I took this young lady aside and asked her if she'd be willing to play along. Yes, she was game. So I said, "If Captain Pendleton asks you if you've ever had hearts of palm salad, respond this way: 'Yes, Captain, I've had hearts of palm salad, and let me tell you about my salad dressing for it.'" Having committed the recipe to heart by now—how could I not have?—I passed it on to her.

Sure enough, Captain Pendleton did ask her to sit next him, and just as we'd suspected, during the first course he asked her if she had ever had hearts of palm salad. The young lady responded like a trooper, giving him the exact measurement for each ingredient in his precious dressing. He was crushed, and he hardly said a word for the remainder of the dinner.

We had all wanted to get his goat, but I felt bad for him afterward.

———*∿*———

A few weeks after we had completed the submarine operation, I had a chance to meet with Vice Admiral Reginald L. Kauffman, who at that time was commander of destroyers in the Pacific. You'll recall that I had met him in Florida when I was at the Sub-Chaser Training Center and that I had had great fun with his daughter, Betty Lou, who loved to dance. Through some channel or another, Admiral Kauffman had heard about the subs we had sunk and the fact that I had conned the ship during the attack runs.

"John," he said, "I think you ought to get a Navy Cross out of this." "Admiral, I'd like to see the ship get a Presidential Unit Citation. As far as I know, what we did is unique in naval warfare, and it wasn't one person who did it. It takes a team, a good team, to do what we did. I think each and every man on board should be rewarded." "Well, I agree with you, John. I'm going to recommend that your ship get a Presidential Unit Citation. What about individuals? Who do you think deserves what?" "That's a tough one, Admiral," I said, "because there are so many deserving men. First, I think Captain Pendleton should get the Navy Cross. The skipper's been regular navy for a long time and he's had very little recognition for his accomplishments. Now he may not be the best leader in the world, but he's a stickler for equipment maintenance—and the fact that our equipment was in such good condition had a lot to do with our success. Furthermore, he has a fine character. He let us run the ship as we felt she should be run; he recognized that he had good officers and men, and he put his faith in us. I would like to see him get the Navy Cross."

I paused. It was a tough question, being asked to assess your own performance. "As for me, if I got a Navy Cross too it wouldn't seem right, since I was the exec, not the skipper. Furthermore, I'm just a reserve and I'll probably be getting out of the navy after the war. So I would recommend that the navy give me a Legion of Merit for Combat." At that time, the navy's highest awards were the Navy Cross followed by the Legion of Merit, the Silver Star, the Bronze Star, and the Letter of Commendation. Since that time, however—and unfortunately for me!—the medal relationship has changed; now the Silver Star is second to the Navy Cross and the Legion of Merit comes third.

I recommended our antisubmarine officer, Gus Dailey, and Soundman First Class John Prock for the Bronze Star, and Soundman Second Class Roger Burnhardt and Soundman Third Class Paul Ayers for the Letter of Commendation. In retrospect, I wish I had recommended Dailey and Prock for the Silver Star and Burnhardt and Ayers for the Bronze Star. They certainly deserved them for their outstanding performance. So many other people, including the hedgehog gun captain Charlie Ober and his assistant, Ralph Norman, did outstanding jobs that I could have recommended many more medals than I did, and now I regret not doing so.

The medals were awarded, although not until much later. It takes time for medal recommendations to wend their way through the bureaucracy. On August 21, 1944, Admiral Halsey recommended the *England* for the Presidential Unit Citation, Captain Pendleton for the Navy Cross, and me for the Legion of Merit. It was after I had made lieutenant commander that the actual awards were made. Prock and Dailey were awarded Bronze Stars, and Burnhardt and Ayers, commendation medals.

Oh, yes, and one other medal was given out, to Commodore Thorwall. I had made a point of not recommending him for anything, in light of his supernumerary status and the fact that Commander Pendleton had had to threaten to send him below because he was interfering with our actions on the bridge during an attack run. Nevertheless, someone saw fit to award him a Bronze Star because he was on our ship.

Incidentally, after we sank the six submarines Thorwall gave up any thought of slapping Captain Pendleton and me with a court-martial. He knew that with our record there was no way the navy would even consider court-martialing us. In fact, he wrote a letter in which he recommended that I be given a Bronze Star for conning the attacks that sank the submarines. He also requested that the *England* receive a Presidential Unit Citation. Following is a copy of his letter, dated 16 June 1944:

CONFIDENTIAL
FIRST ENDORSEMENT U.S.S. ENGLAND (DE 635)
on CO, USS ENGLAND
ltr. DE635/P15,
Serial No. 025 of
16 June 1944.
c/o Fleet Post Office,
San Francisco, Calif.,
17 June 1944.

From: The Commander Destroyer Escort Division Forty
To: The Commander in Chief, U.S. Pacific Fleet

Via:(1) The Commander Third Fleet

1. Forwarded.

2. Commander Destroyer Escort Division Forty was on the bridge of USS England during all the attacks and carefully observed the performance of all officers and enlisted men involved. Every man on every battle station performed his duties with the utmost efficiency.

3. Upon return on 28 May 1944, ComCortDiv 40 sent an airmailgram to ComSoPacFor recommending that ENGLAND be awarded a Presidential Citation for outstanding performance of duty. This airmailgram further stated "Performance of each man aboard, including staff personnel, was superlative with no individual outperforming others."

4. If individual awards are to be given it is strongly urged that the Bronze Star also be awarded to Lieutenant John A. Williamson, D-V(G), USNR (96906). The Commanding Officer made the first four firing runs on Sub #1, the first firing run on Sub #2, and the first firing run on Sub#3. Hit was

obtained on his second run on Sub #1. Lt. Williamson was conning officer and made all the other attacks. The following summarizes his attacks and the results achieved:

Sub #1 hit on his first firing run.
Sub #2 hit on his first firing run.
Sub #3 hit on his first firing run.
Sub #4 hit on his first firing run. Second salvo was fired on underwater disturbance.
Sub #5 Missed on his first and second firing runs.
Submarine was then attacked with depth charges.
Sub #6 hit on his first firing run.
Sub #7 hit on his first firing run.

C. A. THORWALL.

You remember Sub #5 was not a submarine at all. It was the poor whale we attacked and could not kill with hedgehogs. We killed him with the depth-charge attacks.

I guess I should have appreciated his putting in a good word for me, and in truth I was grateful that he recommended the *England* for the Presidential Unit Citation. But Commodore Thorwall was bent on revenge, something he would later go to great lengths to try to exact.

At any rate, the *England* received the Presidential Unit Citation, and everyone on board was thrilled to read these words from Secretary of the Navy James Forrestal on behalf of the President of the United States:

The President of the United States takes pleasure in presenting the PRESIDENTIAL UNIT CITATION to the

UNITED STATES SHIP ENGLAND

for service as set forth in the following citation:

"For outstanding performance in combat against enemy Japanese forces in the Pacific War Area from May 19 to 31, 1944. Utilizing to the full all available weapons and equipment for anti-submarine warfare, the U.S.S. ENGLAND skillfully coordinated her attacks with other vessels and with cooperating aircraft, striking boldly and with exceptional precision at the enemy's vital undersea craft. In a sustained series of attacks, she destroyed six hostile submarines within twelve days, effecting this devastating blow to enemy operations during a particularly crucial period and disrupting attempts by the Japanese to supply or evacuate key units located in the Bougainville—New Britain—New Ireland areas. By this heavy loss to the enemy, the ENGLAND contributed substantially to the undetected and unmolested advance of the United States Fleet, pointing toward the subsequent seizure and occupation of the Marianas islands by our forces. A gallant and daring fighter, superbly ready for combat, the ENGLAND has achieved an outstanding record of success, reflecting the highest credit upon her gallant officers and men and the United States Naval Service."

For the President
Signed by,
James Forrestal
Secretary of the Navy

I was also thrilled to read the citation to me for the Legion of Merit, again signed by Forrestal on behalf of the president:

For exceptionally meritorious conduct in the performance of outstanding services to the Government of the United States as Executive Officer of the USS *England,* in action against enemy Japanese forces in the Bismarck Archipelago area, from May 15 to May 31, 1944. Skilled and courageous, . . . (then Lieutenant) Williamson contributed vitally to the success of his ship in this brief and critical period of the war and during which the *England* contacted, tracked down and was largely responsible for the destruction of five Japanese submarines and the probable sinking of a sixth. His excellent seamanship, skillful and accurate conning of the vessel and unfaltering devotion to the fulfillment of his duty added greatly to the success of each engagement and upheld the highest traditions of the United States Naval Service.

Lieutenant Commander Williamson is authorized to wear the Combat "V."

The Legion of Merit could be awarded for noncombat performance as well as for combat. If it was for combat you wore the Combat "V."

Though these medals weren't awarded until much later, the *England* had already become a famous ship, if not in the eyes of the American public (our actions were secret and had not yet been released to the media), then at least in the view of naval commanders in the Pacific.

On August 30, while we were still in Milne Bay for repairs, Lieutenant Commander Pendleton was transferred back to the States, promoted to commander, and given command of a division of destroyer escorts. I mentioned earlier that a skipper on one of the ships in his division told me later that all Commander Pendleton ever talked about was the *England.* I laughed, recalling that when he was on the *England,* it seemed as if all he ever talked about was hearts of palm salad dressing. I could understand why the *England* replaced salad dressing in his affections. After all, it was on our ship that he had made his reputation, received a Navy Cross, and earned his promotion to commander. Being regular navy, this meant a tremendous amount to him, and it made up for what he felt had been unfair treatment by the navy over the years. Yes, Commander Pendleton loved the *England* and her men. The feeling was mutual. We were all delighted about his promotion.

At the same time, I became commanding officer of the *England,* with Lieutenant George Brines relieving me as executive officer. It was thrilling to take command, even if the challenge was no greater than before on account of my having been de facto skipper since the time of the *England's* commissioning. I was proud to carry the title of commanding officer of this great ship.

I appointed Lieutenant Phil Goode as gunnery officer, Lieutenant Knight as communications officer, and Lieutenant Howard Engleman, who had been communications officer, as assistant gunnery officer and navigating officer. I felt that the executive officer already had enough to do without being saddled with navigation duties as well. That's why I appointed Engleman as navigation officer. It was a good choice—he became proficient at that job after only a few weeks.

———∽∾∽———

As I mentioned, at the time of these changes we were still in Milne Bay, New Guinea, undergoing repairs. New Guinea was a fascinating island. In the late 1930s, while exploring the island's upper jungle plateaus, explorers found native tribes whose existence nobody had been aware of. The Milne Bay area of New Guinea was governed by an Australian magistrate. One afternoon several officers from the *England* were invited to tea at his home, located several miles from the base in the hills. We borrowed a jeep from the navy transportation pool and drove through jungle. On the way, we came to a clearing that housed a small church. A service was in progress, led by a missionary and attended by dozens of native men. When we pulled into the clearing they were singing hymns, and though we couldn't understand the words we did recognize the tunes. The sound was unearthly in its beauty, and for several minutes we sat there, spellbound and silent. Then we resumed our journey. We enjoyed our visit with the Australian magistrate, who filled us in on the history of Milne Bay, but it was that native singing, not the historical facts, that stuck with me over the years.

On September 14, with the *England* again ready for sea, we said good-bye to exotic New Guinea and MacArthur's Seventh Fleet and got under way for Treasury Island. There we rejoined Nimitz's Fifth Fleet as part of Escort Division 40, which was still commanded by Commander Thorwall, who had left the *England* and was now embarked on the *Forman*.

Over the next week and a half we spent much of our time anchored at Treasury. We conducted training and exercises with the destroyer escorts *Forman* and *Willmarth* and sometimes went searching for floating mines that might have drifted from an enemy minefield in the Shortland Islands area. When we came across a mine, we destroyed it with small arms.

The *England* had been in the Pacific since February 14, 1944, and now it was the middle of September. Our men had not had any liberty except on the Coconut Islands, where all they did was play a few games of soft-ball on the beach and have a few beers. Since we were pretty much twid-dling our thumbs at Treasury, I felt it was high time to request some rest and recreation in a real city—Sidney, Australia. Sidney was Australia's larg-est city and had a reputation as an outstanding place for liberty.

At this time Thorwall's Escort Division 40 was part of a task group commanded by Admiral Arleigh "31-Knot" Burke. Admiral Burke had ac-quired the moniker 31-Knot after his destroyer task group intercepted five Japanese destroyers that had just delivered fresh troops to Buka, in the Solomons. Burke's force sank three of the enemy ships and, racing along at 31 knots, chased the others almost all the way back to Rabaul. This spelled the end of the Tokyo Express supply line, and for the rest of his life, he was known as Admiral 31-Knot Burke.

Hoping to get liberty for my men, I sent a dispatch directly to Admiral Burke and copied his boss, the commander of our task force, requesting ten days of rest and recreation in Sydney. Sydney was couple of thousand miles away, which I didn't think was too far a distance since we wouldn't be joining any significant operation for at least several weeks, if not a couple of months.

The very next day I received a reply from Admiral Burke: "Reference your numbered dispatch, negative, repeat negative." In other words, Hell no, you aren't going to Sydney. The day after that, however, we received a copy of a dispatch from the task force commander to Admiral Burke saying, "Recommend you approve sub-killer *England's* request for rest and recreation in Sydney, Australia." Hooray!

And then my heart sank. We received a copy of a dispatch to Commander Thorwall directing him to designate one ship in his division to accompany the *England* to Sydney. "You can bet your bottom dollar he wants to go to Australia, too," I grumbled to myself. Commander Thorwall fancied himself a ladies' man. When he'd been with us on the *England* he would brag about his prowess with women, saying he could get any girl to go to bed with him if he had a date with her. "I'm one of the best 'cocksmen' around," he used to say. I could just imagine him dreaming of all those Aussie women awaiting his arrival on their shores.

Sure enough, Commodore Thorwall designated the *Forman* to accompany us to Sydney. So at midday on September 25, in company with that ship, we headed off for Sydney. Four days later we pulled into port. Since Sydney lies below the equator, September is springtime in that city. Spring fever was upon us; we were raring to go.

Prior to getting under way for Sydney, the captain of the *Forman* and I had discussed the logistics of liberty for the crew. The navy had a rule that a third of the crew must remain on board at all times while we were in Australia. We decided to let a third go ashore each day at noon for a forty-eight-hour liberty. They would return for twenty-four hours of duty, and then go off for another forty-eight hours. On day one section 1 would go on liberty, on day two section 2 would go on liberty, and on day three section 3 would go on liberty. This staggered system would allow our crew the maximum amount of liberty possible while we still kept a third of the crew on board.

En route to Australia, Commander Thorwall threw a monkey wrench into this plan. He sent a message to me and the captain of the *Forman* ordering us to keep one-half of our crew on board at all times while in Sydney. This restricted us to twenty-four-hour liberty slots. One-half of the crew would go for a twenty-four-hour liberty, and then they would report back to stand a twenty-four-hour watch while the other half went on liberty. This wouldn't be nearly as much fun as leaving the ship for forty-eight hours at a shot. I didn't know how I was going to circumvent this order, but I figured there had to be some way.

When we tied up at the dock, all sorts of officers and enlisted men swarmed on board to offer us their help getting supplies, ammunition, and fuel. Right away, I had the supply officer put in a request for lettuce, tomatoes, and ice cream, and I gave orders that these were to be served for breakfast, lunch, and dinner while we were in port—a popular move. At sea it was difficult to get our hands on fresh food.

The men who crowded onto our ship to help were also brimming with advice about entertainment in Sydney. According to one officer, opportunity abounded; since most of Australia's young bucks were away at war, the Aussie gals were lonely, and they'd taken a shine to U.S. Navy men. He said there were lots of places for the enlisted men to go. As for officers, the best place to meet women was at the tearoom in the Australia Hotel. Apparently most young Australian women worked. When they turned seventeen, if they didn't get a job that contributed to the war effort, they would be drafted into canning factories. If we went to this tearoom about 1700, he assured me, there would be plenty of ladies there after work who would be glad to have dates with officers of the U.S. Navy.

"What about officers clubs?" I said.

"The best one is run by a group of patriotic Australian ladies," he replied. "They set it up to provide a top-rate facility for visiting officers as well as Australian officers."

Suddenly I had an idea. "Where is this club?" I asked. Then I went over to the *Forman* and told the skipper we had urgent business. We caught a taxi to this officers club, and when we got there we asked to speak to the manager, one of the well-bred ladies who had founded the establishment.

"We've got a serious problem," I announced. "There's a senior officer on board who's in his mid-forties, and we need to get rid of him for ten days." I explained the whole liberty mess to her. "You wouldn't happen to know of a young lady who could take charge of this guy for ten days and keep him away from the ship, do you? We'll pay her anything she wants, as long as she keeps him out of our hair." The captain of the *Forman* and I had already agreed that we would pay this lady out of the ship's service fund, since the matter was crucial to our men's well-being.

Naturally, the manager of this officers club was shocked at our request. In addition to being well bred, however, she was also very practical. "What you're proposing *would* help boost the morale of the U.S. Navy," she conceded. Patriotism thus putting to rest any moral qualms, she began mulling over possible candidates for the job. Finally she decided on a lady she knew quite well whose husband had been in the Australian army and had been killed fighting the Japanese. She was about thirty-five years old, a tough but attractive woman. "Go ahead and call her," we said. It just so happened that the woman was at home and available to come over to the officers club.

We met her and took an instant liking to her. She was attractive and looked as if she could handle herself. After explaining the situation and its ramifications for the Allied war effort, we let her think it over. "Okay," she finally said, agreeing to undertake this patriotic duty. "I'll do my best to entertain him and keep him away from the ship for ten days. But how will we meet?"

We decided that the best way would be for the officers club ladies to get the captain and me dates for the night; we could invite Commodore Thorwall along and say we had a date for him also. So the captain and I went and told Thorwall that we had been down to a nice officers club and lined up some dates. Would he like to join us for dinner? Just as I'd suspected, the self-styled cocksman jumped at this opportunity.

That night we met our companions for a pleasant dinner at the club. Commodore Thorwall was very pleased with his, especially after the meal, when the captain and I returned to our ships and his date invited him to come along with her. He glanced at me as if to say "You see what I mean; they really do go for me" and snapped up the invitation.

That woman's word was as good as gold! They didn't see Commodore Thorwall for ten whole days on the *Forman*. I happened across him a couple of times in nightclubs when I was out on dates, and each time he was pretty tanked up. When his lady friend returned him to the ship—right on schedule, two hours before we sailed—I went out to see her. "You can't imagine how much we appreciate this," I said. "How much do we owe you?"

"Captain," she said, "you don't owe me a dime. I kept him drunk most of the time and he wasn't much trouble. I did this for the United States Navy and to help defeat the Japanese."

My heart was brimming with gratitude. I have no idea how she accomplished this mission. Whatever her secret, it was effective and she performed a valuable service, if not for the whole U.S. Navy, then at least for the deserving crewmen of two destroyer escorts. With Commodore Thorwall thus preoccupied, we were able to keep one-third instead of one-half of our men on board at any given time.

I ask you: Should a naval officer never disobey the order of a senior officer?

This was the second time I had disobeyed his orders. He didn't know about this time!

The second night we were in Sydney, some of us officers went to the Australia Hotel tearoom to see what kind of ladies we might meet there. At 1700 the place was crowded, mostly with women in their late teens or early twenties. Men prospecting could choose between "nice" and "loose" girls. There were women who would shack up with you for the duration of your time in Australia and others who made a point of announcing, after you'd asked them out to dinner or to go dancing, "When the dancing's done I'm going *home*"—in other words, "You're not jumping into my bed, sailor."

That night at the tearoom, I spotted an attractive young blonde and asked her if she would permit me to buy her a drink. She said she would be delighted and moved over to our table. Her name was Nadia Gundry. I found out after dinner that she was a good dancer, and since I loved to dance I considered myself lucky to have met her. That night Nadia took me home to meet her mother, who was divorced, and that night I went back to the ship.

Nadia became my unwitting tutor in Australian English. One time we went out dancing after dinner. We had just finished doing the Hoochie Koochie, which took quite a bit of energy, and she said, "Boy, am I knocked up!"

"What do you mean?" I said, alarmed.
"I said I'm really knocked up."
Then it dawned on me. "Does that mean what it means back in the States?"
"What does it mean there?"
"You know," I whispered, "in that way."
She burst out laughing. "Here, 'knocked up' means really tired."

Though I hadn't done anything to get her in that condition, I was relieved nonetheless. It was a source of good fun for both the Americans and the Australians to hear one another's odd expressions. In Australia if someone performed well, for example, you didn't say "well done" or "good job." You said "good on you, mate." In the ten days there I almost learned to speak Australian.

And yet, despite different accents and expressions, there existed a true bond between us and the Aussies. They were outgoing, warm, and friendly—great hosts who treated our guys like royalty. We left Australia with a love for that country, feeling as if the Australians were more like Americans than any other people in the world.

Three of my men fell in love with more than just the country. Four or five days into our stay, each one of them came to me individually to seek permission to tie the knot. (They had to have permission from their commanding officer before they could get married.) Not knowing whether marriage on the heels of a whirlwind romance was the best thing for them, I suggested that they wait for three months. If they were still game after that, I would get them leave to come back to Australia to get married. This also would give the fiancées time to plan weddings. All three guys thought it was a swell idea.

After we left Australia, the officers had to censor mail from the ship to be sure no secrets were divulged to the enemy. One enlisted man wrote to his buddy on another ship: "We've been somewhere where we have had ten days rest and recreation. I cannot tell you where we have been. We did not get much rest, but good God what recreation!" Eventually such euphoria died down. Can you imagine: after three months not one of the enlisted men who had come to me asking permission to get married wanted to tie the knot with the girl he had fallen so madly in love with?

——◆——

After our wonderful liberty in Sydney, we got under way for Treasury Island, where we refueled on October 15 before proceeding to Hollandia, on the southeastern end of New Guinea. There we reported to the commander of Task Force 76, Seventh Fleet, and were told that we would probably be sent out on October 27 with a convoy for Leyte Island in the Philippines.

Because of the grounding incident, our starboard propeller shaft was still out of line, which caused the *England* to vibrate and posed a risk to the starboard main engine. Therefore, we were given a tender availability. The shaft was partially straightened with the application of heat; now instead of being 91/1000 out of line, it was 13/1000. As soon as this repair was made we conducted trials and found the vibration negligible. The *England* was now available for unlimited operational duty. In a future overhaul the shaft could be replaced—at least, that was the intention. Little did we know that this repair would never be made. At any rate, with the pending Philippine operation marking a critical stage in the war, we had more important things to think about.

11

Prelude to the Philippines

AFTER THE MARIANAS, THE NEXT stepping-stone in the American advance on Japan was Peleliu, in the western Caroline Islands. Once this was secured, the United States set its sights on the Philippines, which MacArthur had had to evacuate back in 1942 when those islands fell to the Japanese, and to which he had dreamed of returning ever since. It was in the Philippines that Nimitz's westward-moving drive and MacArthur's drive up through the islands of the southwest Pacific converged for the final assault against the Japanese home islands.

In September 1944, American carrier-based aircraft crippled Japanese airfields in central Luzon, and by mid-October, when a force of some seven hundred U.S. ships gathered east of the Visayan Islands for the invasion of Leyte, the Americans had more or less gained control of the air over the Philippines. On October 20 the invasion began; in a characteristically dramatic gesture, MacArthur waded ashore proclaiming, "People of the Philippines, I have returned." Within days the Americans gained a solid foothold.

But success was not easy to come by. Japanese naval commanders, increasingly desperate as their losses mounted, decided to make yet another attempt to bring down the curtain on the U.S. Fleet. The plan was to use three forces: a decoy force, the Central Force, and the Southern Force. The decoy force would lure away one of the two U.S. forces supporting the landing, while the Central and Southern forces would converge on the remaining force in Leyte Gulf and pulverize it. The ensuing encounter, the Battle for Leyte Gulf, turned out to be the greatest sea battle in history.

The battle, which began on October 24, didn't go as the Japanese had planned. Admiral Halsey's Third Fleet did indeed fall for the ruse, leaving the gulf in hot pursuit of the decoy force instead of remaining to support the landing, which is what it was supposed to do. But Admiral Thomas Kinkaid's Seventh Fleet blocked the Southern Force at the southern approach to the gulf. The Japanese lost twelve ships. Belatedly realizing that Halsey was nowhere around, Kinkaid, his fleet stretched to the limit, dispatched a force of six slow escort carriers and seven other undergunned ships under Rear Admiral Clifton Sprague to guard the northern entrance. Presently, Japan's Central Force entered the gulf from the north, hoping to pinch off the U.S. force. But Sprague outsmarted the enemy. He launched all his planes and sent up smoke screens over his disadvantaged ships, which threw the Japanese into confusion. After two hours, the enemy force turned away in defeat.

The Japanese ended up losing twenty-six warships—including all of their remaining carriers—to the Americans' six. So much for the hope of delivering a final blow to the U.S. Fleet. This hope had been thwarted twice before, at Pearl Harbor and in the Marianas. After the Battle for Leyte Gulf, it died for good.

But that didn't mean we Americans were in for an easy time. Despite early successes, MacArthur's land campaign to liberate the Philippines would drag on until the end of the war. At sea, the Japanese, woefully short of ships, submarines, and aircraft, resorted to suicide attacks to try to prevent their enemies from further advancing on the home islands. While the land battle raged, kamikazes began popping out of the clouds with a vengeance, peppering down on ships of every size and type. No vessel was immune from the threat of men willing to lay down their lives for Japan. It turned Philippine waters into a killing field, and the *England* was about to sail right into its midst.

———⟋∿∿⟍———

On October 22, Commander Thorwall shifted his flag back to the *England*. Four days later we got under way with the *Forman* and the destroyer USS *Edwards* to escort two hospital ships to San Pedro Bay in Leyte Gulf. We followed a zigzagging course so that in case the enemy launched an attack it would be harder to target us. Surface and air traffic to and from the Philippines was heavy, reflecting the scale and significance of the

170

Philippine operation, but we encountered no enemy and arrived safely in San Pedro early in the morning of the thirtieth.

For the next two days, with Japanese aircraft busy opposing the Philippine invasion, we were at general quarters much of the time. Some planes were dropping bombs; others, flown by kamikazes, were crashing into their targets. The area's officer in tactical command would indicate what type of fire control to use. "Flash red, control green" meant that we should shoot at any plane we saw because there were only enemy planes in the air. "Flash red, control yellow" meant that we should fire only at identified enemy planes because there might be friendly planes overhead. Whenever an air attack was launched—and there were numerous attacks that day and the next—we would get under way in order to more easily evade the enemy.

During these air attacks no Japanese plane got close enough for us to shoot at it. The enemy had bigger fish to fry. There were many large U.S. ships in the area, and they were much more attractive targets than our humble little destroyer escort. Still, we had to be on high alert at all times, for although the *England* might not be under direct attack, any one of the planes within three thousand or four thousand yards could turn and attack us at any time.

On Halloween we set sail to escort the hospital ship USS *Tryon* to Humboldt Bay, Hollandia, New Guinea. We arrived after an uneventful passage and made arrangements for full testing of our propeller shaft, the one that was still slightly off-kilter. In early November we got under way with a maintenance specialist to test the *England* under all conditions, including full-speed runs and back emergency full astern. With no detectable vibration, the *England* was considered fit and ready to go on full operational status.

Earlier, I had told Commodore Thorwall that I wanted the *England* to have a military inspection to confirm the ship's combat readiness. If we failed, I would take the consequences; if we were proved proficient, let it be. He refused the military inspection. The reason, I suspected, was that he knew we would come out good.

While the *England* was undergoing these tests, Commodore Thorwall called in the senior yeoman (ship's secretary) and told him he wanted to write a letter.

The commodore said, "I'm going to dictate a letter to you. Now this letter is about your captain and I want you to swear that you won't show it to him." So the staff member took an oath that he would not show me this letter.

After the yeoman had written the letter, he came to me and said, "Captain, Commodore Thorwall has written a letter about you that's filled with lies. He made me swear that I wouldn't show it to you, so I can't; however, there is an extra copy in the bottom right-hand drawer of the ship's office desk." I retrieved the letter and read it. The letter was a terrible indictment of me and my exec, George Brines.

Thorwall had requested that Brines and I be relieved from our duties. During the period from April 21 to June 20, he claimed, "the ship excelled in antisubmarine warfare but in all other respects was below standard. The ship was extremely lax in the enforcing of discipline, wearing of uniforms, personnel cleanliness, military courtesy, observance of safety precautions, standing of war cruising watches and in training of personnel." He went on to say that he had made various recommendations to improve these alleged deficiencies, all of which he claimed had been disregarded.

Then he recounted the grounding at Seeadler Harbor, without mentioning the extenuating circumstances leading up to that event, and aired several other grievances, among them the following:

On 16 September the Division Commander boarded the ship for one day. He found the Officer of the Deck unshaven, wearing Marine working trousers and wearing no insignia of rank. The crew were in a varied assortment of uniforms including marine caps, army boots, troop coveralls and aviator jackets. Clothing was torn, dirty and mutilated.

On the above date the Division Commander found a war cruising lookout and a number of ready gun crew asleep on station. Punishment for one was a warning and for the other ten hours' extra duty.

From 7 July to 30 July the ship lay at anchor at Emirau and from 1 August to 14 September remained in port at Manus and Milne Bay undergoing repairs caused by grounding. Despite this extended stay in ports the Commanding Officer sent a dispatch requesting ten days' leave for the ship at Sydney, Australia.

The letter concluded by recommending that I be detached and sent to the commander of destroyers in the Pacific for further assignment and that Lieutenant Brines be detached and sent to the *Forman* as gunnery officer. "Copies of this letter together with unsatisfactory fitness reports have been submitted to Lt. Williamson and Lt. Brines for their statement," he concluded.

That was a lie. Commodore Thorwall did not give me a copy of this letter until several weeks later. According to navy regulations, he should have given me a copy as soon as it was written so I would have a chance to respond. No doubt he was hoping I would be relieved before I could respond. And he knew if I could respond, I would be able to rebut most of what he had said. He also knew I would request a military inspection, which would in all likelihood disprove his claims.

I had to act quickly, because we were leaving for the Philippine operation the next day. It so happened that at that time the navy's Southwest Area headquarters were in New Guinea, where the *England* was having her propeller shaft tested. And it so happened that the commander of destroyers in the Pacific was Admiral Reginald Kauffman, the father of my friend and favorite dancing partner, Betty Lou. The naval headquarters were located about ten miles from Humboldt Bay, up in the hills about a mile from General MacArthur's headquarters.

I borrowed a jeep from the transportation pool, headed for the hills, and handed Admiral Kauffman a copy of Thorwall's letter. When he finished reading, he turned to me and said, "John, this is horrible. Tell me about it."

"Admiral, the whole thing is filled with lies. Most of Commodore Thorwall's accusations can be disproved by the ship's log. Prior to him writing this letter, I requested a military inspection to supply proof that he's wrong about all these complaints, but he refused to allow it." I paused, carefully considering my words. "As you know, we're leaving for the Philippines tomorrow. I'd like to request that you not do anything about this letter until we return and that you order a military inspection for the *England* at that point. If the inspection bears out what Commodore Thorwall says, I'll stand to be relieved and I won't argue about it. But if the inspection is positive, then I'd like to retain command of the USS *England*."

"John, you go ahead and take your ship to the Philippines. I promise you'll have a military inspection."

Several weeks later, Commodore Thorwall was making preparations to switch his flag to the *Whitehurst*. Before he left, he called me in. "Williamson," he said, "I just want you to know that I've written a letter that will be delivered to you within the next day or so. You're not competent to command this vessel and I have written this letter to the proper authorities recommending that you be relieved. The only thing I regret about this is the fact that you'll get to go back to the States and not me." Then he took his bags and left the *England*. Little did he know that I'd already read his letter and had taken action on my own.

In addition to talking to Admiral Kauffman, I had fired off a letter to the chief of naval personnel. My first point addressed Commodore Thorwall's order, when I was still executive officer, concerning regulation uniforms:

> I requested Commander Thorwall to tell the Captain his desires in order to avoid any friction in the chain of command. Commander Thorwall then informed me that he could not tell the Commanding Officer anything as the Commanding Officer had been in the Navy too long. Commander Thorwall continued to give me orders without taking them through the Commanding Officer. It was easy to see that a situation such as this could, and soon did, become almost intolerable.

I mentioned that after the successful antisubmarine operation, Commodore Thorwall had recommended me for the Bronze Star, and then I went on to say that the commodore's subsequent complaints about my perceived unwillingness to enforce discipline probably reflected our different ideas about discipline:

> I have never had any trouble whatsoever in getting orders that I issued to the officers and men under my command carried out. I believe that unless a ship is a happy ship it will be neither efficient nor ready to fight. Since ComCortDiv 40 issued orders to get into uniform the crew has been put in the uniform designated. Occasionally a man will be seen out of uniform,

but this is the exception, not the general rule. ComCorDiv 40 insists that this uniform be enforced and that men found not in uniform be regularly punished. I do not believe in nagging my men about little things while there are as many big things to think about as there are under present operating conditions. However, since the order regarding uniforms must be strictly enforced there have been several men given extra duty for being out of uniform according to ComCortDiv 40's orders, when men on every other ship in the harbor were permitted to do the things for which my men must be put on report. Since his coming aboard it is considered that the morale of the officers and men has dropped to a new low in the history of the *England.*

As for Thorwall's complaints about cleanliness, I said that I had been aboard several destroyers and destroyer escorts since coming to the southwest Pacific and had seen very few that compared to the *England* in this regard. Furthermore, the *England* had never been criticized by an officer in tactical command for her maneuvers or execution of signals, and she surpassed many other destroyers and destroyer escorts in efficiency and training.

"If the chief of naval personnel takes any action on this unsatisfactory fitness report by Commander Thorwall," I concluded, "it is respectfully requested that my previous fitness reports be checked against this one. . . . I strongly believe that this report is unjust and in error, and . . . that under normal conditions of wartime operation I can fully satisfy officers that may be placed over me in regard to my duties as commanding officer of a destroyer escort."

———◦∿◦———

On November 7 we got under way at approximately 1330 to sweep the harbor entrance prior to the sortie of our convoy. We had been given orders by the commander of Task Force 76 to accompany a convoy composed of thirteen fleet support ships with tows, one liberty ship with tow, and one army repair ship. The escorts were the *England* and eight sub-chasers. En route to the Philippines, once again we encountered heavy surface and air traffic. Fortunately for us most of it was friendly, a sure sign that the war was moving in the Americans' favor.

On the morning of the eighteenth, as we were nearing the Leyte Gulf southwest of Homohan Island, a sub-chaser ahead of the convoy spotted a floating mine close aboard. Ordering this ship, the SC 745, to circle the mine and keep the convoy ships away from it, we hoisted a signal for an emergency turn to starboard and gave a fifteen-second blast on the siren. The convoy failed to turn, oblivious to our warnings. But the SC 745 continued to circle the mine, forcing the convoy to split, with two columns passing on her starboard side and two on her port side, thus avoiding disaster. Commodore Thorwall then instructed the SC 745 to destroy the mine.

After we entered San Pedro Bay, our job with the convoy was finished. We spent the rest of the day alternating between being at anchor and getting under way, for Japanese planes were still hammering away at fleet targets. Adrenaline was streaming through our veins; we maintained a state of high alert, ready to open fire at any minute, never losing our edge. Looking back on it, I marvel at the stamina and determination of our men as well as the sailors on other ships.

On November 19 at about 0700, we heard by voice radio an urgent report of Japanese planes in the area and went to general quarters. It was a cloudy day, with cloud cover at about 2,500 feet. Ten minutes after going to general quarters, I spotted a plane come popping out of the clouds. It appeared to be an Oscar-type Japanese fighter, which carried no bombs. The aircraft took a steep dive and went boring through the air toward a merchant ship anchored about three thousand yards on our port beam. Bull's-eye! Only a second after making its debut, the plane erupted in a plume of flame and billowing black smoke, and with my binoculars I could just make out the ship's frantic crew racing across the deck. Shortly afterward two more planes shot out of the clouds and went diving toward two merchant ships nearby. By now on high alert, these two ships managed to get some 20-millimeter fire into the air. You had to shoot quickly and accurately to down a plane whose pilot was determined to dive on your ship. Luckily, each defender hit something—either plane or pilot—for both aircraft missed their target and crashed into the sea.

Though we'd heard about kamikazes and knew they were operating in the area, this was the first time we'd actually seen suicide planes. It was a real shock—young men sacrificing their lives in the name of their emperor. Japan had reached the point of desperation.

On November 22 we were ordered to join a convoy of eight merchant ships and two navy tugs being escorted by seven ships under the commander of Destroyer Squadron 14 in the destroyer *Caldwell*. Carrier Division 29 provided air cover. Three days later the convoy split up. We continued on our way with two other screening ships and seven merchant ships, arriving in Hollandia on the twenty-eighth.

In early December, under orders from the commander of Task Force 78, we arrived at Manus Island in the Admiralties, along with the rest of Escort Division 40. On the afternoon of the fifth, a nice-looking barge approached the *England*. The gangway watch called me and I went out to meet it.

An officer climbed the ladder and introduced himself as Captain W. Craig, a representative of the commander of destroyers in the Pacific. "I'd like to talk with you for a few minutes," he said, so I accompanied him into the wardroom. "Williamson," said Captain Craig, "I plan to come aboard tomorrow at 0600 with my staff to give your ship a military inspection."

"I'm delighted, Captain. I've been looking forward to this. We'll be ready as possible."

Having been in the Philippines for over four weeks, and in port for just a day or two, we hadn't had much of a chance to get the *England* shipshape, but I wasn't worried. I discussed the inspection with my officers. "Men," I assured my officers, "I think we're well prepared. I don't want you to lose sleep over this—we'll come out just fine." I didn't discover until the next morning that most of our officers and men had stayed up all night getting the ship as clean and shipshape as possible in that short time.

The next day, December 6, Captain Craig and his staff of officers and enlisted men came aboard and put us through a full military inspection that lasted from 0600 until 1800. They ran us through every drill and exercise imaginable. On December 8 Captain Craig sent a report to W. K. Phillips, commander of destroyers in the Pacific Fleet, that contained this assessment:

Engineering	Excellent
Damage Control, C&R	Excellent
Gunnery & Torpedoes	Excellent
Sonar, Radar & CIC	Excellent
Communications	Excellent

Supply	Excellent
Medical	Excellent
Personnel	Excellent
State of Training	Excellent
General Quarters Drill	Excellent
Cleanliness	Excellent
Military Courtesy	Excellent
State of Discipline	Excellent

"The Commanding Officer, U.S.S. ENGLAND, is deserving of special credit," Craig concluded. A copy was sent to the commander of Escort Division 40.

When Commander Phillips received this report from Captain Craig, he wrote the following to the chief of naval personnel:

> Subject officer assumed command of the U.S.S. ENGLAND (DE 635) on 30 August 1944, having served on board as Executive Officer for approximately nine months prior to that date. During his tour of duty as Executive Officer, the U.S.S. ENGLAND performed outstandingly in actions against the enemy and special credit is due Lieutenant Williamson therefore.
>
> Reference (a) is a report of a thorough surprise inspection of the U.S.S. ENGLAND conducted on 6 December 1944. This report indicates clearly that the ship commanded by Lieutenant Williamson is, to his special credit, being well maintained, well trained and well disciplined in all departments.
>
> It is requested that this letter and the enclosure be made a part of the official record of Lieutenant Williamson. It is also strongly recommended that he be temporarily promoted to the rank of Lieutenant Commander in the Naval Reserve, to hold such rank while serving in command of a destroyer escort.

In the end, it was Commodore Thorwall who went back to the States, not me. He was relieved of his command by dispatch. I believe Admiral Kauffman had him dismissed for several reasons besides this incident with me. Not the least, Thorwall had ignored Admiral Halsey's explicit order not to break radio silence when we were in the middle of the sub-sinking operation between Manus and Truk.

To replace Thorwall as the commander of Escort Division 40, the Navy

Department chose Commander Frederick Hause, who had been commanding officer of one of the ships in our division. Hause took charge immediately after Thorwall left, and on 6 March 1945 he wrote a letter to the chief of navy personnel recommending me for a spot promotion to lieutenant commander, which I was given. I deeply appreciated Hause's gesture; without it, and that of Captain Craig, a promotion probably wouldn't have been granted me for another six months to a year.

Thankfully, I never ran across Commander Thorwall again. I did hear about him, though. Some months later I was in Pearl Harbor and I happened to be introduced to a senior officer on the staff of the commander of destroyers in the Pacific (this was no longer Admiral Kauffman, who had since moved on to another command). "Williamson," he said, "you had a division commander by the name of Thorwall."

"Yes sir."
"What can you say about him?"
"He was a good seaman."
"Is that all?"
"Yes, Captain, why do you ask?"
"Well, the other day we got a letter from him requesting that the Bronze Star he received for being on your ship during the submarine-sinking operation be exchanged for a Navy Cross. He said he was primarily responsible for the sinking of those submarines."
"That's interesting, Captain. What did you do?"
"I wrote on the request 'Bullshit' and gave it to the admiral. He wrote 'Concur,' and we sent it back to him!"

Things were looking up. The *England* had been vindicated. I was commanding officer of what I believed was the best ship in the Pacific Fleet, with the finest crew imaginable, and everyone was delighted to have Commander Hause as our new division commander.

—⟨≈⟩—

On December 9 we got under way to escort the attack transport *General C. G. Morton* to Guadalcanal. We arrived on the twelfth, went to Tulagi and Treasury Island to pick up ammunition, and then returned to Seeadler Harbor on the fifteenth. At Sceadler we had a five-day availability for general maintenance, during which Commander Hause shifted his pennant from the *England* to the *Forman.*

We remained in Seeadler Harbor until December 26. As far as we knew there was no place nearby to get Christmas cards to send home, but there was a picture floating around the ship of a big buxom Pacific Island native with nothing on but a grass skirt. Someone had the thought that this would make a great Christmas card, so I went over to the *Piedmont,* a navy destroyer tender that was supplied with reproductive equipment, and asked them to make copies of this picture. We pasted the picture on a sheet of white paper. Underneath the picture we wrote, "Dreaming of a White Christmas."

During the war various entertainers traveled around the world putting on shows and plays for the troops, and it just so happened that Irving Berlin, who had written the song "White Christmas" and put together a show called "This Is the Army," was on the *Piedmont* when I went to retrieve the pictures. "John," said the executive officer, "you've got to meet Irving Berlin and show him this Christmas card."

With that, he took me in to meet Mr. Berlin. "I'd love to have one of these to send my wife," the musician said when he saw the card. "She would never believe that one of my songs could end up like this." So I gave him a copy. Later I went ashore with a number of my crew to see his show, which was a rare treat—it was the only show I saw during my entire time in the navy.

Christmas Day was spent at anchor in Seeadler Harbor. It was hard to have a fantastic Christmas so far away from home, but we managed. Some of the crew went ashore and picked up some little bushes whose branches resembled those on pine trees. The men took a broomstick, put holes in it and stuck these branches in, and then sprinkled them with metal shavings that our machinist's mate had made to simulate tinsel. *Voilà,* a Christmas tree! And the cooks in our galley did themselves proud. Able to get their hands on fresh provisions, they prepared roast turkey, dressing, and all the trimmings. For that one special day we forgot all about the war and our hearts were filled with peace and love, especially for one another.

12

Combat Plus

IT WAS NOT UNTIL EARLY January 1945 that MacArthur's forces finally landed on Luzon in the Philippines. They went ashore and began the longest ground campaign of the Pacific war, one that would drag out until Hiroshima and Nagasaki were bombed. Meanwhile, Nimitz's forces were gearing up for landings on Iwo Jima and Okinawa that would bring the Americans ever closer to the Japanese heartland.

But that was in the future. For the rest of December 1944 we remained at Manus, entering the new year without much of a celebration. Although the war had clearly turned in our favor, the Japanese were determined to defend their homeland, and with fierce fighting likely on the horizon I was bent on keeping the *England* battle-ready. The importance of training, drummed into my head at the Sub-Chaser Training Center in Miami, had been more than brought home to me during the twelve days of submarine attacks we'd launched. I'd never forgotten that people who know how are far more effective than those who don't. We took advantage of training our ship at every opportunity, going ashore to practice simulated submarine attack procedures, getting planes to tow sleeves past our ship so we could fire at them, and firing star shells so our machine guns could shoot at the bursts. Whether we were at sea or in port, we took every advantage to conduct practices and drills of all kinds. We did far more than our share of training, and I believe that it made a tremendous difference in the results our ship obtained.

We spent the first two weeks in January escorting the attack transport *Yarmouth* between Manus and Ulithi in the Caroline Islands. In mid-month, while we were at Ulithi, I received an invitation from my old friend

Captain E. F. McDaniel—Captain Mac, whom you may recall had been executive officer on the destroyer *Livermore* and later the dynamic commanding officer of the Sub-Chaser Training Center. Since I'd last seen him, he had been reassigned as executive officer on the cruiser *Biloxi*.

Captain Mac found out that my ship was anchored in the southern end of Ulithi, and he sent a message asking me to come have dinner on his ship and to spend the night. He would provide transportation. Now, Ulithi was a huge harbor—from the northern end where the larger ships were anchored to the southern end with the smaller ships was twelve to thirteen miles—so I figured Captain Mac would send a boat to fetch me. I was in my cabin getting dressed to go when my messenger came in and said, "Captain, your plane is here."

"What?"
"Your plane is here."

I threw on a fresh uniform and went out, and sure enough, back off our starboard quarter, there was a seaplane waiting for me. I got in the whaleboat and climbed into the plane, which took off for the northern part of the harbor. When it landed it was lifted by a crane, and we were deposited onto Captain Mac's ship. I felt like royalty. That night we had dinner and I spent the night on Captain Mac's ship. We had a delightful evening together, the fruit of shared memories and mutual respect. We talked of the *Livermore* and times in the North Atlantic, the Sub-Chaser Training Center and the amazing things we accomplished there. I told him how his leadership had influenced my life. We talked until the wee hours, and then he provided me with a private stateroom and I fell into a deep sleep.

After breakfast the next morning I got into the plane, which was plopped back into the water by crane. On the trip back to the southern harbor I looked down and noticed that the *England* stood out like a sore thumb, with her high-visibility paint. At that time there were two different paint schemes for the outside of navy ships. One was gray-blue paint that made the ship difficult to see at night. The hull was painted a darker shade, the middle part of the superstructure a lighter shade, and the upper structure the palest shade. In the other scheme, the ship was painted black, white, and gray in splotches all over. This camouflage was supposed to make it difficult for an attacking surface ship to judge the target angle of its prey.

The *England* happened to have the splotchy, high-visibility paint job, the only ship in the southern part of the harbor that did. And in three days we were going to sea where we'd be a sitting duck. After landing I summoned Bob Webb, our first lieutenant. "Bob," I said, "how long would it take us to completely paint the exterior of our ship?"

"We could do it in five days, Captain," he replied.

"Well, I was just flying overhead, and the *England* stands out like a sore thumb with this high-visibility splotch job. If I was a Jap suicide plane and I looked down at a convoy of ships, I would pick out the *England* to dive on. We're getting under way in three days, you know."

"Captain," he assured me, "we'll have the ship painted by then." He was true to his word. When we departed three days later, that ship had been transformed from a painted lady to a modest, low-visibility vessel with a far better chance of eluding the enemy.

On January 15, while escorting another ship back to Manus Island, our sound gear went out. It seems that our projector was inoperative because of a damaged ground that couldn't be repaired at sea. This did not affect our listening sound gear, so we switched from active pinging to listening watch, which greatly curbed the protection we could give the other ship. We suggested that she zigzag during daylight for added protection, but the captain didn't consider this necessary. The entire way I felt exceptionally vulnerable without our full range of sound gear, and I sweated over it until we arrived at Manus and went into dry dock for a day-long repair.

Every time we steamed through waters under enemy threat and reached our destination, we thanked our lucky stars. And every time we set out once again, we knew our luck might run out. No matter how experienced, or how well trained, we couldn't help but view our movements as an extended game of Russian roulette.

After the war started my sister married a young guy by the name of Johnny Richardson, whom I'd met on my way to the Sub-Chaser Training Center. Sis and Johnny boarded a train with me in Opelika, Alabama, and rode as far as Montgomery, Alabama, before getting off. After they married Johnny joined the marines, and now he was with the First Marine Division on Peleliu in the Palau Islands. In the fall of 1944, Peleliu had been bombed by U.S. naval and air forces and had been captured by amphibious assault after bitter fighting. The landing had been an especially tough operation for the marines, and Johnny had survived it. I was anxious to get there and see him.

It just so happened that while we were anchored at Manus, Escort Division 40 was ordered to provide an escort for a supply ship heading to Peleliu, so I volunteered the *England* for the job. We got under way on February 1 and arrived on the fifth, my twenty-seventh birthday. I reported to the port director at Peleliu, and we were told to patrol for enemy submarines off the island's west coast while awaiting orders about a return trip to Manus. Our guys could patrol off the coast as well without me as with, so I took off to see Johnny. Prior to their heading off for that duty, I got in our whaleboat with a case of chocolate milk in tow—doubting that the marines had any chocolate milk there—and went ashore to try to find Johnny. I knew his company number and found him easily.

We clapped each other on the back, joyous at this rare chance to reunite in the faraway Pacific after so many months of devastation and war. And Johnny was just as happy to get that case of chocolate milk as he was to see me. I spent most of the day with him, and then returned to the *England* while she was still on patrol. There was no ship to take back, so we returned to Manus on our own. I couldn't have had a better birthday present than to see my brother-in-law, who had survived the bloody landing at Peleliu.

Back at Manus, the *England* went into limited availability to have her boilers cleaned. While this was being done I was summoned, along with the commanding officers of other ships in Manus, to the ship of the senior officer present afloat for a briefing about the next operation, the Battle of Okinawa.

Okinawa and the island of Ie Shima, just to the west, had a large contingent of Japanese military personnel as well as a couple hundred thousand civilians. Since Okinawa was only about 340 miles south of Japan, we would be in easy range of land-based Japanese planes. Another challenge for the navy, army, and marines would be the heavy defenses on Okinawa, where seventy-seven thousand Japanese army troops were stationed with twenty thousand local military. The Japanese would put up maximum resistance since they dreaded the thought of Americans taking over that island and using it to launch air attacks against the homeland. "It's going to be a fierce struggle," the captain briefing us warned. "Your ships will be under heavy attack by Japanese torpedo planes, bombers, and kamikazes." After capturing Okinawa, the briefer went on, U.S. forces would be landing on Kyushu, the southernmost of Japan's four home islands. With a pointer, he indicated the landing spot on a map.

"That's Indian country, isn't it?" one of the commanding officers said. "You're damn right it's Indian country," the briefer responded. "But I'm told we have to go in there if we're going to win this war once and for all."

This was before any of us knew about the atomic bombs that would actually bring the war to an end. The Japanese had fought to the death on islands throughout the Pacific, costing thousands of American lives, and there was every reason to believe that their resistance would be even fiercer on the home islands. It made us shiver to think about the landing on Kyushu and all of the men who would die. Would it be hundreds of thousands? Our only hope, it seemed, was if the Japanese realized they were defeated and surrendered before that time came. I prayed they would.

I went back to the ship determined to do everything I could to get the *England* ready for Okinawa. I put in an immediate request for two planes towing sleeves. I wanted two sleeves so that the two machine-gun groups could fire separately, enabling us to better judge their results and correct deficiencies. The request was granted, and on the morning of February 15 we headed to sea for antiaircraft practice. After the planes finished towing, they would drop the sleeves and we would pick them up to check the hits. Our gunners did an excellent job.

The rest of February was relatively quiet—the calm before the storm—with just a couple of escort assignments. At one point, while we were in Ulithi, I received a message from my friend Eddy Duchin, the piano player who had been my exec on the sub-chaser in the Atlantic. Eddy had been transferred from sub-chasers to a cruiser, and he happened to be in Ulithi while I was there. Upon discovering that the *England* had arrived, he sent word asking me to meet him on the recreation island. At most ports the navy would clear one of the islands for recreation. There wasn't much to do, but you could play sports and have a beer.

All these old friends I was running into—Captain Mac, my brother-in-law, and now Eddy Duchin! Eager for another reunion, I went ashore by whaleboat and met Eddy on the beach. He had brought along a quart of bourbon, and we sat under a palm tree on that island and proceeded to drink, reminiscing about all the good times we'd had in New York in the old days, going from club to club and hobnobbing with the crème de la crème. We watched the enlisted guys playing softball, watched the sun setting in the west, and then returned to our respective ships—both a little more than unsteady from polishing off that quart of bourbon.

That was the last time I was to see my good friend. After the war I received the sad news that Eddy had died of cancer.

In mid-March, while we were back in Ulithi, Commander Fredrick Hause, our new division commander, was directed to report Escort Division 40 to the commander of Task Force 54 for duty. We were to have the division ready for sea and extended operation by daylight on March 21. Meanwhile, the *England* received a voice message from the commander of Task Force 54 to report to the commanding officer of the *New York,* one of the older battleships, for duty as an escort to the Okinawa area.

We got under way on the twenty-third in company with the destroyer *Leutze* and the destroyer escort *Whitehurst,* a three-ship escort for the *New York.* The battleship's skipper was designated commander of the task unit. En route the escorts had to refuel from the *New York.*

With the Battle of Okinawa on the horizon we were about to enter dangerous waters, but refueling posed its own special risks. The *New York* hoisted her signal flags to indicate a refueling speed of 8 knots. The *Leutze* was first in line. She went alongside the battleship and refueled at 8 knots. Then it was our turn. We took station astern of the *New York* and made ready to come alongside when suddenly the battleship hoisted another signal flag indicating a change of speed to 15 knots. He was more anxious to get to Okinawa than I was. I wasn't confident about refueling at such a high speed, but rather than argue I increased our speed to 20 knots and we came alongside smartly, slowed to 15 knots, and then tried to get close enough to reach the *New York*'s fuel hose.

When we were about twenty yards short of our goal, the bow wave of that big battleship hit our bow and we began edging away. "Right 5 degrees rudder," I called to the helmsman, but that didn't bring us any closer. "Right 10 degrees rudder!" Still no results. I was hesitant to increase rudder any more than that, thinking we might get caught inside this bow wave and be slammed against the side of the battleship. The *New York* had at least twelve to fourteen inches of armor plate—she would crush our little thin-hulled ship. So I ordered the rudder increased by small increments, but still we got no closer.

The captain of the *New York* was standing on the port wing of his bridge and, because we were going to fuel port side to the battleship, I was on the starboard wing of my bridge. When he saw that we were getting no closer, he lifted his megaphone and bellowed, "Goddamn it, Skipper, give it some rudder!"

"Damn it, Captain, I already have on right full rudder. What do you suggest?" Seeing my frustration, he turned to his signalman and a flag hoist went up: "Speed 08," meaning slow to 8 knots. That took care of the problem and the *England* sucked up the fuel thirstily.

———⟋⟍⟍⟋———

With both the Americans and the Japanese fiercely determined to possess Okinawa, the battle for this island would prove to be the most costly and complex operation of the entire Pacific war, as well as the last, though we had no way of knowing that at the time. Over half a million American troops would be committed to the operation, along with a huge armada of 1,213 warships. The landings on Okinawa were preceded by landings on the Kerama Islands, which lay off Okinawa's southwest coast.

The initial landings on the Kerama Islands had commenced on March 26. About midnight on the twenty-seventh we entered the dreaded whirlwind, approaching the southern tip of Okinawa with Kerama Retto to our west. Our standard formation speed was 16 knots, with the *Leutze* in station one ahead of the *New York*, the *Whitehurst* on her port bow, and the

England on her starboard bow. Presently we began seeing antiaircraft fire to the west and northwest, and we went to general quarters. There were so many ships passing us that we had to use our surface radar just to clear them. The *New York* would change course now and then, and we would change our position to remain on her starboard bow.

The man who had briefed us on this operation wasn't kidding when he said it would be intense. We had just given all our guns, caked with salt from heavy weather en route to Okinawa, a thorough cleaning in anticipation of a melee. Within two hours of our initial approach to the island, at about 0230, the *Leutze* reported an enemy plane bearing 290 degrees true, five miles and closing. A few minutes later she opened fire with her radar-controlled 5-inch 38-caliber guns, and the plane changed course.

That was just the beginning. Hardly had an hour gone by when we got a real taste of what the Battle of Okinawa was going to be like. At around 0340, two enemy planes broke from the clouds and came zeroing in on our formation. With cloud cover only partial, the moon was visible to the west of us at about 15 degrees elevation, and its light shining on the water made us easily visible to the enemy. On account of the dozens and dozens of ships milling around the area, our surface radar was crowded with pips, and it failed to distinguish the planes from the other traffic. Our air search radar was equally useless, since the attackers flew in low. None of the other ships in the area picked them up, either.

Imagine my shock when suddenly, in the midst of this traffic circus off Okinawa, I heard the drone of a plane overhead, looked up from my position on the bridge, and moments later spotted an enemy plane about five hundred yards off our starboard quarter releasing its cargo. As it went skimming past us, another plane passed off our starboard side at about one thousand yards; luckily for us, this second plane didn't attack.

In mute horror, we watched the weapon from that first plane embark on its path, unsure whether it was a bomb or a torpedo. Then we heard a propeller noise on our sound gear, the telltale sign of a torpedo. No sooner had the thing hit the water than it went racing astern of us, in the direction of the *New York*.

I snatched up the voice radio: "*New York*, torpedo coming your way! Repeat, torpedo coming your way!"

While we listened in vain for a response from the *New York*, the torpedo continued on its run, now heading for a position between that ship and the *Leutze*. Then all of a sudden, *ka-boom!* The weapon erupted in what appeared to be the wake of the *Leutze*.

"What was that explosion?!" came a voice from the *New York*.
"A Japanese torpedo," I explained. "It was dropped at us but missed its mark. I believe it exploded at the end of its run."

Having narrowly escaped disaster, and more than shaken, our little task unit proceeded along its course, now passing south of Kerama Retto, where the initial landings were taking place, and then turning north and heading for Hagushi Beach on Okinawa. Between 0620 and 0700 we observed air attacks against battleships and cruisers from Task Force 54, several planes shot down, and two suicide planes diving onto ships. No enemy planes came within firing range of the *England* or the *New York*.

Having successfully escorted the *New York* to her destination off Hagushi Beach, at 0720 we received a visual message from her releasing us from duty. Lacking instructions, we remained in the area and took station to the southwest of Fire Support Unit 5. At 0830 the battleship *New Mexico,* some five thousand yards northeast of us, reported torpedoes fired at her from the north. The source of the torpedoes was unclear. Guessing that they came from either tubes on the beach or midget subs close to the beach, we changed speed to flank and began searching for a possible sub. Meanwhile, the *New York* reported torpedoes fired at her. We passed north of the *New Mexico* and searched the area to within three thousand yards of the beach in company with the destroyer escort *Miles*. Jittery about the possibility of mines—this water had not yet been cleared by minesweepers—we didn't go in any closer to the beach. The *Miles* made a depth-charge attack on a dubious contact, which was subsequently declared not to be a submarine.

We had been plunged into the fog of war, with ships milling all over the place, planes crisscrossing the skies, antiaircraft fire going off all over, and unseen dangers lurking beneath the surface of the water. It was a daunting, alarming, awesome experience. At 0900 the destroyer escort *Bennion* directed us to screen to the west of the battleships and cruisers, and as we took station the firepower we witnessed far exceeded any that had unfolded before our eyes in the months preceding.

About two months before the Battle of Okinawa, I had quit smoking and made a $5 bet with Bob Webb, our first lieutenant, that he would light up a cigarette before I would. By the time the *Bennion* gave us that screening order, I was so ready for a cigarette I could have chewed one up. Since 0100 Bob had been with the repair party below deck, where he couldn't witness all this action firsthand, so I got on the telephone and asked him to come up on the bridge. "Bob," I said, "you've been below now for hours. I thought you might welcome the opportunity to see what's happening." For about fifteen minutes he stood there and gazed out at the spectacle that filled the sky. That was enough for Webb. "Captain," he said, turning to me, "let's call off our smoking bet."

"That's exactly what I wanted to hear," I replied. "Let's have a cigarette." We canceled the bet, lit up, and kept smoking for the remainder of our time off Okinawa.

Around noon we received a dispatch to proceed with the *Leutze* and the *Whitehurst* to Ulithi for another escort duty back to Okinawa. We had formed column astern and were heading out when the *Leutze* had a possible submarine contact and directed us to stay clear while she made an attack run. The contact fizzled out—a non-sub—so we continued on our way to Ulithi. Needless to say, we weren't sorry to be leaving Okinawa behind, if only for the time being.

After a rough passage through heavy seas and winds of typhoon intensity, we arrived at our destination on March 30, only to turn around the next morning to escort the cruisers *Mobile* and *Oakland* back to the battle area. We arrived three days later, reported to the commander of Task Force 51, and were directed to take screening station A24, southwest of Kerama Retto.

Among the hundreds of ships off Okinawa and Kerama Retto were troop transports, supply ships, older battleships, cruisers both heavy and light, as well as destroyers and destroyer escorts. Battleships and cruisers and a few destroyers shelled targets as called for by marines on the west side of Okinawa. Other destroyers and destroyer escorts took up screening stations around the islands of Okinawa, Kerama Retto, and Ie Shima to protect the larger ships from submarine and aircraft attack. Some screens were placed closer to the island for antisubmarine warfare; others lay farther out to spot and if possible shoot down enemy planes and to report raids coming down from Japan.

Station A24, to which the *England* was assigned, was an antisubmarine screen. The antisubmarine stations were generally seven thousand yards apart, so we would run from one point to the next point seven thousand yards away, and then turn around. We patrolled for submarines using active pinging.

The larger ships pounded the beaches and the Japanese installations on Okinawa continuously—16-inch shells from the battleships, 8- and 6-inch shells from the cruisers, and 5-inch shells from the destroyers—while carrier aircraft reinforced their efforts. The barrage went on for so long that it was hard to understand how there could be any enemy left to resist. The Japanese, however, knew how to defend themselves. In the island's southern area, enemy troops were dug into a series of rugged coves virtually invulnerable to air and sea bombardment. When marines and army troops landed on April 1, Easter Sunday, the response was stiff and deadly.

At 0300 on April 4—one of those bright moonlit nights whose beauty we had come to fear—an unidentified single-engine plane approached from the north and passed close enough ahead of the *England* that we could see it, but not in time to open fire. It was skimming over the water at one hundred feet. The plane opened to the south of us at about three miles and changed course so as to silhouette the *England* in the path of the moonlight. There might as well have been a spotlight shining on us, we were such a perfect target. As the aircraft started toward us, I turned the ship and headed straight for it. We opened fire on a radar bearing. Our fire wasn't accurate, but with it we effectively bared our claws. Warned off, the plane swerved away and opened to the south.

Two days later, we proceeded to Hagushi Beach and reported for a fueling assignment. On the sixth we were ordered to join some other destroyers and destroyer escorts to take a convoy of thirteen transports to Saipan. That same day Admiral Toyoda, commander in chief of the Japanese First Mobile Fleet, launched Operation Ten-Go, and the first of ten massed kamikaze attacks called *kikusui* (floating chrysanthemums), which involved hundreds of aircraft, was unleashed against the U.S. invasion armada. Meanwhile, the smaller kamikaze raids continued.

No sooner had we gotten under way than the destroyer *Lang* and one other destroyer left the formation to return to Okinawa. So many ships had been damaged at Okinawa from heavy air attacks that these two ships were sorely needed. The screen commander was in the *Lang*, and before his ship departed he entrusted command of the screen to me. No doubt he thought that Lieutenant Commander Pendleton was still our commanding officer, for among the destroyer escort skippers left in the screen I was the most junior. Fortunately, despite my lack of experience as a screen commander, we made it to Saipan without mishap.

On April 17, after helping escort a convoy of tank landing ships and support landing craft to Okinawa, we were back on antisubmarine duty. By now U.S. troops had reached Okinawa's northernmost point and were in the process of securing the Motobu peninsula as well as Ie Shima, the island to the west.

Over the next few days we joined screens at various positions off the island, following up on elusive submarine contacts. In one incident, a submarine was spotted by a PBM—an antisubmarine patrol airplane—about fifty-five miles from Okinawa. We proceeded in company with the destroyer escort *Abercrombie* to conduct a retiring search curve, but we found nothing.

Before daylight on the twenty-fourth, we made sound contact with what we thought was a submarine. Passing near the area where the initial contact was made, and unable to get another sounding, we took the *England* on a firing run and unleashed a pattern of hedgehogs. The pattern was off target to the right. When we started in another run, the contact disappeared. In company with the destroyer escort *Oberrender*, we searched on a retiring curve and made no contact. After looking at the recorder traces of the contact, we decided that it was not a submarine at all but our old nemesis, a big fish. Again, shortly after daylight, we made a sound contact some five miles from the previous one, and again we were unable to regain contact.

By April 27 we had joined an antisubmarine station south of Kerama Retto and to the west of Okinawa. The destroyer *Ralph Talbot* was on station some seven thousand yards astern of us. That night, air attacks were heavy and we remained at general quarters throughout. It gave us a taste of what we were in for the following night, April 28—a night that no one on the *England* would ever forget.

———

On April 28 there was a brilliant full moon, making the crafts of the U.S. Fleet a bunch of sitting ducks for the eighty-six air raids that would rain down on it in the hours ahead. A raid consisted of anywhere from four to thirty aircraft, most of them torpedo planes or kamikazes, and there were so many in the area that, as on the previous night, we remained at general quarters with adrenaline coursing through our veins.

At about 2200, the inevitable occurred. Our air search radar picked up a raid of some four or five planes thirteen miles to the northwest and closing on. A few minutes later they were five miles away, bearing 310 degrees. By the time we determined that there were four planes, not five, they were three miles from us. A minute or two later we saw a plane flashing a light, hoping we would open fire so that the three other incoming aircraft could target more clearly and dive on us. We didn't open fire, nor did any of the ships nearby.

The *England* was tense, all hands ready. Suddenly an incoming plane dived on the *Talbot* seven thousand yards astern of us. A split second later a fire erupted from the side of her hull. We couldn't tell if it was a hit or a close miss.

We didn't have time to speculate. Radar reported a plane "Lost overhead and closing fast!" That could mean only one thing—the plane was diving on us. Immediately I yelled down the voice tube: "ALL AHEAD FLANK AND RIGHT FULL RUDDER!"

There was no question that the helmsman knew this was an urgent command.

I knew the kamikaze was diving just ahead of our wake in order to hit the fantail. Four to five seconds later a Japanese fighter believed to be a Tojo came roaring out of the sky with his engine at top speed. Fortunately our fantail had swung about thirty yards to the left of our wake and the plane splashed close alongside our starboard quarter. He had missed.

The plane hit the water so hard that parts of the plane and its gasoline afire flew into the air, coming down toward our fantail. The splash of the plane hitting the water went up about 150 feet in the air, came down, and completely blanketed the fire.

There was dead silence on the ship. We all knew how close we had come to death and destruction. That pilot knew in his last seconds of life that his was a mission in vain. Coming in at an 80 degree dive, the plane was lost to radar and we didn't site it until just before it hit the water, forward of our wake but on our starboard side. At the very last moment we dodged our enemy as he slammed into the water.

But this was no time to celebrate—as far as we knew, there were still two planes overhead. Normal screening speed was 15 knots, but when planes were within four miles it was standard practice to slow down and thereby reduce the wake effect. Immediately after the crash, then, I slowed to 5 knots and had our fantail crew turn on the smoke generators in the hopes of obscuring our wake. The after repair party assessed the damage and found very little. The starboard fire main, next to where the plane hit, had burst. It was turned off and repaired within an hour or two. And we had some damage in the engine room—broken gauge glasses and a leaking fire main, which was temporarily repaired with a wooden wedge.

The fantail scheme didn't work. With the ship at 5 knots, and wind coming from the north while we were proceeding south, most of the smoke flowed back over the deck, choking the fantail gang. Presently the rear gun crew asked us to secure the smoke generators, which we did. Conscious of those planes overhead that hadn't yet made a dive, I still maintained our slow speed.

While all this was going on, a second plane came diving in and hit the destroyer *Talbot*. Her engines still operable, she proceeded to Kerama Retto, and an unidentified destroyer replaced her on station.

The raids were coming in one on top of another now, so many that we remained at general quarters in the hours that followed. For a while no plane threatened us directly. Then at around 0250 we picked one up on the air search radar about eleven miles away and closing in. When he was nine miles away we lost contact; moments later, our surface radar picked him up flying low over the water and zeroing in on our starboard beam. As we were almost at the end of our patrol area, I decided to turn the *England* around with full rudder to bring the plane on our port beam. After the turn we would have more room to maneuver.

At around 0259 the plane was reported at 310 degrees, range 4.5 miles. He had us directly in the path of the moon, but as before, we couldn't see the enemy. Moreover, our hands were tied. With radar fire control, the guns could have trained on the target miles away—but we were without it, and so we couldn't yet fire. Surface radar reported the contact as being "as big as a boxcar." To better maneuver as he homed in, I changed to flank speed. Every few minutes, surface radar updated its report—4,000 yards away, then 3,500, then 3,000, then 2,500. . . . At 2,000 yards the plane finally came into view, a twin-engine Betty torpedo bomber directly on our port beam, skimming about twenty-five feet above the water.

All of our guns were on target and commenced a barrage of fire—1.1- and 20-millimeters using tracer control and the 3-inch using local control with open sights, since the plane could not be seen through a lighted sight. The lighted sight was primarily a daylight sight that, like a telescope, magnified the target. As the plane approached on our port beam I turned hard right, bringing my stern to his nose. Under a hailstorm of fire, the pilot banked left and began paralleling our course, keeping close to our port beam. Now that he was so close we could see our shells flashing all over him like points of light on a Fourth of July sparkler. All at once the plane went nose down and hit the water about eight hundred yards off our port beam.

The sight of that twin-engine death machine slamming into the sea sent a huge cheer through the crew—our first enemy plane shot down! As soon as it hit, flames came roaring up from the site of the crash, a conflagration that would last until just before daylight.

"Top Hat, are you hit?" came a voice over the radio. Top Hat was our code name. The voice originated from another destroyer escort, on the station just north of ours.

"No, we aren't hit. We just splashed a Betty."

A few minutes later, as the fire burned on, the voice crackled over the radio again. "Top Hat, *are you sure you aren't hit?*"

"Yes, we're not hit! Repeat, that's the Betty we just splashed a few minutes ago. But thanks for asking."

A half hour before daylight we picked up another single plane some seven miles to the north, altitude hovering around 300 feet. As we tracked him intermittently on surface and air radar, he closed from the north and merged with the ship on our station, closing to within 4,000 yards, then changed course and mixed with the ships on a station 4,500 yards to the east of us, then veered back toward our station. He never did come within firing range. This was the last plane we had on our screen until the next night, and no ships reported being attacked by it.

Late in the afternoon of April 29 we saw a Betty torpedo bomber attack the destroyer minesweeper *Butler* some 6,000 yards northwest of us. Another Betty attacked the destroyer minelayer *Wiley.* Both planes were splashed by beautiful gunnery.

—◦◦◦—

The night of the twenty-ninth was another prolonged battle of nerves. Around 2330 we picked up a raid of four to six planes some thirteen miles away. Their approach was almost identical to the one the night before: When the planes came to within three miles, one turned on an orange-colored light, apparently to draw our fire and give the kamikazes a clear target. The lighted plane passed astern of us at an estimated 2,500 yards, but we didn't dare shoot.

Roughly two hours later we picked up a single low-flying plane bearing 320 degrees true, distance nine miles. By this time we had begun to believe that discretion was the better part of valor, and rather than waiting to bring him astern when he was close enough for us to fire at him, we turned and gave him our stern when he was three miles away. He closed to within two miles, then changed course to get back on our beam. As he did so, we changed course as well, playing a cat-and-mouse game to keep him directly astern, where he would have less of a target. He followed our turn through 90 degrees, struggling to get on our beam while maintaining a range of four thousand yards.

Giving up, he changed course and headed for two destroyer escorts on Killer 4, the screen next to ours. As he flew through the path of the moonlight, he was sighted and identified as a twin-engine bomber, probably a Betty. Having no success with Killer 4, he eventually changed course and disappeared into the smoke screen of Ie Shima. About three minutes after he disappeared into the smoke, we heard an explosion. Judging from the sound, we surmised that he had fired his torpedo blindly while in the smoke.

For the rest of the night we remained at general quarters, and while a number of raids passed close to the *England,* none singled us out for attack. At daylight we received an order to proceed northwest of Ie Shima and provide an antisubmarine screen for the *Wiley* and a destroyer minesweeper while they transferred ammunition. This assignment was easy, one that any of our officers was capable of handling. Exhausted from two successive nights of being at general quarters, I decided to catch some shut-eye. "Wake me up when the screening is done," I said to the officer of the deck. "We have another assignment lined up afterward." Then I went to the sea cabin next to the combat information center and conked out.

Presently the officer of the deck called down through the voice tube, "Captain, we're done screening. What are we supposed to do now?"

"Head northwest," I mumbled and fell back asleep.

About fifteen minutes later, I woke up and went to see what was happening. Arriving on the bridge, I discovered to my horror that we were all alone, heading northwest in the direction of Japan. As far as I knew, we had come closer to the homeland than any other ship in the U.S. Navy up to this point. "What in the hell are you doing?" I said to the officer of the deck. "If the Japs fly down from there we'll be the first ship they spot and the first one they attack!"

"But Captain," he replied, "you *told* me to head northwest." And indeed I had. I'd been in such a deep sleep I didn't remember issuing the order. I thanked my lucky stars that I'd woken up in time.

It didn't take us long to turn the *England* around and head to Kerama Retto, where we were scheduled to get fresh provisions. Though we had just been through two of the hardest nights we'd experienced in the Pacific, we weren't shaken enough not to look forward to ice cream, lettuce, tomatoes, and real eggs and potatoes. It was time to stop and take a deep breath before heading back out into the melee around Okinawa.

13

A Suicide Bombing

THOUGH BY EARLY MAY THE Americans had secured most of Okinawa, the kamikaze attacks continued relentlessly, and resistance on the island's southern tip, where Japanese troops were holed up in their caves, remained fierce.

The early days of May we spent on escort and patrol duty around Nakagusuku Wan, an inlet in the southeast coast of Okinawa and the main harbor that the U.S. Fleet held on that island. On the third, we were assigned to a berth in Nakagusuku Wan that put us in a screen with several destroyers and destroyer escorts around three battleships and a cruiser. That night it was dark and overcast, the bright moon that had put us at such peril in late April having disappeared. The darkness was broken intermittently as the larger ships fired at targets ashore.

Though Nakagusuku Wan was a harbor, it wasn't a safe haven. The inlet was teeming with ships, making it a rich target for Japan's desperate zealots. There were reports from other ships of suicide swimmers and suicide boats in the inlet, and we posted a watch to fend off this latest threat. A mine-toting swimmer could seriously damage a ship if he managed to slip close to the hull and detonate his weapon. Another danger in Nakagusuku Wan was navigation. It was difficult to maneuver inside that crowded harbor without colliding with another ship, and whenever we headed out for patrol or escort duty we had to inch forward until we reached the harbor entrance. It was so dark that we had to navigate completely by radar.

On the morning of May 4 we gingerly proceeded toward the harbor mouth to join an antiaircraft screen around transport ships in the area. Air traffic wasn't as heavy as in late April; on this morning we saw only one enemy plane, coming in from the eastern side of Okinawa and running a gamut of heavy antiaircraft fire. We were amazed that it continued advancing, considering the heavy defensive barrage being thrown up in the air. The plane kept on advancing, and we could hear the drone as it went into a vertical spinning dive and crashed into the light cruiser *Birmingham*. Although the cruiser was damaged, it was probably still operational.

Two days later, on a screening station off Kerama Retto, we sighted a person floating in the water. Coming closer, we discovered that it was a Japanese corpse. We retrieved the body, which appeared to have been in the water for less than twenty-four hours, and stripped it of a map and several photographs of a Japanese plane. After reporting this information to the commander of Task Group 51.5, we were directed to turn the material over to the intelligence officer in the amphibious force flagship *Eldorado* upon completion of our screening assignment.

While we were still on the screen, some of our machine gunners reported that a bird had landed on the shield of the number 3 gun with a message of some kind tied to its leg. It had been raining hard; apparently the bird had sought out our deck as a refuge. Having heard that Japanese communications were breaking down, we thought that maybe they had resorted to birds for conveying messages and that this bird might be carrying some valuable intelligence. So I dispatched three men with shotguns to catch the courier.

The poor thing was so wet it could hardly fly, and there was no need for guns. The men scooped it up and removed the message, which was enclosed in a rubber tube that had been wrapped in scotch tape and tied to the bird's leg by wire. Slowly, so as not to damage it, we unwrapped the paper. On it was typed "8 May 1945 liberated by US Naval Forces." Slightly disappointed at not having intercepted more intelligence material, we liberated our soggy captive, completed screening duty, and delivered what information we did have from the Japanese corpse to the *Eldorado*.

The morning of May 9—May 8 in Europe, the day the Germans and Italians surrendered unconditionally to the Allies—dawned bright and clear. We didn't have time to celebrate the hard-won victory in Europe. Clear skies were ominous. As hard experience had taught us, they often signaled impending air attacks. That morning we were directed to a screening station about halfway between Kerama Retto and Tonachi Shima, an island to the northwest of Okinawa. At dusk, as feared, reports came in of

Japanese raids approaching our screening area, and we went to general quarters.

One raid was forty-eight miles from us, and another was reported farther north. At 1853 we picked up three planes on our air search radar bearing about 26 degrees true at a range of some seven miles. Friendly aircraft were close to the Japanese planes, trying to shoot them down. All of these were closing on the *England*. We changed speed to flank, 23.7 knots.

Prior to the Okinawa operation, I had talked to some American aviators about the best defense against Japanese suicide planes. They indicated that if a plane was coming in at a steep dive, say, 70 to 80 degrees, we should try to force the pilot to increase his dive angle. That was because once a plane had committed to such a steep dive at full power, it was extremely difficult to further increase the dive angle. The aviators also told me that a plane coming in at a 20- to 30-degree angle had good control; in that case, the best thing we could do to avoid getting hit was to shoot it down. This advice wasn't very heartening.

I analyzed the situation. If a kamikaze were to dive at a 20- to 30-degree angle and we were unable to shoot him down, where would be the best place for him to hit from our point of view? Obviously, we would be at general quarters when the plane came in. And that meant that the emptiest part of the ship would be the wardroom area, under the bridge. If I could maneuver the ship to make the plane hit there, it would probably kill fewer people than if it hit anywhere else. If at all possible, I decided, that was what I would do.

At 1854 the planes were still closing. Thirty seconds later, we sighted three aircraft bearing 260 degrees true. One, flying about three miles ahead of the others, was identified as a Val, a light bomber. At the time of sighting his position angle was about 30 degrees bearing 060 degrees relative on our ship. Our ship course was 200 degrees.

As the seconds ticked by, a sense of foreboding came over the *England*. We could see the Val in the clear blue sky as he zeroed in on us; he was approaching in a gliding dive. At 1855 we opened fire with the main battery guns and shortly thereafter with the 1.1 heavy machine gun. When the range closed, our 20-millimeter guns erupted and we began evasive maneuvers at flank speed. Trying for the lesser of evils, I gave left full rudder to bring the Val on our quarter so that if he did hit, casualties might be minimized.

With all the planes that had targeted us since the beginning of the Okinawa operation, it was just a matter of time before one hit. This was the one. Early in his approach, the Val appeared to be heading for the bridge, and for a second it seemed as if he might miss. Then his port wing nicked the forward boat davit and the plane slammed into the ship. He crashed into our superstructure at frame 55, just above the main deck.

Meanwhile, the other two enemy planes were heading for the *England,* and it was hard, despite my scheme to try to keep the damage down, not to think that the *England* was doomed. What could a small destroyer escort do, outnumbered three to one? Fortunately the other two attackers were shot down by marines flying F4U fighter planes.

Before the Val hit, we could see it was carrying two Japanese aviators, one in the forward compartment, slumped over his controls as if dead, and the other in an after cockpit, who was apparently piloting the plane. By the time it slammed into the *England,* the plane had been seriously damaged by our gunfire—one wheel shot off, the engine burning and smoking. It wasn't clear whether the pilots were kamikazes; most Japanese suicide aircraft were fighter planes without bombs. This was a light bomber, however, and though I didn't realize it at the time, it was loaded. Had the plane not already been damaged, it might have dropped its bombs but not struck us.

Later, among the debris in the wardroom, we found two unarmed bomb-nosed fuses believed to be from some type of firebomb. The bomb that did the damage was thought to have been a five-hundred-pound delayed-action weapon. Flung from the plane by the force of the crash, it hit the main deck at the wardroom's forward bulkhead, bounced four feet into the air, and detonated just off the centerline to port, under the forward part of the pilothouse and the number 2 gun.

When the plane hit and the bomb exploded, the flying bridge lost all control and communications, burning gasoline sprayed all over that area, and nearly all the ship's phone circuits went dead. Almost instantly, smoke and flame engulfed the bridge, and I gave the order to abandon it. Some men on the signal bridge and those who had stumbled out of the combat information center jumped overboard, taking with them several wounded who probably would not have been saved otherwise. Other men on the bridge clambered down the number 2 life raft and from there swung down to the main deck while men below sprayed them with water. I climbed to the top of the sound shack. From that view I was amazed, shocked, and dismayed. It was only then that I realized a bomb had exploded.

From that vantage point I saw my gunners on the 20-millimeter machine guns hanging dead in their gun straps and the loaders lying dead beside them. Clearly, the deck had blown out from under the after part of the number 2 3-inch gun. The amount of destruction was unbelievable. Though distraught, shocked, and in despair, I still had to act as fast as I could to get the ship under control and to see that we fought the fire.

Along with two other men, I jumped from the top of the sound shack to the pilothouse deck, and there our paths split. They saw one escape route. I saw another. They went to the port side of the bridge where others were climbing down, while I stood on top of the sound shack, assessing the destruction below.

The number 2 gun was a level below the pilothouse, and since the deck aft of the gun had been blown away, I couldn't jump. Instead, I slid down the barrel of the number 2 gun, which was angled up at the starboard quarter.

One of our gunner's mates, a great guy by the name of Bricker, was badly wounded. I tried to pick him up and hand him down to the men at the number 1 gun a level below, but he weighed over two hundred pounds and was so heavy I couldn't lift him. "Get your men together and get a stretcher for Bricker," I called down to Ralph Norman on the number 1 gun. "He's in a lot of pain; he'll need some morphine."

With that, I jumped onto the main deck and scrambled aft, 20-millimeter shells from the clipping room exploding all around me. When I reached the number 1 gun I could better assess the damage, which was extensive. In addition to swallowing up the pilothouse, combat information center, and radio room, smoke and flame had also spilled into wardroom country, my cabin, the radio room, the galley, and the ship's office, among other spaces. My primary responsibility was clear: get control of the ship, stop her, and be sure the fires were put out as fast as possible, before they spread to ammunition stores. Without losing another second, I directed the men to start dumping ready hedgehog and 3-inch ammunition overboard. Some of the ammunition from the number 2 gun had already been blown over the side by the bomb.

Proceeding past the burning bridge, I found one of the officers directing the crew to abandon ship. "Cancel that order!" I yelled at the top of my lungs. "We are *not* going to abandon ship. Repeat, we are not abandoning this ship. We are going to save the *England!*"

When I reached the after control room, the ship was going in circles at flank speed with left full rudder. The guns that were undamaged were still ready to open fire.

It was crystal clear what I had to do in order to fight the spreading fire: we had to stop the ship or at least slow down. I opened a hatch on the main deck above the engine room and shouted, "Go to two-thirds speed!"

At 1909, only twelve minutes after the crash, a minesweeper approached us from astern, at which point I decided to stop all engines and await her arrival. The minesweeper could lend us some extra hoses and provide radio communication. We needed to report the damage, get assistance for the wounded, and round up a ship to retrieve the men who had jumped overboard.

Much to our relief, at 1930 the minesweeper *Vigilance* moored alongside to port. She sent firefighting parties aboard with hoses and gasoline pumps, and we began to transfer the wounded to her. Meanwhile, a whaleboat from the minelayer destroyer *Gherardi* arrived with a firefighting party, a doctor, and a medical team, which was a tremendous help to us.

Within the next few hours we got additional assistance from several other ships: a landing ship (the LSM 222), an unidentified patrol escort, and the seagoing tug USS *Gear*, which was going to tow us to Kerama Retto. We were very grateful for all the dedicated officers and men who arrived to lend us a hand. Thanks to their help, by 2130 we had the worst of the fires under control, and the *England* was restored to a state of manageable chaos.

Ours wasn't the only ship that had trouble on the evening of May 9. A number of other vessels had been damaged at sea by kamikazes and towed into Kerama Retto. As the *Gear* led us in, we could see a heavy dome of smoke hanging over the harbor. As soon as the air raids were reported, ships with smoke generators had circled the area and completely smoked in the harbor to make it more difficult for Japanese bombers and suicide planes to attack the ships anchored there.

We arrived about 0130; the *Gear* anchored with the *England* tied alongside. We were dead tired but had a few fires still smoldering. Firefighters from the *Gear* told us to get some sleep—they would keep any remaining fires under control. All hands from that ship were generous with their help, and our officers and crew were deeply grateful. While our visitors fanned out to do their work, I walked around the ship trying to comfort my men and get them settled down. Because the officers quarters were completely destroyed, some officers spent the night in the chief's quarters, while others slept wherever a vacant bunk turned up. The captain of the *Gear* invited me to spend the night on his ship.

I still didn't know how many men had been killed or how many wounded had been transferred off the *England*. All I knew was that I'd lost many good men, and along with my officers and crew, I was devastated. "Captain Williamson," the *Gear's* skipper said, "you've been through enough. Before you go to sleep I want to give you some brandy for medicinal purposes." So that night on the *Gear* I drank a glass of brandy, the only alcoholic beverage I ever had on a ship in the U.S. Navy. I was deeply grateful for that drink. It helped me fall asleep and forget, for a few hours at least, the great grief that engulfed me.

—◁◊▷—

The next day, May 10, was a time of accounting and cleanup. That morning we began the grisly job of figuring out who was killed, who was missing, who was wounded, and where they were. It was vitally important that I inform the Navy Department of casualties so that families could be notified. In addition to this, there was the terrible job of removing corpses to another ship for burial on Kerama Retto.

The final tally of dead was thirty-seven, including those who were missing and presumed dead. (The men who had jumped over the side of the ship had been picked up by another ship.) Forty men had been wounded, including Lieutenant Bob Webb, our first lieutenant. Some of them were transferred to hospital ships or to the hospital at Kerama Retto. Others were treated aboard the *England* by our pharmacist's mates and doctors from other ships.

Most of the dead had been killed as a direct result of the bomb, which, as I mentioned, exploded under the forward part of the pilothouse, wiping out all the men on the machine guns above the pilothouse and just about everyone on the number 2 3-inch gun. Since it blew out the main deck, all of the people in the repair party below were killed instantly.

The attack transport USS *Gosper* was a big help during the gruesome business of assembling a roster of missing and killed. Her skipper supplied a boat and a working party to remove bodies—or what remained of bodies—to Zamami Shima, an island near Kerama Retto where the navy cemetery was located. All of our known dead were buried there. I don't know what happened to the missing men, of whom there were ten. Some may have been killed instantly and blown over the side from the force of the explosion. Others may have jumped over the starboard side and been sucked into the propellers, since at the time of the hit I had the ship on left full rudder.

One of the victims was Lieutenant Knight, our communications officer. He was heading to his battle station in the radio shack, having just descended a ladder onto the second deck, when the plane hit. The flames came shooting up through the stairwell and engulfed his body right there outside the radio shack. We figured he had died in a matter of seconds.

When the bodies were being removed, one of the men came to me and said, "Captain, we can't move Lieutenant Knight. He's baked like a roast." I went up to see him and winced at the sight. "Go get a sheet and cover him up," I said. Once the sheet had been placed over Lieutenant Knight, I helped the men carry his body to the ship that was carting away our dead. I joined in the effort not because another pair of arms was needed, but because the men needed encouragement. It was emotionally devastating to dispose of the corpses of people to whom we had grown so close during the many months of war.

Another great loss was our chief boatswain's mate, Frank Manlove. Manlove was the person who had been designated King Neptune when we crossed the equator. A few months earlier, I had a dispatch from the States indicating that Manlove's mother had died. I called him into my cabin and relayed the sad news to him, asking him if he wanted to be released to go back to the States. "We'll be able to get you air transportation, Chief, but it'll take five to six days to get home, perhaps even more." He said he wanted to think it over. A few hours later he came back to my cabin. "Captain, it'll take so long to get back to the States that my mother will already have been buried. My next of kin is my sister. Much as I'd like to visit with her at this time, I know if I do go back to the States I'll be transferred to another ship. I'd rather stay on the *England,* so I choose not to go back."

Little did he know that that decision would spell his doom. As soon as I had time, a couple of weeks after the hit, I wrote a letter to the next of kin of those men killed in action. It seemed the right thing to do. A personal gesture might bring them some comfort; at the least, it would give them more information about their loved ones than they would receive in a dry telegram from the Navy Department. So I wrote Frank Manlove's sister. She wrote back: "I knew that Frank was killed even before I received the telegram from the Navy Department. On the night of May 9 I had a dream in which I saw Frank and Mother walking hand in hand and they were both smiling. I knew they were together."

As the day wore on we continued removing the dead. In addition to grief, we felt a heavy sense of responsibility, as if somehow we had failed in combat. In our heart of hearts, however, we knew that the odds had been stacked against us, and we were still proud of the *England* and all we had accomplished on behalf of the United States of America.

As we moved methodically through the ship collecting bodies, we also began a more thorough job of damage assessment. First and foremost, of course, was fire damage. Fortunately, the previous August while the *England* was in Milne Bay, all the men and officers had been sent for a refresher course in firefighting, and that training had proved invaluable in coping with the fire that erupted as soon as the Val struck our ship.

Twenty seconds after the plane hit us, repair party number 2 had water on the fire. Speed was critical. We were under flash condition red, with Japanese planes still in the vicinity; the fire had to be under control and not visible after dusk if we wanted to evade enemy planes, which had a tendency to dive on damaged ships. Moreover, the flames were particularly difficult to fight. The base of the fire lay in spaces near the explosion as well as in the wardroom, the passageway just aft of the wardroom, and the ship's office, where reams of paper were stored. The smoke from burning paper was so thick that no single person close to it could man a hose for more than a minute at a time. Moreover, it was difficult to reach the base of the fire on account of bomb damage forward and, aft, flames shooting down the passageway. Another difficult fire to put out was in the after mess hall. We couldn't get in there because both the port and starboard access hatches were blocked by fire.

Despite these drawbacks, hoses from the boat deck and from the starboard side of the main and superstructure decks helped immensely in fighting the flames. As these hoses took effect, additional hoses were eventually worked from all the ship's plugs, except those connected to the ruptured forward main. In addition, we used several handy billys (small gasoline-powered water pumps) and four streams from the *Vigilance*'s fire main. Two hoses were run directly to the signal bridge once the men regained access to that area. The fire there was so hot that five-inch-deep water on the pilothouse deck was boiling.

The fire on the signal bridge was under partial control within an hour of the hit. The fire in the radio shack and captain's cabin, however, was still going until about 2230, though it wasn't visible to enemy aircraft. Damaged bulkheads prevented anyone from getting beyond the passageway entrance to those spaces. Because the early fire was a gasoline fire, we used fog applicators, which are more effective against gasoline, for the first half hour, and then we switched to a solid stream.

All but one of our phone circuits were out. The engine room circuit was shorted out by damage in the forward part of the ship. Working quickly, Chief Engineer Heiler scrambled topside to locate the source of the damage, then had this one circuit cut out from the junction box in the number 1 engine room. This fix, which took only four minutes, rapidly restored communication between all engine rooms and the firerooms.

The electrician's mate stationed in the information center (IC), though he couldn't figure out where we'd been hit, saw that the gyro was shorted and shut it down together with all the shorted circuits. By the time he was done, the IC was heating up like a kettle on a stove, so he came up through the scuttle into the after mess hall. The fire there had been put out. He took one glance at the water sloshing over the mess hall deck, some four feet deep, and dogged down the scuttle to the IC to prevent flooding. Then he tried to squeeze through a partially opened hatch at frame 58. Debris had fallen on the hatch and it wouldn't budge any further. "Help!" he yelled. "I'm stuck in here!" A firefighter heard his cry and trained a hose in his direction while another man opened the hatch and pulled him through.

Our investigation showed extensive but not serious water damage. So much water had been used to fight fires that in addition to the after mess hall, the engineer's storeroom, another storeroom, the ice machine room, and both cold storage boxes were completely flooded. Water sprayed into the wardroom ran down the inboard passageway and washed debris up against the coamings and entrance to the machine shop, creating a dam that resulted in a buildup of more than a foot of water in the passageway. It took ten men to remove the debris. Once it was cleared away, two submersible pumps were used to drain water into the engine room, where it was pumped overboard by the main circulating pumps.

As for damage from exploding ammunition, we found evidence that some of the 3-inch ready ammunition on the number 2 gun that had not blown overboard had exploded and that one of the ready boxes had fallen from the gun into a burning mess hall, where several of the shells cooked off. Twenty-millimeter ammunition in the forward clipping room had also exploded; the fires from this had been quickly subdued by streams of water played into the clipping room from the main deck.

Once the damage assessment was completed and we had pieced together what had happened throughout the ship, I felt crestfallen, thinking that somehow I had failed. I strongly believed that had the *England* been outfitted with the sort of armament that newer destroyer escorts were being given, which included the quad 40-millimeter machine gun and two 5-inch 38-caliber semiautomatic guns, and if she had had the benefit of radar directors on the main battery and 40-millimeter guns, we would have shot down the Val bomber that slammed into us. But those thoughts were excuses. I didn't need excuses; I needed time to weep over my lost men and my seriously damaged ship. But I didn't have that time! There were too many things that urgently needed to be done.

Also upon completion of the damage assessment, the pride I had in my men deepened. Nobody on the *England* had abandoned ship other than the men on the bridge and the signal bridge, and they jumped overboard out of desperation, because it seemed as if they were completely trapped. They took with them several wounded men who otherwise could not have been removed from the bridge. The chief pharmacist's mate and the second-class pharmacist's mate, who toiled tirelessly to deliver the best care, tended to other wounded. They had able assistance from several other crew members until help arrived from ships alongside.

In the aftermath of the attack the air was filled with bogies, some coming within five miles of the *England*. The men on the 1.1-millimeter machine gun, various 20-millimeter machine guns, and the number 3 main battery gun remained at general quarters throughout all the chaos and uncertainty, steadfastly manning their stations. Meanwhile, all repair party personnel and everyone involved in the firefighting effort—not just firemen, but also many men from the forward guns and those who could be spared from the engineering spaces—did an outstanding job. Despite the intensity of the fires they were fighting, I never had any doubt that the conflagration could be brought under control.

Almost all the officers who had remained on board proved themselves deserving of the leadership roles to which they had been entrusted. Though wounded, our first lieutenant, Bob Webb, had fought the fire for thirty-five minutes before he collapsed and was carried to another ship. The executive officer, George Brines, slightly burned and suffering from shock, took charge of the fantail, and after I arrived he remained there to control the guns if necessary and to maintain ship control while I was occupied with other tasks. The assistant engineering officer, Ed Hughes, and Chief Machinist's Mate Karl Kasca were ordered to remain in the after engine room and to take main engine control there, while Chief Engineer Fritz Heiler came topside to help fight the fire. This organization left the gunnery officer, Walt Kabbes, fighting fire forward, and the engineering officer fighting fire aft. The assistant first lieutenant saw that hoses and handy billys were in the right place at the right time.

The strenuous efforts of these men had left me free to watch what was happening all around the ship and in the air. Only two officers disappointed me—the man who had ordered "abandon ship" and another who had come apart at the seams, unable to carry out the simplest order in the hours after the attack and in the days to follow.

All in all, the crew of the *England* had done an outstanding job of controlling the damage and getting the ship secured as quickly as possible. As skipper, I had every reason to be proud.

During the time we were in Kerama Retto there were almost continuous Japanese air raids, and it seemed as if we were forever going to general quarters. Day and night, boats would crisscross the harbor throwing up billowing clouds of smoke to veil us from enemy eyes. Thus covered, we often heard the Japanese planes, but we rarely saw them. The canopy of smoke was like a warm blanket pulled over us on a cold night.

Despite all the activity overhead, the closest any Japanese plane ever came to us while we were lying damaged in the harbor was about twelve hundred yards away, which was a good thing on account of our limited firepower in the wake of the May 9 attack. Because we weren't under direct attack and it was almost dark, we didn't open fire. As I've mentioned, firing into the air had the effect of disclosing a ship's position to enemy planes, making the ship a better target. There were two conditions under which a ship could fire at an enemy plane in the Kerama Retto area. Under "flash yellow" a ship could fire only on a positively identified enemy plane. This policy was meant to protect friendly aircraft. Under "flash red" a ship could fire on any plane as long as that plane appeared to be attacking it.

With the air assaults so relentless, it was no surprise that there were a lot of trigger-happy gunners in the harbor who sometimes failed to adhere to the letter of this policy. However, I recall only one occasion when quick fingers actually brought down a friendly plane. While under heavy air attack, one of the carriers anchored at Kerama Retto decided to launch some of her fighters to help protect her and the other ships in the harbor. The first plane took off from her deck and had flown a thousand yards when some zealous fellow from who-knows-what ship opened fire on it. That set off a chain reaction; others saw his guns going off and assumed that the aircraft in question must be Japanese, so they joined the fray, opening with their own guns and downing the valiant fighter. In the meantime, the second plane was already taking off from the carrier. Happily, it slipped through the curtain of flame and lived to tell the tale.

We remained alongside the *Gear* until May 11, at which time she towed us over to the auxiliary repair ship USS *Egeria* for emergency patching up. The speed of these preliminary repairs was impressive. One week later we fueled and proceeded to the southern anchorage at Kerama Retto, awaiting orders for departure to the Philippines. There the *England* would receive additional emergency repairs, enough to enable her to limp back to the Philadelphia Navy Yard for a complete refitting. It was a long way to go in a damaged ship, but all the navy yards on the U.S. West Coast were already crowded with other ships that had been damaged off Okinawa.

And more damaged ships were to come—by the time Okinawa was finally declared secure, on June 22, a whopping 368 U.S. ships would be crippled in the operation. Even more devastating, 4,900 American seamen would be killed and almost the same number wounded, and 36 U.S. ships would be sunk. Much of this devastation was the direct result of the 1,900 kamikaze attacks launched between April 6 and June 22.

While the *Egeria* patched us back together, I was tremendously busy, so much so that at times I wondered if I could get everything done. In addition to informing the Navy Department about the killed and wounded and notifying their families personally—a wrenching task, since I had developed a sense of deep affection and concern for my men over the eighteen months since the *England*'s commissioning—I had to write an official damage assessment report and make recommendations for repairs. This became a full-time job for me and several of my officers and petty officers. Among other things, we recommended that the entire superstructure between frames 36 and 59 be replaced; that parts of the main deck be replaced between frames 35 and 47; that our armament be updated with a quad 40-millimeter machine gun, two twin 40-millimeter mounts, and 5-inch 38s; and that the *England* be given a general overhaul, since she had been in continuous operation for sixteen months.

The prospect of going back to sea was daunting, to say the least. We had no radar and no radio save for a small one with a scant radius of about a hundred miles that the *Egeria* had given us. The best we could do with it was to communicate with ships close by. Limited as it was, however, this radio would come in handy later.

Moreover, much of our gun power had been knocked out. We had lost our number 2 3-inch gun and several forward machine guns, and for the time being, at least, we lacked ammunition for our forward number 1 gun. In addition, we had no sound gear—that effectively cut off our ability to engage in antisubmarine warfare. We did have the forward hedgehog, but we had thrown the ammunition for it over the side, and even if we had had the ammunition we couldn't have used it for the simple reason that we had no sound gear. We also had depth charges, but they too were useless without sound gear.

Complicating the situation, we had no communications from the open bridge, where we would have to conn the ship since the pilothouse had been completely knocked out. We were able to rig a special telephone line that went from the bridge to the engine room and the after steering space. We would have to send ship's course down to the helmsman and relay engine speeds and start and stop orders to the engine room.

I felt as if we would be crossing the Pacific with our hands cut off, and I was a little skeptical as to how the return trip would work out.

14

Home at Last

BEFORE OUR DEPARTURE FOR Leyte Gulf in the Philippines, we were saddened to see our beloved ship stripped of much of her remaining defensive
and offensive capability. The *England*'s air radar and surface radar antennas
were removed and given to the commander of Service Squadron 10 in case
they were needed for other damaged ships. And because our hedgehog and
a number of our guns had been destroyed by the bomb explosion, much
of our ammunition was removed. However, all of our depth charges remained on board. Though we had no operable sound gear, should we happen to spot a submarine by periscope we could take a stab at sinking it by
dropping depth charges—a slim, but fighting, chance.

Thus pared down, our pride tested but still intact, we got under way for
Leyte Gulf on May 22 in company with the battleship *Colorado* and the
destroyer *Bebas*. Although we proceeded in a screening position for the
battleship, it was something of a charade, since we could do so little to fend
off a submarine on the prowl. We took some measure of comfort in the
fact that the *Bebas* had sound gear.

Three days later we limped into San Pedro Bay in Leyte Gulf. I remained on my battered ship, still consumed by the responsibility of getting
her back into functioning order, but I gave the crew a long-overdue liberty.
They must have had one heck of a time, or else been sorely in need of a
break, for seven of them were AWOL. I held a captain's mast to dole out
their punishment, which was mild on account of what my men had endured: the loss of eight days of liberty plus twenty-four hours of extra duty.

The USS *Dixie,* a destroyer tender, was assigned to bandage up the
England. Members of her crew took a half-inch steel plate from a captured
Japanese ship and welded it to our open port side. The plate ran from the

number 2 gun to where the side of the bridge was blown out, about forty feet. This did not completely enclose the damaged area, but it did give us some protection from waves coming over the side.

The repair officer from the *Dixie* explained to me that his people had tacked on this plate and strengthened it as much as they could with the available equipment. "We think you'll be able to stand a 40-degree roll without the bridge coming off," he said. My heart sank. If we took a bad roll and the bridge did come off, the *England* would probably roll over—almost certain disaster for all hands, unless another ship was in the vicinity to pick up survivors. "What I recommend," the repair officer went on, "is that you avoid rough weather—any area where you might encounter a roll of more than 40 degrees."

Is he joking? I thought. Like all destroyer escorts in tempestuous seas, the *England* had often rolled 40 degrees or more. Steeling myself, I determined to do my utmost to steer clear of storms, however difficult it might prove. We were fortunate in that we still had a good engine room and could still make 24 knots, our top speed prior to the attack. With enough warning, maybe we could outrun bad weather.

—⚓—

On June 3, 1945, we set out on the long voyage to Philadelphia, a much subdued but wiser ship. Behind us we were leaving thirty-seven men—ten missing and twenty-seven buried on an island in the Pacific. We were much more experienced and much more knowledgeable in the ways of war. Along with our sadness and wisdom came pride. Having achieved a historic record by sinking six submarines in twelve days, the *England* had left her mark on the Pacific.

As we crossed the ocean, I agonized over the loss of all those men and over the wounds that so many others had received. Should I, or could I, have done anything differently to prevent that Japanese Val from hitting the *England*? For many months I would mull over the circumstances of those few short minutes of combat that had brought on irreversible tragedy. On the one hand, I couldn't justify my actions as correct; on the other, I couldn't say that what I had done was wrong. The plane hit the *England* where I had planned for it to hit—the problem was, I hadn't counted on it carrying a bomb. Most Japanese suicide planes *don't* carry bombs, I told myself time and again. Had it not been for the bomb our casualties would have been minimal—perhaps as few as eight.

Well, I finally decided, I did the best I could with the knowledge I had, and I did what I thought at the time was best for my ship. This reflection didn't get me anywhere—it still doesn't, more than five decades later—but there was nothing I could do about it. The thirty-seven men were lost and many of the wounded were back with us, recovered. It was time to try to put the past behind me. Though combat was still raging in the Pacific, a U.S. victory seemed certain, and it was possible that for the *England,* the war was over. We were headed back to the United States, the land of the free and the home of the brave, the shining city on the hill.

We got under way for Eniwetok Island in the Marshalls with the attack transport USS *Carteret* and the destroyer escort USS *Ahrens,* our anti-submarine escort. Their assignment was to escort us through the danger zone where Japanese submarines and planes were still operating. It was strange and mildly humiliating to be the escorted ship after so many months of escorting ships ourselves, but the memory of our record in the Pacific helped us hold on to our pride. Once we were through the danger zone, the *Ahrens* left and we took station ahead of the *Carteret,* as if we were the screening ship. A Japanese submarine observing us from a distance wouldn't know that we were incapable of fighting and wouldn't know that our sound gear was out—they might think we weren't pinging because we were in a listening mode.

En route to Eniwetok, the *Carteret* slowed to 6 knots and we went alongside for provisions, fresh meat, and the ever-popular ice cream. We also exchanged movies, the main recreation for the crew outside of a combat area. Usually, ships would show a movie at least once a day, often after dinner. Observing the blackout rule, we showed movies in the crew's mess hall. Most of the men who were not on watch would attend, even if it meant losing sleep.

On June 10 the *Carteret* said farewell and we arrived at Eniwetok to refuel. To everyone's delight, while we were there, Lieutenant Webb, who had been treated for wounds at Kerama Retto, rejoined us. We gained one and lost another—I detached an officer who would be flying to Philadelphia to deliver our battle-damage report to the navy yard. We had been asked to send an officer ahead with the report so that advance preparations could be made to rebuild the *England* as soon as we arrived at Philadelphia. I had decided that the best candidate for this job was the officer who had become a blob of Jell-O in the aftermath of the attack. He was a terrible disappointment, unable to carry out the simplest order, and when I sent him trotting off to Philadelphia with the battle-damage report I was as happy to see him go as he was happy to take his leave.

After refueling, we headed for Pearl Harbor in company with the destroyer USS *Fox*. On June 16 we arrived at Pearl for a short stopover of three days. While there, we had a chance to visit with one of our guys who had been wounded at Okinawa. Badly burned, he had been treated on a hospital ship at Okinawa and then transferred to the navy hospital in Pearl for further treatment. He was a courageous guy, much loved by the crew and fully deserving of the Purple Heart he'd been awarded. I filled him in on all the things that had happened to our ship since that fateful day of May 9. "Captain Williamson," he said, "I wish I could return to the States on the *England*."

I felt a lump in my throat. "I wish you could too, but the most important thing is for you to get better." He was in a bad way, and I had to wonder if he ever would fully recover. Years later I was overjoyed to see him at one of our *England* reunions. He had recovered fully except for some scars.

When we departed Pearl for San Diego, it was in the company of the carrier USS *Tulagi*. So slim was the chance of encountering an enemy submarine on this leg of our journey that the Navy Department let us, a ship that could hardly protect itself against large waves much less enemy subs, serve as the antisubmarine screen for an important carrier.

On June 25 we followed the *Tulagi* into San Diego Harbor, wondering what kind of welcome was in store for us. I had read sometime before about a British destroyer that sank three German submarines on a single cruise in the North Atlantic. When she steamed up the Thames River upon completion of her cruise, the riverbanks were lined with British citizens welcoming this great and heroic ship back home. Would there be thousands of people on the dock waiting to welcome us back because we had sunk six Japanese submarines in twelve days?

First we were directed to the fuel dock, where we refueled, discharged most of our remaining ammunition, and unloaded our torpedoes and depth charges to lighten the ship and make her more stable. At 1720 we were on our way to the pier at the navy supply depot, where I expected at least a welcoming committee. As we approached the dock I looked through my binoculars and saw no one on the pier. We came closer. Still no one. Surely, I thought, some men will appear to handle our lines. But not a single person was there. When the great *England* came alongside the dock, I had to put our own men over to handle the lines. It was a sore disappointment.

The next day I reported to the commander of the San Diego Naval Base to find out what our orders were for proceeding to Philadelphia. When I told him I was the captain of the USS *England,* the first thing he said was, "What are *you* doing here?" He had no idea we were coming and no idea why we were there. I explained that we had been badly damaged at Okinawa by a suicide plane and that since all the West Coast yards were filled to capacity, we were en route to Philadelphia for repairs.

"The damage is extensive, sir," I said. "We have no radar and very little communications capability—just one small radio with a hundred-mile range. We're under orders to travel with another ship at all times."

"Well," he said indifferently, "we don't have any ships going east. Everything we have here is going west to fight a war. You'll have to go to Philadelphia, or at least to the Canal Zone, by yourself. When do you plan to leave?"

As soon as possible, I felt like saying.

Despite the cold welcome, it was a great thrill to be back in the States after so many long months of hardship and combat. Understandably, my men were chomping at the bit, and I arranged leave for as many of them as possible. With the chance of an enemy encounter now nil, it wouldn't take a lot of hands to handle the *England* from this point on. The men on leave could rejoin us in Philadelphia.

As for me, it had been many months since I had had a proper date, much less talked with a woman, and I was acutely aware of the fact that my old flame Barbara Hale was in Hollywood, California. I called her and she seemed glad to hear from me. Since we were leaving in a day or two I couldn't ask her down, nor could I go to Hollywood. No doubt if I'd seen her I would have fallen in love all over again, but too much time had gone by, too much experience had intervened. Maybe I'll visit that beautiful gal again someday, I thought. But I never did.

—⁓⁓—

On June 27 we set off on our lonesome for Balboa in the Panama Canal. I combed the ship's maritime books to find out all I could about weather patterns in the area. Generally the weather was decent. The main danger came from hurricanes spawned off the Gulf of Tehuantepec on Mexico's southwest Pacific coast, but they weren't common, and as we got under way that morning in late June I wasn't particularly concerned. We steamed south in calm, beautiful seas—the sort that had given birth to the name Pacific, which means mild or peaceful—staying some hundred miles off the coast of Mexico so that we could navigate with star sights and sun lines.

At San Diego I had slept in a bunk in the chief's quarters. Now at sea and worried about my decrepit ship, I put a cot underneath the gun director deck, about four feet above the deck of the open bridge. Sleeping there, I could be near the officer of the deck and the ship's controls in case of emergency.

"Wake me up if the barometer drops more than four one-hundredths of an inch in an hour," I told the various officers of the deck. On July 1, at around 0330 on the mid-watch, Lieutenant Gus Dailey dutifully woke me up. "Captain, the barometer's dropped five one-hundredths of an inch in the last hour. The wind has shifted to an easterly direction and is currently blowing at about 25 knots."

"Okay, report back to me in thirty minutes with an update," I said.

At 0400, after Dailey had been relieved, the new officer of the deck reported that the barometer had dropped three one-hundredths in the previous thirty minutes and that the wind had picked up to about 35 knots. It was still blowing in an easterly direction and was fairly steady. I climbed out of my cot and headed for the bridge, concerned that we might be headed into a hurricane. We were some four hundred miles northwest of the Gulf of Tehuantepec. With the wind off our port bow and the *England* steaming in a southeasterly direction, the center of the hurricane, if there really was one, would be on our starboard bow.

We held our course for the next two hours. Wind velocity increased to about 50 knots, the seas grew rougher, and it started raining—all signs that we were on the fringes of a hurricane. At 0545 I ordered the ship slowed from 16 to 14 knots, and eventually to 12 knots. The wind was steady for several hours, meaning we were either heading toward the hurricane's center or it was heading toward us. At 0705 we changed course to 060 true, steaming northeast toward land, which I hoped would get us out of the wind and to the east of the hurricane's center. The last thing I wanted to do was to go through the center of a hurricane; after all, we'd been told not to roll more than 40 degrees. A roll that severe might put us in great peril.

All that day I continued to change speed and course to minimize roll and get us out of the area. It was difficult to predict what this hurricane was going to do. Hurricanes spawned in the Gulf of Tehuantepec would sometimes come straight up the coast of Mexico and later turn out in the Pacific near California, but there was always the chance that they would turn out to sea closer to the gulf.

Hurricanes are circular storms. In the northern hemisphere, they circle in a counterclockwise direction and tend to travel in a northerly or northwesterly direction, though they can change direction without notice. The eastern semicircle of a hurricane in the northern hemisphere is more dangerous than the western semicircle. That is, if a hurricane with winds of 100 miles an hour is moving at 15 knots in a northwesterly direction and you are in the eastern half, then the wind will be 115 miles per hour. If you are on the western half, the wind will be 30 knots less. This hurricane tended to move in a northwesterly direction. My plan was to escape it completely or at least enter the less dangerous western half.

I finally decided that the best plan was to turn around and run away from the hurricane as fast as we could safely go. Eventually we would do one of two things. If the storm was proceeding up the coast, we would head out to sea after getting well ahead of it, then turn southwest and ride past it. If, however, the hurricane turned out to sea, we would go back down the coast of Mexico.

Late in the afternoon, we headed in a northwesterly direction at a speed of 16 knots to position ourselves well ahead of the hurricane. I had the engineering plant put water into all of our empty fuel tanks to minimize roll. All hands were ordered to don life jackets. For the rest of that day and most of the next, July 2, we ran at 16 to 18 knots, and eventually the winds calmed somewhat.

In the meantime, I kept trying to reach another ship with our limited voice-radio capability. Finally I got through to a carrier and reported our estimated coordinates—we hadn't been able to get a navigational fix for forty-eight hours—to her meteorologist, who would have a better idea of the hurricane's movement. "It seems to me," I told him, "that the storm is moving up the coast. I believe the best plan would be for us to head to sea, pass ahead of the center, and get in the less dangerous semicircle. What do you think?"

"Give me a few minutes to look into this," he replied. A while later he reported back to us. "I think your plan is the best bet," he confirmed. So I decided to change from a northwesterly to a westerly course, still at a speed of 16 knots.

I was pretty certain we'd been blown off course, but because we couldn't get a navigational fix I wasn't sure by how much. I estimated that at most we could be fifty miles off course. Not knowing our precise coordinates posed a problem. There was a group of islands off the coast that we wanted to avoid, and I had to make a decision before midnight to turn and either head southwest or back toward the coast of Mexico, depending on the caprice of the winds.

As we continued west, the winds changed, suggesting that the hurricane was heading up the coast and would pass behind us. Betting on this, at 2303 I ordered a change of course to the southwest, 0235 true. Alas, the fickleness of hurricanes! No sooner had the *England* made her course change than the storm took a sharp turn and began barreling out to sea. My hands were tied. Afraid to switch to a northwesterly direction where the islands might be, I couldn't do anything but remain on our southwesterly course. The wind had picked up and steadied to an estimated 90 miles per hour. We were headed for the center.

On this course the wind was almost directly astern of us. We maintained a high speed of 16 knots to minimize rolling and increase control. I was almost sick with worry. Though the *England* had endured terrible storms at sea, she had never been handicapped as she was now, unable to sustain a severe roll. If we capsized, not all the men could abandon ship, certainly not those in the engineering spaces. Moreover, we wouldn't have time to release life rafts or launch our two boats. We would be in life jackets some 150 miles off the Mexican coast, in shark-infested waters, with no means of notifying anyone.

This fickle hurricane could spell disaster. After all she had gone through in Pacific battles, would our gallant little ship and what was left of her crew end up in an anonymous grave in a Pacific storm?

At about 0020 what we had dreaded all along happened—we entered the eye of the hurricane. Abruptly, the wind ceased blowing and it was dead calm. We slowed to 10 knots. The barometric pressure dropped precipitously and crewmen began getting headaches. Eerily, despite the lack of wind, the waves were still churning, now in mixed, unpredictable directions. We began rolling every which way, 20 degrees, 30 degrees, 40 degrees—the maximum roll the repair officer from the *Dixie* had felt the *England* could sustain without her bridge coming off. His words kept ringing in my head: "Avoid any area where you might encounter a roll of more than 40 degrees."

As noted, our bridge structure had been badly weakened by the bomb explosion, and the forty-foot steel plate used for an emergency repair did little to strengthen it. The plate was merely designed to keep out waves that might wash over the side and fill the empty spaces below. Imagine how we felt, then, when our brave ship, which had taken out six Japanese submarines and been struck by a suicide bomber and lived to tell the tale, began rolling 45 to 50 degrees. With a roll like that, it seemed as if the metal plate were no better than stapled on.

No matter what course we chose, the *England* continued to bob wildly in the eerie stillness of the hurricane's eye. We gritted our teeth, praying that the roiling seas wouldn't tear the bridge off and cause the *England* to turn turtle. Navigating through this perilous dead zone required all of our seamanship skills. It was 0020. We slowed further, to 5 knots, and over the course of the next hour changed course from 235 degrees to 170, 190, 130, 110, and finally 070 true. At 0121, when making this final course change, we resumed a speed of 10 knots. Hallelujah! We had entered the less dangerous side of the hurricane, where the wind was blowing some 60 to 70 knots. It seemed as if we had made it.

Gradually the wind lessened, and with it our sense of relief grew. Finally, after hours of battling high winds and rough seas with a makeshift bridge, we left the hurricane behind. Picking up speed to 15 knots, we steamed in an easterly direction toward the coast of Mexico. After doing all that extra running around we were dangerously low on fuel, and though it was possible we could make Balboa on what was left, rather than take a chance it seemed best to look for the closest fueling place. We decided to pull into a little port that appeared on our emergency fuel list, Manzanillo, a village in Mexico's Colima State.

We reached Manzanillo on the morning of July 4, and by far we were the largest ship that had ever pulled up to its dock. The dock was so rickety we weren't sure it would hold our lines. The Mexicans could speak little to no English, and we could speak no Spanish, which didn't help as we approached the dock. But with the weather calm there was little danger, and in the end we pulled alongside without incident.

Manzanillo was an old walled town that exported coffee and hides. The locals were extremely hospitable, and while we were fueling, the mayor, who could speak reasonably good English, arrived to welcome us. I indicated that I was planning to get under way immediately after fueling. "But Captain," he said, "this is the Fourth of July, your national holiday. Why don't you let our town give you a Fourth of July welcome? We would appreciate you staying and letting us do that."

I thought about it for a minute—about how generous the offer was and how much fun it would be for the crew to get off the ship after that harrowing hurricane and celebrate the Fourth of July. "You're extremely kind," I said to the mayor, flashing him a big smile. "We would be honored to accept your invitation."

The town put on a rousing show for us—the local women in picturesque costumes of bright yellow and red, the men in sombreros with guitars strapped to their shoulders. They played songs and danced. Their hospitality was in inverse proportion to the size of their town, and when we departed, it was with a profound sense of gratitude to the citizens of Manzanillo.

We got under way at around 0700 the next morning, continuing our voyage to Balboa that fortune, both bad and good, had postponed. On the fifth all went well until about noon, at which point we entered an area of moderate storm intensity. I thought to myself, Not another hurricane, please! Once again, we tried various courses and speeds to outmaneuver the storm and to minimize our pitch and roll. As it turned out, the storm wasn't as bad as the hurricane. I decided to ride it out, and by midnight we had resumed our original course toward Balboa.

We arrived on the ninth and cruised the channel to Balboa Harbor, Panama Canal Zone. About 0948 the port director and an ensign supply officer came aboard by small boat to direct us to tie alongside pier 2. We refueled, obtained fresh provisions, and remained moored until the next day.

All of us were excited about going through the canal. In leaving the Pacific, we were leaving war behind, for the conflict in the Atlantic had ended. Though in reality the U.S. West Coast was no more war-torn than the East Coast, there was something official about crossing from one ocean to the next. The Atlantic side of the world signaled peace.

At 0710 on July 10, the Panama Canal pilot came aboard with three lock seamen. As the *England* rose through the locks, our excitement mounted. We were heading east, where the sun rose and hope for the future lay! At 1225 we anchored in Gatun Lake; three hours later we left the anchorage, and by 1812 we were through the canal. While the pilot and his three lock seamen took a small boat ashore, we got under way from Cristobal and headed toward the Caribbean.

It was dusk, and for the first time in many months we were able to turn on our running lights and deck lights. Now, no matter how dark it was, we could all move about the ship in complete light. This sounds like a simple pleasure; in fact, it was an incredible thrill to men who had lived in darkness night after night for as long as we had been in the war zone. Those bright lights gave a physical dimension to the peace we were so keenly aware of as we entered the Atlantic. Another benefit of being out of harm's way was that now we could show movies on the spacious fantail instead of in the cramped, claustrophobic mess hall.

On July 12 we passed Haiti, and four days later we approached Delaware Bay. That afternoon a lieutenant from the navy yard and ten civilians came aboard to go over the damage as we headed up the Delaware River for Philadelphia. At 1530 we moored at Fort Mifflin, Pennsylvania, to unload ammunition; two hours later we were tied up at the Philadelphia Navy Yard. At last!

We had planned ahead of time to hold a memorial service for the deceased and lost members of our ship's company, and we lost no time. Minutes after tying up, with chaplains aboard, we held a service in memory of all those cherished souls. Once that was done, we changed berths and began preparing for the long-awaited repairs to our gallant *England*.

———

Alas, our ship's days were numbered. The navy had decided to convert the *England* from a destroyer escort to an APD, a high-speed transport, and the repairs proceeded in that direction. The ship's company all felt a little sad about such radical surgery; the *England* as we knew her would no longer be. In fact, however, the *England* had ceased to be her true self as soon as that Val nosed into her and one of its bombs ripped out part of her port side.

None of us wanted the *England* converted to an APD. But we had no choice in the matter. The navy had made the decision, and we couldn't buck it.

At any rate, the *England* never received her makeover. On August 6, an American B-29 dropped an atomic bomb over the Japanese city of Hiroshima, and because the Japanese refused to surrender, three days later the United States dropped a plutonium bomb on Nagasaki. After almost four years of bloody conflict in the Pacific, the war came to an abrupt end. And with its end, all work on the *England* stopped. The navy had to determine if the ship was worth repairing or so badly damaged that she should be scrapped. The final decision was to scrap her.

Before Hiroshima and Nagasaki, I received news that I was to be relieved by Lieutenant Commander Phil LeBoutillier. Following leave, I was to take command of a more modern 5-inch-gun destroyer escort and head back to the Pacific. I wasn't sure if I was ready. Though I had loved commanding the *England*, I didn't relish the thought of returning to the Pacific. Maybe I've used up all my luck, I thought. This time around I would head off to the Pacific with fear and apprehension, emotions I hadn't felt the first time. And I would have to muster every last ounce of energy to face the trials of war once again—storms, suicide bombers, blackouts, and food shortages. . . .

Happily, with the war's end these anxious thoughts evaporated into thin air. In addition to the general thrill I felt about being back in the good old United States of America—back to civilization, with wholesome American girls and all the incredible hospitality shown to fighting men returning from war—now there was this news. It was over! I was elated, along with everyone else. The day word arrived of the Japanese surrender, there was dancing in the streets, music playing, and parties everywhere.

On several occasions after arriving in Philadelphia, I dated a charming young lady named Sandy, whom I'd met at one of the local officers clubs. On the night of the surrender, one of the officers from the *England* invited us to his apartment for drinks and dinner. All of us were in high spirits, and I had too much to drink, so much that Sandy had to pack me onto a train and take me to her suburban home, where she and her mother nursed me back to reasonable health. The next morning I dragged myself back to my hotel room, ruing my bad judgment but still exhilarated over America's return to peace.

I went home to Alabama on leave, and while there I got a call from a navy captain in Norfolk, Virginia, who wanted to know whether I planned to stay in the navy. Although by this time my temporary promotion to lieutenant commander had been made permanent and I loved going to sea, I wasn't sure.

"Captain," I said, "I'm considering it, but I can't give you a definite answer yet."

"The reason I called you, Commander," he said, "is that if you decide to stay in we'd like you to take command of antisubmarine training for the Atlantic Fleet. This would be an outstanding opportunity."

"Thank you, sir," I said. "It's a great honor to be asked. I'll think about it and call you back."

For several days I pondered the offer. It was indeed a great honor, and I was deeply grateful to the U.S. Navy for all the training, experience, and opportunities it had given me over the years. But I wasn't sure what I wanted to do, other than get married and have children. The thought of moving them around from one navy base to another wasn't very appealing.

Moreover, that terrible letter from Commodore Thorwall was lurking in the shadows. Even with the outstanding report from the *England*'s military inspection, could the Thorwall episode keep me from someday making admiral?

If I was to stay in the navy, I didn't want anything to hinder my rise to the top.

So with a sense of mild regret, I called him back. "Sir, I want to thank you from the bottom of my heart for offering me this great opportunity, but I've decided to return to civilian life and join the Naval Reserves." The phone made a click as I hung up, a tiny noise that marked the end of a hectic wartime career. During its course I had experienced both the joy of success and the agony of defeat. I had learned that in war, victory comes with a great cost in blood, sweat, and tears. The United States had prevailed, but only after great toil and strife, and many precious lives lost. Amid the victory shouts could be heard the silence of mothers who had lost their sons; wives, their husbands; children, their fathers. At the young age of twenty-seven, I felt as if I had experienced both the worst and the best that life had to offer.

Index

Toyoda, Admiral Soemu, 109, 119, 145, 190
Trinidad, 73
Tryon, hospital ship (APH-1), 170
Tulagi, carrier (CVE-72), 215
Tunney, Gene, 17
Tuscaloosa, cruiser (CA-37), 4, 5, 11
Tustem, merchant tanker, x, 45, 47

Uda, Lt. Shigehira, 122
underwater demolition teams, 59
Ungar Buick Co., 57

V-7 Program, 4, 5, 6
Val, Japanese bomber, 199, 213
Vaughn, Hank, 91-92
Victorious, HMS, carrier, 18–19
Vigilance, minesweeper (AM-324), 202, 206

Wagner, boat engineer Glenn, 117
Wasp, carrier (CV-7), 12, 18
Webb, Lt. R. D. "Bob," 93, 113, 115, 182, 189, 203, 208, 214
West Virginia, battleship (BB-48), 90
Whitehurst, destroyer escort (DE-634), 83, 173, 185–186, 189
Wichita, cruiser (CA-45), 5, 11, 38
Wiley, destroyer (DD-597), 195–196
Williamson, Rebecca, 1, 182
Williamson turn, 62–63, 78
Willmarth, destroyer escort (DE-638), 161
Wolf, Capt., 45–47
wolf packs (German submarines), 22, 26, 32, 89

Yarmouth, attack transport, 88, 180
YMCA, 4
YWCA, 7